THE ZUNI
ENIGMA

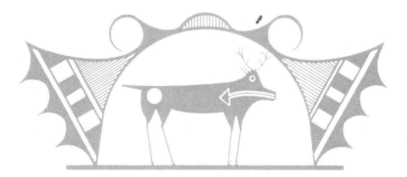

THE ZUNI ENIGMA

By Nancy Yaw Davis

W. W. Norton & Company New York • London

Since this page cannot legibly accommodate all the copyright notices, pages
295–98 constitute an extension of the copyright page.

For information about permission to reproduce selections from this book, write to
Permissions, W.W. Norton & Company., 500 Fifth Avenue, New York, NY 10110

The text of this book is composed in Veljovic Book
with the display set in Herculanum
Composition by Allentown Digital Services.
Manufacturing by The Hadden Craftsmen, Inc.
Book design by Dana Sloan
Cartography by Jacques Chazaud

Library of Congress Cataloging-in Publication Data
Davis, Nancy Yaw.
    The Zuni enigma / by Nancy Yaw Davis.
      p. cm.
  Includes bibliographical references and index.
  ISBN 0-393-04788-1
  1. Zuni Indians—History. 2. Indians of North America—Transpacific influences.
  3. America—Discovery and exploration—Japanese. I. Title.
  E99.Z9 .D38 2000
  970.01'9—dc21

                                                                99-38955
                                                                CIP

W.W. Norton & Company, Inc., 500 Fifth Avenue, New York, N.Y. 10110
www.wwnorton.com

W.W. Norton & Company Ltd., 10 Coptic Street, London WCIA 1PU

1 2 3 4 5 6 7 8 9 0

Dedicated to the Zuni Tribe,
their descendants, and their Asian relatives

"I always wondered why I spoke Japanese so easily."

Zuni council member, veteran, World War II
May 1988

CONTENTS

LIST OF ILLUSTRATIONS

FIGURES

MAPS

TABLES

ACKNOWLEDGMENTS

W illiam E. Davis has shared his whole married life with me—and this theory. Somehow he knew when to help and when not to, a treasured gift of thoughtful insight. Our children have come to understand my passion for research, and for that I am most pleased—and relieved. Without the solid grounding of my family I know I could not have completed this multiyear project.

I am warmly grateful to friends who puzzled over my commitment, worried about the toll it took, but never said "Don't do it." Suzan Nightingale got me started on the serious business of writing on October 18, 1994, when she said, "The pain of writing is finite; the pain of not writing is infinite." She was right. John McKay's timely advice led to a recommitment I'm glad I made. Helen Fisher recommended that I contact Mary Cunnane at W. W. Norton when I was ready to tackle the book. I did, and Mary initiated a process in New York that both startled and challenged me; her initial editorial perspective and suggestions are appreciated. Katinka Matson helped me through the first two versions of the manuscript with seasoned advice for a first-time author. Someone told Edwin Barber that I was the "Crazy Lady from Alaska" and I am grateful to them both—to one for the distinguished title; to Ed for sticking with me as my editor just anyway. Skepticism can sharpen one's effort to document rigorously even when it entails seemingly endless endnotes. Mary Babcock's sharp copyediting combined with the special skills of many others on the Norton team brought a messy manuscript to neat resolution. I remain in awe of the entire publishing world and am grateful the potential of this new idea was recognized and encouraged by the right people at the right times.

A special note of thanks must be offered to all my colleagues in anthropology who so vigorously objected to my theory, especially those in linguistics and in Southwest studies. Of course, the book would have been better had I been able to engage them in discussion (but then, it probably would never have been written). Now I hope those conversations can take place and energy can be directed to the delight of exploring and debating new ideas, even fuzzy ones. Anthropology as a whole is a complex field but it has much special perspective to offer the world in the third millennium.

Of the handful of anthropologists who did not visibly shudder at my audacious theory, the strongest support has been provided by Betty J. Meggers, whose keen theoretical questions kept the idea of transoceanic influences alive. Her friendship, encouragement, and careful reading of a draft manuscript heartened me, especially during the lean times. Others who have commented constructively include: Nancy O. Lurie, Charles Hockett, Karl Schwerin, Robert Humphrey, Bill and Karen Workman, Bernard Siegel, and James Gibbs. Jeffrey Mass, Bill Durham, David Botstein, and Luca Cavalli-Sforza provided questions and references that sharpened my thinking and added to the larger questions. Rita R. Colwell inspired me by her scientific presentations and words of encouragement to hang in there—and keep the references.

Special merit should be given to all the librarians of the world who cheerfully assist scholarly mavericks in pursuit of strange, surprising topics. I am especially indebted to Laura Holt at the Library of the Museum of Indian Arts and Culture in Santa Fe.

The continuing interest and fresh perspective given by friends and neighbors who are not anthropologists played a significant role, too. George Grant and Käna Van Pelt, Ginni Davlin, Effie

Graham, Diane Brenner, Tay Thomas, Dale V. Sellin, Lyle and Dalene Perrigo, Jack and Martha Roderick provided the kind of uncritical cheering section that I surely needed. Atsuko Yamamoto and Kiyoko Gallaher guided with patience as I struggled to learn the basics of Japanese. Tomoko Miyanishi kindly assisted me on our adventure to the National Museum of Japanese History.

Alaska Native friends, especially Alberta and Leo Stephan and George and Susie Ondola, have helped me endure the discipline it has taken to complete this project by giving me perspective about the troubled twentieth century we now leave. Their intelligence, resilience, strengths, and refreshing sense of humor—despite the pains of the past—encouraged and inspired me. They keep me humble as we share this magnificent land together. Cheenan.

It is difficult not to apologize to the Zuni. They certainly did not ask for visits from yet another Anglo anthropologist, but I was compelled to come and share what I was learning that touched on their history. Each of ten short visits (one to four days) gave me a feeling of how this new idea might be perceived in the Pueblo.

I will be forever grateful for the wonderful hospitality and friendship of Josephine Nahohai and her family, especially Milford, whose gifts include a cheerful and open sharing of his knowledge of Zuni art in its many forms. Jim Ostler and Tom Kennedy added their help over the years as I struggled with how to make sure the Pueblo benefits from this book.

Four different councils have allowed me time to inform them of the status of my research. Given the utter complexities and urgent matters of governing a modern tribe, hearing about a book with Zuni in its title surely was not the favorite topic of recent councils. But at least this book will not be a surprise, and I hope that with this forewarning it can be supportive of the directions the tribe chooses to go in the twenty-first century. To all the Zuni who remember me and made me feel welcome even if I was an anthropologist (writing a book, no less!), I wish you great success with the continuing dignity of a strong identity and healthy economy. You are, indeed, a very special Native American tribe. Ela'kwa.

Nancy Yaw Davis
Anchorage, Alaska
September 1999

FOREWORD

BEFORE TIME: THE A:SHIWI AT THE BEGINNING

Our tribal traditions concerning our origins and emergence from the four worlds below are not stories, fables, or fairy tales. We consider them as true historical accounts. Unlike stories, fables, and fairy tales (which we also have) told only in the wintertime, "The World of the Beginning" can be told at any season because it is not a fable.

According to our elders, in ancient times the earth was soft, and there were no humans in this world. Every day Sun Father came up in the East to bring a new day. He traveled high over Mother Earth, pausing briefly at high noon overhead. He then descended into the western ocean, and it became night. All night long he traveled under Mother Earth to reach the eastern ocean in time to bring another new day. But the days were empty. There was no singing, no joy, no dancing, no prayers, and no gifts. The world was empty.

Every day, as Sun Father traveled high over Mother Earth, he could hear the cries of his children deep in the womb of Mother Earth. One day, as he paused at high noon, he saw two columns of foam at the base of a waterfall. With his great power, he put life into the forms, thereby creating the Twin Gods. This gives the Twin Gods their great power. They are the creations of *uwanami,* rain spirits, and Sun Father.

Sun Father said unto the Twin Gods, "Go, go into the womb of Mother Earth and bring forth my children up to my light and warmth." The Twins obeyed and entered the womb of Mother Earth. After many tries, the Twins succeeded in bringing forth the People. This was the Beginning, *hon chimi k/anap kya.* This was our Beginning. We were born out of Mother Earth. We were not created.

At the direction of *hon a wona wil lap ona,* the spirits who guard our life roads, we traveled for many years in search of the "Center Place." We moved every four days (actually every four years—some say eight, counting day and night—because we had not yet established a calendar, or the various societies).

After many years of travel, the Elders in Council, requested the help of the Water Spider, *K/an asi te pe,* who was asked to reach out to the four corners of the world. Where his heart rested would be the *Itiwanna,* the Center Place. The Water Spider reached out to the edges of the world and his heart came to rest at *Halona Itiwanna,* present-day Zuni, *Shi win a.* That is The Word of the Beginning.

Some of the villages we occupied during our search for the Center Place—all now in ruins—are known and named in the longer account of The Word of the Beginning.

Hawikuh (the meaning of this name is lost; it cannot be directly translated) was one of our six named villages occupied at the time of the first-documented Spanish encounters. Estavanico, a Moor from Azamora, who had been a servant of Antonio Durantes on an ill-fated Florida exploration, and Fray Marcos de Niza, who was a Franciscan priest of French ancestry and had earlier been in Peru among the Inca with Francisco Pizarro, arrived in about June 1539. They were followed in 1540 by Don Francisco Vasquez Coronado. They claimed they had found the A:shiwi (we didn't know we were lost). This was *Eno:te,* Ancient Time to our people.

These were the first- and last-recorded contacts between the native and foreign cultures until the American period, some one hundred years later.

The A:shiwi, the name we call ourselves, have lived in the Zuni River drainage area for over fourteen hundred years. We are at the crossroads of all the archaeological cultures in the Southwest: the Mimbres, the Hohokam, the Mogollon, the Sinagua to the south, and the Anasazi to the east and north. Our culture, named a Puebloan culture, is a composite of all these major archaeological cultures.

However, we are unique in one major aspect: We speak the Zunian language, and Zuni is the only place we can speak it for it is a completely unique language. This leads me to believe, strongly, that the A:shiwi not only came in contact with many other different language groups in their travels in search of the Center Place, but also were joined by others during their long journey. Present-day Zuni is a kaleidoscope of different cultural elements from the Southwest and, perhaps, beyond.

But why are the Zunis so unique in language, physical variations, and some material cultural aspects? What happened in about 1350 at Hawikuh? Dr. Davis addresses these and other questions in the following pages.

The mythology of the Melika, the "White People," tells us that we Native Americans came across the Bering Strait, in small groups over a long period of time, perhaps even thirty-five thousand years ago. If this is true, why couldn't others have come across later—or earlier? According to some, the Vikings came to Greenland (or Vinland) many years before Columbus. Artifacts found in archeological sites along the West Coast give hints of earlier travel across the Pacific Ocean. The Polynesians traveled to all of the major Pacific islands long before the time of Columbus; they discovered the Hawaiian island group circa A.D. 200.

The Conquistadors traveled from Spain, to Mexico, to Hawikuh in less than fifty years after Columbus. Then came the "Pilgrim Fathers," in search of a new kingdom, perhaps their very own "Center Place," when they showed up at Plymouth in the "New World." My point is that if we have some knowledge and documentation of all these early voyages from nearly all of the world, how many unknown or undocumented voyages might have occurred?

This brings us to the matter at hand (the topic of this book): What happened about the year A.D. 1350 in the Zuni area? Were people migrating into the area? Was the migration by a party who may have sailed across thousands of miles of open seas in search of their "Center Place"? And, if there was a cultural contact, what material, linguistic, cultural, and physical evidence remains in the 1990s? This book is the first major effort to answer these important questions, made by a person who has courage enough to ask them out loud.

Dr. Nancy Yaw Davis lays the questions before us. It is an anthropological detective story with many tantalizing, intriguing clues. Some A:shiwi will be skeptical, as I once was; others will enjoy it and wonder about the far-flung relationships we have in this world we occupy. This book is a thought-provoking resource for those who wish to learn more about Native cultures and human prehistories.

And can, or will, the academic community respond, or is it going to scoff at the idea of cultural contacts over many hundreds of miles, over open seas, and over a long period of time? Will readers take a serious look at the tribal oral histories and examine and explore to see whether traces of an "intruding" culture are visible in the present-day cultural matrices?

Let us look and see with an open mind and a clear heart. If there is nothing here, at least we will have rattled the cage and possibly caused some rethinking of the subject. And at the very least can open the door and start to unravel some of the questions.

Edmund J. Ladd, Shiwi
Late Curator of Ethnology
Museum of New Mexico
Museum of Indian Arts and Culture
Santa Fe, New Mexico

PREFACE

During the five years I worked on this book, hidden away in my office about a mile from my Alaskan home, terrible things were happening in the larger world. Racism was continuing its large and ugly effects. Ethnic differences were fragmenting our species into bitter, warring groups. Religions whose themes at one level enhanced human compassion, at another level were providing doctrine for murder. The world was becoming a bloody mess and getting worse.

Somehow the Zuni tribe in New Mexico countered all that misery as its people vigorously maintained their unique language and validated their religion with ceremonies and powerful dances. Perhaps I indulge in romanticizing this peaceful tribe in the American Southwest, but there seems to be a wholesome human thread there, uniting many clans at their center of the world, a drawing together of diverse groups with a commitment to be A:shiwi, the people who live in the Pueblo of Zuni. Respecting different origins yet uniting under a common rubric of a shared identity provides the Zuni a quality of humanity with a larger message. Our ancestors, like theirs, have moved and migrated, merged and mixed, many times over in our collective hominid past. If we recognized—indeed if we celebrated—that fact, could we too be more peaceful? Can we humans be more respectful of the rich quality of variations that different peoples of the world bring to our consciousness, to our schools, and to our neighborhoods?

As I venture to present evidence of an unusual migration that occurred seven hundred years ago, I wonder, What broader insights and validation about our shared humanity might emerge?

INTRODUCTION

May 26, 1988, the day I announced my theory with a thousand themes. I was one scared anthropologist as I stood in the tribal chambers and looked across the table at seven distinguished council members of the Pueblo of Zuni, New Mexico. I was there to present my controversial ideas about a connection between the Japanese and the Zuni to the Zuni people themselves.

Introductions were made. To my left and at the head of the long, polished table sat Governor Robert Lewis, and to his left, Lieutenant Governor Pesancio Lasiloo. To the governor's right, Head Councilman Barton Martza. Four of the other five council members were seated along the far side of the table, facing me: Virgil Wyaco, Sr., Angus Mahooty, Rita Enote Lorenzo, and William Tsikewa, Sr. (Edward Beyuka was absent on business that day.) I explained who I was: an anthropologist from Alaska who had stumbled across evidence that gave birth to a startling theory about the Zuni, their famous and much-studied tribe.

The council members were courteous and attentive. I relaxed and began:

> *If I am wrong about what I present today, we can all have a good laugh. At first it may seem quite outrageous.*
>
> *But, if I am even partly right, this is a part of your history. And even if it is only a small part of your history, I believe you should know about it.*

I went on with my presentation outlining my initial discovery in 1960, the subsequent history of surprising confirmations, and the recent invitation I had received to present a paper in San Francisco at a small conference called "World Cultures of Ancient America." But before I could give a public presentation, I explained, I felt I must first inform them of my findings. Even if my hypothesis is ultimately proved wrong.

I handed out a chart outlining similarities between Zuni cosmology and the Japanese version of yin-yang, a complex Chinese system for organizing the world into directions, seasons, colors, and numerous other specific characteristics. We looked at another chart summarizing striking similarities between certain Zuni and Japanese words in categories of environment, kinship, and religion. Next, I reviewed the persistent, unanswered questions concerning the archeology of the region, including changes in settlement patterns suggesting the arrival of a new population in approximately the late thirteenth century A.D. A copy of a 1904 drawing of the Zuni deity Bitsitsi was passed around the table. Cautiously, I pointed out the similarities between the word *Bitsitsi* and *Butsu,* a Japanese word for Buddha.

Next I distributed a table that summarized a comparison in dental morphology, and pointed out that the frequency of certain cusp patterns was more similar between Zuni and Japanese than between Zuni and other Native Americans, suggesting genetic admixture of two distinct populations. Then I reviewed a chart comparing certain blood features that raised questions about their unusual and unexplained frequencies, especially the presence of type B of the ABO system. Further, I discussed studies of skeletal remains from thirteenth-century archeological sites that reveal significant structural differences, also strongly suggesting there were two distinct populations present in the area at that time.

After two hours of presenting the data and entertaining a lively discussion, I summarized my theory: The Zuni of New Mexico are distinct from all other Native American people in language, culture, and biology partly because by the thirteenth century a group of Japanese reached the west coast of North America and migrated eastward in search of the middle of the world, ultimately settling in the Zuni valley. There these pilgrims from the Pacific found it—Itiwanna, the very exact center of the world where they hoped there would be no more earthquakes and no more wars.

Part of this theory is congruent with the Zuni's own oral history. The Zuni's migration stories include detail about other peoples who joined their pilgrimage to this spiritual center, merging their forces and participating in the search. Some migrants from the combined assembly traveled north and went too far east; some branched south and they also went too far east. Eventually, these groups and associated clans turned back and rejoined the people coming to the middle, the very exact middle: Itiwanna.

I believe that the people who came together, who consolidated and settled in six direction-oriented villages at Zuni about A.D. 1350 were unique in many ways then; and that the modern population is still distinctive—Native Americans and Japanese, together, merged into one tribe with a unique language and exceptionally complex cultural and religious systems.

I am stating this theory with greater confidence now than when I spoke about it in 1988 to the council. In the intervening years, I have undertaken substantially more research, including spending the year 1990–91 in the libraries at Stanford University as a visiting scholar and taking a short, validating trip to Japan in 1998.

Additional pieces of the puzzle keep emerging unexpectedly. The Zuni many-petalled "sacred rosette," for example, appears remarkably analogous to the Japanese national imperial symbol, the chrysanthemum; the motifs also share similar meanings related to water, to the center, and to Buddhism. The sudden appearance of thirteenth-century glaze on pottery first found just west of Zuni has not yet been explained. Zuni ties to the abandoned Anasazi civilization to the north appear strong, suggesting, as we will see, even earlier Asian influences. New research questions and discussions are now linking changed settlement patterns, population sizes, irrigation technology, and ceremonial centers, sharpening and expanding vision about past events in the

Southwest area. The whole region is rich in detailed, descriptive information—and riddled with unanswered questions, ready for new discussions and alternative explanations.

The findings reported here are far from complete, but I have brought the thesis as far as I can for now. Some parts of it may be disproved, but that does not dismay me. We need new perspectives, new intellectual tools for comparative analysis of human cultures over space and through time, new ways of thinking, new paradigms.

The central challenge here is the larger picture. The accumulation of specific facts from many sources converging to build this one theory invites us to think new thoughts, question old assumptions, and take our understandings about our shared humanity a little further. It was this spirit of opening a discussion that led to my first meeting with the Zuni Council, and now to this book.

At that first meeting in 1988, rather than the hostility, defiance, and dismissal that I had feared, the elected representatives of Zuni indicated a keen intellectual interest in my theory. They knew the Zuni were different from all other Native Americans, including the other nineteen Pueblo tribes in New Mexico and Arizona. They knew no other tribe spoke a language even remotely similar to theirs. They knew their religion continues to be a powerful integrator of their society, and includes great respect for the ancestors; many shrines mark stops and events on their long odyssey to Itiwanna. But the council had not heard previously of this possible explanation—that Japanese genes, ideas, and words had been incorporated into their tribe long ago.

At the end of the session, I handed out draft copies of my paper, "The Zuni Enigma," which was eventually published by the New England Antiquities Research Association in 1992.[1]

Governor Lewis thanked me for coming and closed the meeting. The others quietly, kindly, nodded to me as they filed out of the council chambers.

As I gathered up my materials, Councilwoman Rita Enote Lorenzo lingered, and invited me to the ceremonial dances that night. Pleasantly surprised, and certainly relieved, I accepted. Thus began my own pilgrimage to the "center of the world." Itiwanna. May 26, 1988.

So the first meeting with the Zuni Council was memorable in many ways. I felt my data and theory had been received with great dignity and honest curiosity. (Later I learned four council members were veterans of World War II; two had been prisoners of the Japanese.)

I have not asked the Zuni to *believe* what I set forth here, nor have I ever requested their approval, or "blessing" of the theory. They know who they are and where they came from, as Ed Ladd clearly summarizes in his foreword. The Zuni account of their origins is sacred, detailed, and complex, providing a spiritual identity as powerful for them as the Bible and the Koran do for others. I do not wish this book to challenge Zuni knowledge of who they are; rather I simply add a new dimension to be considered.

Neither have I asked Zuni permission to undertake original research in their community, for the Zuni already are among the most-studied people on earth. My findings are primarily based on a close study of already published documents.

Ultimately, far more important than this theory about Native American and Japanese pilgrims in the thirteenth century A.D. is coming to grips with new ideas about human history and society now. Grappling with the premise of the Zuni enigma, raising questions about migrations and human mobility across lands and seas, and critically assessing the evidence may help usher in a more peaceful twenty-first century. It is my hope that this book will take us beyond the divisive constraints of ethnicity and national boundaries and will encourage us to ponder our shared humanity across our common planet.

THE DISCOVERY

It happened on a dark, rainy night in Seattle in early March 1960. It was a fluke—the accidental juxtaposition of ideas. I was reading *The Mind of East Asia*[2] by Lily Abegg for a graduate course on Japanese personality and culture at the University of Washington. The charts on pages 50 and 51 first looked vaguely familiar, then strikingly like the chart I had prepared for Robert Redfield's course in social anthropology at the University of Chicago in 1957. The charts in the book were based on the ancient

Chinese system of yin-yang; the chart I had prepared was based on the religious system of the Zuni tribe of New Mexico. Both involved directions, colors, characteristics, and elements centered around the concept of the middle. One was a derivative of Taoism and the other, a Southwest Native American Indian cosmology.

As I compared and contemplated the tables and charts that night, there was absolutely no question about it: They were remarkably similar. I had been trained to assume the most likely explanation was simply independent innovation of the two systems. But—*that* similar? The next day, naive but curious, I checked out a Zuni text on religion, and much to my surprise, found three Japanese words within a few pages. Soon I had twenty Japanese-looking words, and knew I had something really hot.

By August 1961 I had written what I thought was a fine draft for my M.A. thesis on the Zuni-Japanese word comparisons, based on an analysis of 625 words. Admittedly my qualifications were modest: one course in historical linguistics and a Japanese vocabulary of about five hundred words at the time of the original discovery. The paper, however, mustered no support at the University of Chicago's anthropology department. "Go back to Alaska and do something *respectable,*" I was advised. Likewise, the chair of my doctorate committee at the University of Washington firmly counseled, "Shelve it."

And I did, sort of. Teaching, family, research, and writing in Alaska kept me busy over the years, but that initial surprise continued to intrigue me. Periodically I checked card catalogs and now computers in various libraries, and tried to keep up on the voluminous publications on the Zuni. Now, nearly forty years later, the idea still surprises me with new pieces of evidence and additional hunches to pursue.

But one mind can only handle the fun of this new idea up to a point. Now it is time to share the theory, present the data, provide the challenge, and cheerfully expose the need for new paradigms to discuss and process evidence of transoceanic influences during prehistoric times. This is a small test case. The intent of this book is to initiate discussion in a challenging way to engage many minds, additional ideas, and alternative explanations.

THE ZUNI
ENIGMA

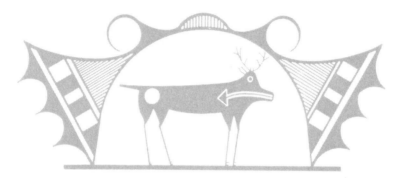

CHAPTER ONE

PORTRAIT
OF A
PUEBLO

Centered in a broad, arid but colorful valley between mesas in northern New Mexico lies what the A:shiwi people call Iti-wanna, "the Middle of the World," place of the Pueblo of Zuni.

Colors are everywhere: reds and whites in horizontal stripes of sandstone, layered into high, flat mesas, unevenly exposed by millennia of erosion. Various intensities of green in pine trees, cedars, piñons, and junipers splay along the thinly forested mountain sides. In autumn the yellow of blooming rabbit brush pops out in patches across the broad valley. The blues and whites of the sky and clouds cut sharply through the clarity of six thousand feet above sea level. Brilliant colors often gently merge, consolidate, and separate into rainbows, arched over the mesas. All seem magnified further during startling sunrises and lingering sunsets.

The Native Americans who live here associate colors with directions: yellow for North, blue for West, red for South, white for East, black for nadir (below), and many colored for zenith (above) and for middle. These colors and directions are also linked with seasons, elements, animals, trees, birds, corn, beans, clans, and religious groups. Directions especially provide an organizational theme to life, centered and balanced at the middle, Itiwanna.[1]

The black and white strip of asphalt of Highway 53 cuts across Zuni reservation lands leading through the Pueblo of Zuni, located near the Continental Divide that runs north and south along North America's mountainous backbone. The reservation, established in 1877, comprises 408,404 acres (638 square miles) in the northwestern edge of the state of New Mexico, with an overlap into eastern Arizona (see Map 1).

The Zuni who live here are unlike other North American Indians, unique even among the other nineteen Pueblo tribes of the Southwest. But the differences are deep, not apparent in the physical appearance of the pueblo. Indeed, on a leisurely drive through town, Zuni appears unremarkable: modern houses, mod-

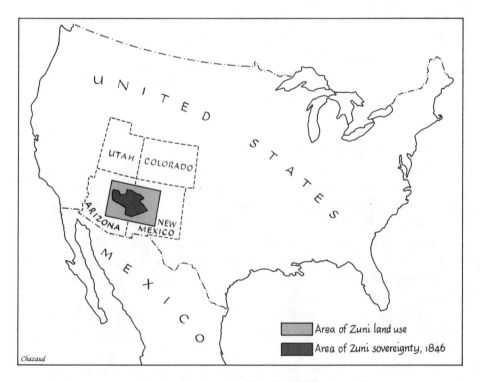

Map 1. *Zuni Traditional Use area.*

ern schools, modern offices and businesses. New trucks and cars reflect successful participation in America's market economy.

The Zuni pueblo, in fact, seems to have all the modern accoutrements of a Native American Indian tribe embedded in America: an airstrip, post office, bank, telephones, faxes, and television; three restaurants, three retail stores, and three gas stations; a museum, a church, public and private schools, a biweekly newspaper,[2] and a branch of the University of New Mexico. Two omissions stand out: There are no liquor stores and no bingo parlors or casinos.

The Zuni suburb called Blackrock includes neat, small government-built houses arranged in rows with equally small yards. A public health hospital,[3] radio station,[4] furniture store, and archeology laboratory[5] are also located here, about two miles from the main town.

But in the older part of Zuni, clustered stone houses and adobe beehive-shaped ovens with wood stacked alongside suggest something of the pueblo's unique character. When the Spaniards explored the American Southwest during the mid-sixteenth century, they reported as many as ninety pueblos in the area.[6] Now there are twenty and Zuni is the largest.

The Tribal Census Office reported 9,448 persons living in Zuni as of December 31, 1994. Of those, 8,740 (about 93%) were enrolled in the Zuni Tribe; other Indians, including Zuni not yet enrolled, numbered 252 (3%), and non-Indian residents, 456 (5%). These figures reflect a tremendous population increase from the low figure of 1,640 residents reported for 1910. The tribal population more than doubled between 1960 and 1994—from 4,190 to 8,740—largely due to improved health care, a high birthrate, and the preference of Zuni to stay where they are.

All generations speak the native language, Zunian. Year-round ceremonies validate strong religious continuity with deep roots in a pre-European past; a separate religious language is used by men during rituals and in their ceremonial chambers, called *kiwitse.* English is also spoken fluently. Overall the community is relatively prosperous. Two main sources of income are wage labor through federal and tribal jobs and the making and marketing of quality jewelry, fetishes, and other arts.[7]

The people of Zuni are handsome, with healthy dark skin and

shiny straight black hair. The height of the men varies more than
the women's, but generally the population is short, averaging about
five feet, four inches.[8] Like other Native American populations,
some Zuni have the "thrifty gene," which was biologically adaptive
in the past, making it easier for the body to store food for lean
times. Now, however, that gene is linked to weight problems and a
high incidence of diabetes. Some Zuni also suffer from a kidney disease (mesangiopathic glomerulonephritis) called locally the "Zuni
disease," one unusually common in Japan. The Zuni are physi-
cally distinctive in many ways—ways that can be partly explained
by considering the admixture of two groups, one Native American
and the other Japanese. And so we begin our exploration.

To visitors familiar with other Native American groups, the
Zuni appear shorter and less Caucasian in mixture than other Indian populations. To people who have traveled abroad, some Zuni
resemble the Japanese, especially those from the Kyoto region, or
relocated Tibetans. Old pictures of the Zuni community, like other
pueblos in the Southwest from the late nineteenth century, depict
Tibetan-like houses in recessed clusters of apartments, many sto-
ried, with wooden ladders connecting the rooftops (see Figure 2).
Zuni women appeared in dresses with a manta at an angle across
the right shoulder—also very much like the Tibetan style. Now, of
course, people wear ordinary Western clothes, except for ceremonial occasions when traditional clothing and many fine items of
turquoise, coral, and silver jewelry are worn (see Figures 4 and 5).

The kinship system seems linked with everything in Zuni society. The Zuni have so many relatives in so many different categories—all in the same town—that they have successfully and
perhaps permanently confused anthropologists. In all, four systems weave people and their relationships into a complex fabric
of social and religious ties: clans, kiva groups, curing societies,
and priesthoods.[9]

First, numerous named relatives are organized in fourteen matrilineal clans. Additional relationships with named "relatives" include persons in religious organizations—six kiva groups, eight
curing societies, and sixteen priesthoods, each with associated responsibilities and ceremonies that occur year-round.

Every Zuni belongs to his or her mother's clan, the primary
kinship affiliation for life. In addition, a Zuni identifies as a "child"

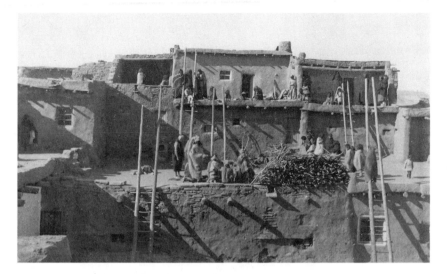

Figure 2. *Zuni pueblo, circa 1895*

Figure 3. *Zuni women by the river, 1903*

Figure 4. *Zuni Olla maidens at the Gallup Indian ceremonials, circa 1972*

Figure 5. *Zuni traditional dress in the modern day.*
Thelma Sheche and granddaughters

of the father's side, which is a secondary relationship but important, especially for males in their religious activities. Membership in the kiva groups—one for each of the six directions—is separate from and cuts across clan membership: All males belong to one of the six kiva groups; no women do. The eight curing or medicine societies are primarily organizations for men who have had a serious illness, were treated, and recovered, thus automatically becoming a member of the medicine society that was successful in healing. A few women are also incorporated through special medical treatment and subsequent survival.

The sixteen priesthoods are exclusively for men and are directed by the rainmakers, called *uwanami*. The highest priest is called Pekwin and is believed to derive his power directly from the Sun Father. In Chapter 9 we will look at the similarities of Zuni religion to Shinto, especially in association with ancestors and shrines. Zuni priests are considered very holy men who must not quarrel and who must remain aloof from worldly affairs, fast often, and go on frequent retreats.

A Zuni man is almost continually preparing for the next religious event, an expensive and time-consuming activity because there are so many ceremonies and dances throughout the year. Hundreds of masks must be maintained and religious regalia repaired in time. The women's participation includes elaborate food preparation,[10] provision of financial assistance and gifts for full-time priests and their helpers, and quietly witnessing the rituals and dances. With few exceptions, women do not dance, nor do they prepare prayer sticks or attend events in the *kiwitse*, which are exclusively men's ceremonial chambers.

In addition to many religious activities, Zuni residents celebrate national holidays such as Memorial Day and enjoy modern sports, especially basketball and volleyball. The A:shiwi Running Club annually takes this traditional sport beyond reservation boundaries to the Boston Marathon, where in 1994 Zuni runners placed in the top 10%.

The Zuni Council manages about sixty programs in areas of administration, health, education,[11] employment, human services, public safety, and law enforcement. The Zuni Cultural Resource Enterprise and Heritage and Historical Preservation Office are also part of its direct responsibility.[12]

Perhaps the most important thing to know about the modern Pueblo of Zuni is the tribe's sense of privacy and religious ceremonial continuity. This does not mean the people are hostile or angry. Zuni sense of the dignity of their "Place" is subtle, refined, and civilized. There are no hotels for overnight stays nearer than Gallup, thirty-five miles away. At selected times of the year, people outside of the pueblo may quietly, respectfully, watch dances from the rooftops encircling the plaza, but without cameras and without pencils. Until recently, the elaborate New Year "Shalako" ceremonies held in early December were also open to the public. But Zuni is nonetheless a very private place and in all likelihood will stay that way.[13]

ZUNI AND THE OTHER PUEBLOS

Questions persist about the relationship of Zuni to other Native Americans, including other Pueblo Indians. How can their distinctive characteristics be understood and explained? Why does Zunian have no known affiliation to any other language in North America? How did the blood allele B get to this pueblo—and not others? Why is the religious system so highly integrated and complex? The Zuni culture is one of the ten most-documented cultures of the world, yet these and numerous other questions persist.[14] Indeed, the complexities of the social, religious, and political system have "occupied scholars and defied interpretation by them since the 1890s," writes Edmund Ladd, a Zunian scholar.[15]

Of course, other Pueblo groups are also unique; together the pueblos comprise a separate cultural area, in many ways puzzling. As Alfonso Ortiz, a Tewa Pueblo Indian and professor of anthropology at the University of New Mexico, noted, "It is essential to stress that the various peoples of the Southwest fashioned unique cultural syntheses from elements of diverse provenance."[16]

Synthesis is a good word to denote a creative ongoing process for all human cultures, but some groups seem to achieve it more easily than others, and seem more responsive to the flexibility required. This capacity for adaptation may be a marker for the whole Pueblo region (see Map 2), not just Zuni. The twenty contemporary Pueblo groups of the American Southwest stand out as distinctive clusters of communities derived from at least seven different language groups, sharing many characteristics, but continuing individual local traditions in pottery, jewelry, and ceremonies. Unlike the nomadic Navaho and Apache who arrived in

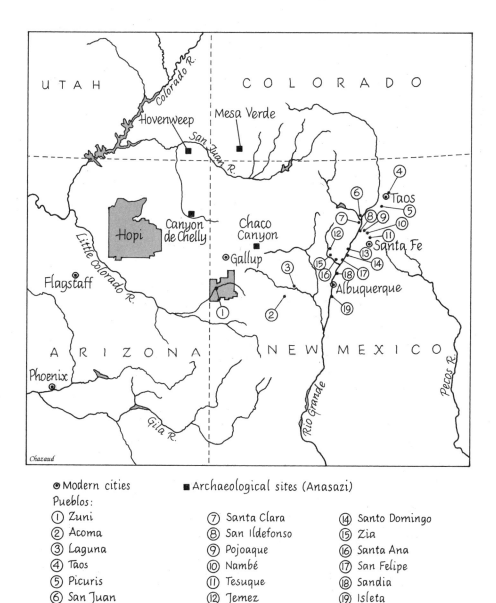

⊙ Modern cities   ■ Archaeological sites (Anasazi)
Pueblos:

① Zuni
② Acoma
③ Laguna
④ Taos
⑤ Picuris
⑥ San Juan

⑦ Santa Clara
⑧ San Ildefonso
⑨ Pojoaque
⑩ Nambé
⑪ Tesuque
⑫ Jemez
⑬ Cochita

⑭ Santo Domingo
⑮ Zia
⑯ Santa Ana
⑰ San Felipe
⑱ Sandia
⑲ Isleta

Map 2. *Pueblo region of the American Southwest.*

the area much later—perhaps as late as the sixteenth century—
and who live in households quite separated from each other,
Pueblo peoples live in consolidated villages and have long been
agriculturalists. In Chapter 9, I speculate on the possibility that the
Pueblo groups as a whole share a common link to the Anasazi civilization, which may have incorporated influences from Asia at an
earlier time than the one considered here for the Zuni.

ZUNI PREHISTORY

The archeological record in the Zuni area indicates that a
flurry of new pueblos was built between 1250 and 1300, but the
Pueblo of Zuni in its exact present location may be quite new—
perhaps as recent as A.D. 1692, after the Pueblo rebellion against
Spanish and Catholic intrusion. The final selection of the exact
middle at Halona on the north side of the sluggish Little Colorado
River was possibly the consolidation of the six pueblos first reported by the Spanish in 1540. A brief reconstruction of the sequence of earlier occupations and influences documented by the
archeological record provides a framework for later discussion of
evidence of the proposed late-thirteenth-century arrival of a pilgrimage from the "ocean of the sunset world."

Clearly, the people who became the Zuni were not the first, or
the only people to come to the Southwest. Between about 9500
and 5000 B.C., the general area was sparsely occupied by a population called Paleo-Indians. The famous fluted stone points—distinguished by deep central grooves—from the Clovis and Folsom
sites in New Mexico are considered representative of one of the
earliest populations in all the Americas. Although details about the
Paleo-Indian period remain murky, the Clovis and Folsom finds
indicate very early occupation in the New Mexico area.

During the next period, called Archaic, from 5000 B.C. to about
A.D. 1, the population of the Southwest increased; hunting and
gathering remained the main way of life. Then, midway through
the Archaic period, about 2000 B.C., corn, and later beans and
squash, were introduced from Mesoamerica, supplementing the
diet and supporting a growing population.

Distinctive semisubterranean structures called pithouses began to appear about A.D. 200, a time when pottery was added to the cultural inventory. The people who settled in the drainage of the Zuni River about A.D. 650 became part of the developing Anasazi cultural tradition to the north.

Archeological sites in the Zuni area indicate continued links with Anasazi communities during Pueblo I, between A.D. 700 and 900. They shared, for example, similar pithouses with granaries and grinding stones. The existence of shells from the Pacific Ocean and the Gulf of California implies a trade network.

After A.D. 900, a new kind of building masonry was adopted; aboveground houses replaced pithouses, and it has been suggested that pithouses changed from dwellings to ceremonial chambers, now called *kivas*.[17] Thousands of small sites associated with distinctive kinds of pottery are identified for this period, called Pueblo II.

After A.D. 1150, the people in the Zuni region shifted affiliation away from Chaco, the major Anasazi ceremonial center in the north.[18] As that civilization mysteriously collapsed, the people in the Zuni River drainage seemed to link more closely with people called Mogollon to the west and south in Arizona. This period, called Pueblo III, continued to be a time of many small pueblos.

Then, between about A.D. 1250 and 1400, a major change in settlement patterns occurred in the Zuni area. People began to aggregate into large, well-planned, plaza-oriented communities ranging in size from 250 to 1,200 rooms.[19] The consolidation of people is associated with intensified agricultural techniques, including irrigated terraces. Sophisticated water control supported the more concentrated populations. During this period, called Post-Chacoan, most communities elsewhere in the Southwest were abandoned, yet the population around Zuni grew; ruins of previous pueblos abound in the vicinity. What happened at Zuni?

This period, the late thirteenth century A.D., is proposed as the probable time for the arrival of Japanese pilgrims—with new language, religion, and genes. If a freeze-frame could capture that event, I believe it would reveal an entourage of people from many backgrounds arriving and deciding this was the exact middle of the universe, and then commencing to build large pueblos, drawing in straggling survivors of the Anasazi civilization.

Of course we have neither a photograph nor a written record of what happened and why such a consolidation occurred. But this is an unusually thoroughly studied area: Sophisticated tree-ring dating, dendrochronology, provides a rich record of when structures were built, and the timing, severity, and length of droughts; skeletal remains indicate significant physical changes in the population; measurements and excavations of ruins reveal major changes in settlement patterns; glaze on pottery suddenly appears.

The archeologists state the present Zuni area was probably founded about A.D. 1350[20] and it is one of six pueblos reported by the Spanish when they arrived nearly two hundred years later.

THE SPANISH PERIOD: 1539 TO 1846

The first Europeans to arrive in Zuni territory were Spaniards in search of "Seven Cities of Cibola" reported to be rich in gold and silver. The first, in 1539, was a black scout from Morocco named Esteban, who came in advance of Fray Marcos de Niza. Esteban offended the Zuni and was promptly killed; Fray Marcos hastened a quick retreat without actually entering any of the villages. The next year an expedition with several hundred armored horsemen under the command of Francisco Vásquez de Coronado explored the Zuni area and other pueblos, but withdrew in frustration in 1541 because no gold had been discovered. Six major villages were occupied at that time (see Map 3).

Four decades later, Spaniards returned to establish mission stations among the Pueblo groups. The first Zuni mission was begun in 1629 at Hawikuh, one of the six named Zuni communities, and another church was added at Halona in 1632. In that same year two priests were killed by the Zunis of Hawikuh, temporarily halting Catholic efforts. Missionary activity may have begun again about 1660 at Hawikuh, but this time it was the Apaches who killed a priest.

By 1680, Spanish exploitation, including attacks on religion, slavery, floggings, and hangings, became intolerable, and the Zuni joined the Pueblo revolt led by Popé, a Tewa Indian from the pueblo of San Juan to the east. All the pueblos joined the effort; missions were burned, priests killed, and the Spaniards expelled.[21]

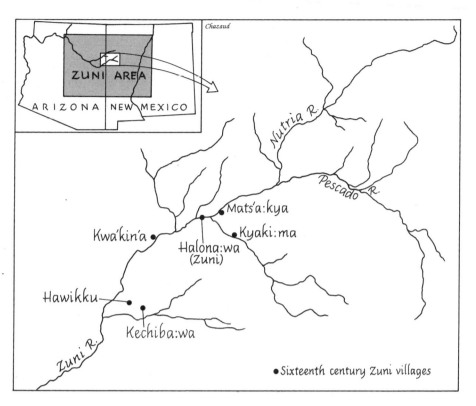

Map 3. *Early historic period: six Zuni settlements.*

Figure 6. *Dowa Yalanne: Corn Mountain*

The Zuni, who had occupied six villages until 1680, retreated to the top of Corn Mountain (Dowa Yalanne) during the revolt (see Figure 6). By 1692, when Spanish control was reestablished, the Zuni had consolidated into one community at Itiwanna, the true middle, also called Halona, the present location. They had been especially resistant to Spanish efforts at Christianization and kept their religion viable throughout this tumultuous period.

Information is sketchy about mission activity after 1703, but we know that three Spanish exiles were killed during this early period by the Zuni.[22] When Mexico threw off Spanish control in 1821, all the Spanish troops and missions packed up and left. Then the pueblos became exposed to new risks: raids by Navahos, Apaches, Comanches, and other Plains tribes.[23]

THE AMERICAN PERIOD: 1846 TO 1950

The Zuni had maintained their self-sufficiency and religious continuity for three centuries, despite Spanish, Navaho, and Mexican intrusion; very few converted to Catholicism. When the American period began in 1846, after the Mexican War, new boundaries were drawn; New Mexico became a territory of the United States in 1848. The next hundred years brought about rapid cultural changes and challenges as external contact intensified and accelerated.

Beginning in the mid-nineteenth century, a stream of expeditions, missionaries, ethnologists, traders, and government officials arrived. Although few stayed, the disruption was significant: Epidemics lowered the population, and deep political factions developed over religious matters.

Until 1934, the Zuni political system was directed by the religious leaders—rain priests, kiva officials, and the sun chief, who appointed the governor (see Figure 7). But the federal Indian Reorganization Act called for an elected council. A new tribal council was duly elected and installed by the established council of priests, and today religious leaders continue to be influential in secular decisions and serve as special advisors.

World War II became a turning point in Zuni history, when over two hundred Zuni men left the pueblo for various military

Figure 7. *Zuni governor, 1925*

services. When they returned as veterans, they had a difficult time reentering the pueblo's social and religious structure, but by 1950 their influence in politics was shaping new developments in the economy, education, and community services. Women in this matrilineal but conservative tribe received the right to vote in 1965.

AMERICAN SOUTHWEST–JAPAN PARALLELS

Since the major theory here is that Japanese influence was one of many contacts in the Southwest, a brief comparative chronology will help align events in the two regions (see Table 1). Just as the Zuni area has a history of a flow of different peoples and ideas arriving from various directions and sources, the peoples and cultures of Japan also experienced a flow of influences introduced from Korea, China, and Southeast Asia.

Japan, like the American Southwest, has a prehistory that includes a paleolithic period, pottery, pithouses, agriculture, irrigation, and new peoples and influences arriving from the south and west. The long Jomon period (10,000–300 B.C.) yields evidence of

TABLE 1
COMPARATIVE TIME LINE: SOUTHWEST AND JAPAN

SOUTHWEST U.S.		JAPAN	
		Paleolithic ca.	150,000 B.C.
Paleo-Indian (Clovis/Folsom)	9500 B.C.	Pre-Jomon (Pre-ceramic) Jomon	10,000–300 B.C.
Archaic	5000 B.C.		
		Yayoi	300 B.C–A.D. 300
Basketmaker	100 B.C.–A.D. 750		
		Kofun (Yamato)	A.D. 300–710
Pueblo I (Anasazi)	A.D. 700–900	Nara	A.D. 710–793
		Heian	A.D. 794–1184
Pueblo II	A.D. 900–1100		
Pueblo III	A.D. 1100–1300	Kamakura	A.D. 1185–1333
Pilgrims to Zuni			
Pueblo IV	1350–1600	Muromachi	1338–1573
Spaniards to Zuni	1540	Portuguese to Japan	1542
		Tokugawa (Edo) (Isolation Period)	1600–1868
Pueblo revolt	1680		
Mexican revolt	1821		
New Mexico territory	1848		
Zuni Reservation	1877	Meiji	1868–1912
		Taishō	1912–1926
Indian Reorganization Act	1934	Shōwa	1926–
World War II 1941–1945			

the earliest pottery in the world, followed by the Yayoi period (300 B.C.–A.D. 300), during which a new population from the west brought rice agriculture, irrigation, and bronze to the islands. Next, another group arrived with the horse, initiating the Kofun (Yamato) period (A.D. 300–710) and the beginning formation of the state. Chinese influences came in small doses for a while, and then in intensive blocks during the Nara period (710–793). The formation of the state of Japan continued through the Heian period (794–1184), about the same time that the Anasazi civilization developed in the American Southwest. The Heian period ended with a military takeover about the time the Anasazi civilization collapsed.

Just as southwestern North America experienced an influx of ideas from Mesoamerica, including the introduction of corn, squash, and beans, so Japan was introduced to rice and terracing from sources to its own south and west. And, in a further parallel, Japan's history was linked periodically with China's, just as the Southwest was sporadically in touch with successive civilizations in Mesoamerica. These parallels are mentioned simply to provide a framework for larger considerations of shared events common throughout the world: Innovations and people have forever moved about in prehistoric times as well as today.

Documented historic events also reveal similarities. In 1542, three years after the Spaniards began exploring the Southwest, the Portuguese reached Japan. Catholic missionary efforts began in 1549 with St. Francis Xavier, but were prohibited by 1629. The emperor of Japan declared an edict in 1635, forbidding foreign influences and establishing a period of isolation that lasted until 1868, the end of the Tokugawa period and the beginning of the Meiji.

Like the Japanese, and of course many other cultures of the world, the Zuni varied in their response to outside influences: sometimes taking in new people and ideas, as described in their migration story in the next chapter, and at other times shutting them out, which is what they did to the Spanish and the Navaho. The Japanese first accepted the Portuguese and the Catholics in the sixteenth century, then excluded them in the seventeenth century. Japan was by size and by isolation in a stronger position than Zuni to impose the edict of 1635 to keep foreigners out of Japan. But the Zuni tried through their participation in the 1680 revolt, and have managed ever since to maintain their religion (see Figure 8).

Shinto leadership in Japan first confronted China and Buddhism in the sixth to eighth centuries. Sometimes the Chinese

Figure 8. *A Zuni celebration called a "war victory dance," 1873*

embassies won converts and the Japanese sent nobility to be educated and to study Buddhism in China, sometimes going as far away as Tibet; at other times local dynasties fought back and reasserted their power. In Japan, this history of relationships with others is partly documented in written records, set down in a combination of Chinese characters called *kanji* and two systems of symbols, *hiragana* and *katakana,* derived from Chinese characters but applied in a uniquely Japanese manner.[24] Zuni history depended on memorized narrative mastered for accuracy and repeated periodically throughout the year.

Thus, the colorful contemporary Pueblo of Zuni is of composite origin; different peoples arrived at various times over a long period. The Native Americans who live there now account for their diverse clans by a long migration story about their search for the middle of the world. I believe Japanese pilgrims provided one source among many that shaped the unusual characteristics of Zuni.

CHAPTER TWO

SEARCH FOR THE MIDDLE OF THE WORLD

Archeological evidence indicates that the Zuni pueblos were settled about A.D. 1350.[1] The Zuni migration story gives evidence of an ancestry of more than one people gathered there: those who came from the west—the "ocean of the sunset world"[2]—in search of the middle of the world; the people encountered along the way who joined the pilgrimage; and residents already living in the Southwest when they arrived. The story is richly documented by a series of publications beginning in 1896 and continues to be narrated in great detail by Zuni priests.

The idea of oceans clearly survives in the modern oral traditions in Zuni,[3] and it is knowledge based on prehistoric links to the coast. Precious shells from the Pacific Ocean are found in archeological sites in the Southwest dating from A.D. 600 and fragments of ancient pottery from the Southwest appear in southern California sites, evidence suggesting that Native Americans moved great distances during prehistoric times, taking goods and ideas with them.

The basic themes of the Zuni search for the middle of the world are of special interest here because they continue to be retold and thus revalidated each year, identifying hundreds of stopping places, difficulties encountered, disasters survived, separations necessary, clans reunited, and the final arrival at Itiwanna.

Fortunately, many printed versions of the migration are available.[4] One prevalent theme in all renditions of Zuni creation stories, after emergence from a fourth level within Mother Earth, is the search for the very center of the world, a place where there would be no more earthquakes and no more war. At Zuni, the true center was eventually found. As the Zunis stated in their book *The Zunis: Self-portrayals by the Zuni People,* "To this day, there still rests in the heart of the village under a building, a rock that is the very place recorded as the middle place."[5.]

T. J. Ferguson, E. Richard Hart, and their colleagues with Zuni elders began documenting Zuni land uses in the 1970s. This led to a detailed atlas of Zuni knowledge published in 1985, which lists a few of the hundreds of stopping places. Of 234 documented land sites that have special uses and meaning, 139 have religious significance, often directly related to the migration story, many marked by shrines and others by memory.[6] From this work we learn that each of the religious groups continues a version of the origin account, so that there are many accounts, not just one; each summarizes tribal history and elaborates different aspects of the shared knowledge.[7]

Map 4 provides a reconstruction of a composite account and names a few of the springs and other places where the people stopped as they moved eastward, searching for the exact center. Some Zuni now consider the origin and migration accounts more symbolic than historical fact. Perhaps some details are being lost with time, and the complexity of the various versions is too difficult to reconcile. But the continuity of the general account validates its significance to the Zuni people today, and it is this continuity and the detail of the chronicles that provide a framework for the questions we are asking about the Zuni enigma. This is Zuni history, similar in significance to them as the Old Testament is to the Judeo-Christian tradition.[8]

The complexity of the story, the diversity of sources, and the recognition that many versions are narrated led me to select a forty-page section in the oldest published version, "Outlines of

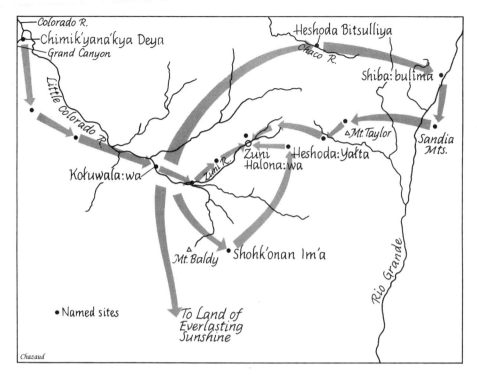

Map 4. *Direction of Zuni migrations.*

Zuni Creation Myths" written by Frank H. Cushing. Cushing was the first ethnologist to visit Zuni, shortly after the reservation was established in 1877. He arrived in 1879 and stayed more than four years. During that time he learned to speak the language and was initiated into the Bow Priesthood, the highest-ranking priesthood. The Bow Priests led the war parties; membership was earned through killing an enemy.[9] These seasoned soldiers also guarded public rituals and enforced the decrees of the council of priests who directed the migration from the west to Zuni. Although Cushing's work was followed by three generations of anthropologists, and is unquestionably controversial,[10] his published account remains the earliest and the most elaborate and detailed. Here is a shortened version of it.[11]

THE MIGRATION

The people who became the Zuni made a great pilgrimage from the ocean of the sunset world to the true center, Itiwanna.

When the world was still young, unripe, soft, dark, and violent, earthquakes were frequent and the Zuni people became wanderers, looking for a stable place. Led by Twin War Gods, they sought the middle of the world under the pathway of the Sun, always moving in the direction of the east.

The first stopping place was named K'eyatiwankwi, Place of upturning, or elevation. The people were still moist, and the world was not yet stable. Here, the Twin War Gods met with the Sun Father and established their relationship: the younger brother to the right and the elder to the left.[12] They were instructed by the Sun Father to cause another earthquake, hoping that the earth would subsequently become safer and more stable.

As a result of this earthquake, the major contours of the world were made.[13] But the earth still trembled and so the people moved on.

Next, the people stayed at Tésak'ya Yäla, Place of nude mountains.[14] But the world rumbled again, and the Twin War Gods led the people into a country and place called Támëlan K'yaiyawan, a place where tree boles stand in the midst of the water.[15] Here they met people already in residence, and from them learned "much of ways in war." (This episode is the first of several that refer to encounters with Native Americans met en route.)

The pilgrims thought they had reached the middle, and so they stopped and built homes. The population increased, but the "earth groaned," and again the conches "sounded warning" and many died in their houses. The Twin War Gods called the people to leave yet again.

Now they had even more people as they moved eastward to Shipololon K'yaia, "Steam mist in the midst of the waters," which may have been a hot springs.[16] Here they encountered yet another tribe, living in "a great assemblage of houses scattered over the hills before them"—the People of Seed. This encounter with a Native American tribe includes a religious motif: The new arrivals, the pilgrims from the west, won over the People of Seed "by wise and peaceful acts rather than by war."

Next, the entourage camped on the borders of a plain "in the midst of cedars . . . and under the shade of hemlocks," and built houses there with the People of Seed. Although no specific times are provided for the stays or length of the moves, some versions of the story suggest four days to four years at each stop. Relatively short stays in each location are also suggested by the numerous archeological sites indicating brief occupations.

From the People of Dew, a second group of Native Americans, the pilgrims learned about planting corn[17] and added a new deity: the flute-playing God of Dew, Paiyatuma.

By then some genetic admixture must have occurred; as the story relates: "Their kin were mingled; thus, their children were one people."[18]

Peace and prosperity did not last at Shipololon K'yaia either. Just when they had almost forgotten about seeking the middle, another earthquake struck. And, the shells sounded warning (see Figure 9).[19]

Hence, many people gathered for the journey, walking east, but they were tired of traveling; they had no horses or wheeled vehicles. So a decision was made to send scouts out ahead to assess the best route to follow in their search for the middle. The leader at this point of the migration was the priest Kawimosa,[20] who is

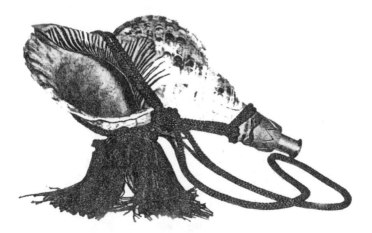

Figure 9. *Conch shell trumpet, Japan*

also credited with the innovation of the sacred dance or drama called *Kaka*.

Kawimosa first sent his eldest son, Kyaklu, to the north. The pilgrims waited for his return. When he did not reappear, Kawimosa sent his next two sons (Anahohoatchi[21]) to the south. They did not return either. Finally, he sent his youngest son, Siweluhsiwa, and his daughter, Siwuluhsitsa, eastward, in search of the best route.

Next, a dramatic story about the incestuous union of this brother and sister unfolds.[22] Their nine children, each with individual characteristics, become the Koyemshi or Mudheads (clowns), who continue important roles in contemporary Zuni ceremonies. Their grotesque features are reminders of what can happen in incestuous relationships (see Figure 10).

After dispersal of Kawimosa's four sons and one daughter to search for the best route to the middle, another earthquake occurred, and the Twin War Gods and their warriors summoned the tribes to journey eastward again. By then, their numbers had grown so great, a three-way split of the entourage was necessary: to the north, south, and east. All three segments took some members from each clan so that the whole group would be represented in each division. The people separated and continued the search, coming together periodically.

Next on their journey, they came to the great divided mountain of the Káyemäshi. The Bear People (clan from the north) were the first to approach, and discovered a broad, murky river separating them from the mountains to the east.[23]

This great body of water may be the Colorado, the largest river intercepting the pilgrims' west-to-east path. Up to this point, the rivers flowed toward the Pacific Ocean.

Tragedy occurred when the people tried to cross: Children were lost and the women did not want to go on. (It is a dramatic story, when the "little ones sank," and the mothers cried for them on the far shore of the river. The Zuni believe those children went to the Lake of the Dead. This event links water creatures such as the frog, turtle, and tadpole to clans, to designs, and to traditions of Zunis today.[24])

Others attempted to ford the river, but turned back. Some clans fled to the south along the bank in search of a better place to cross.

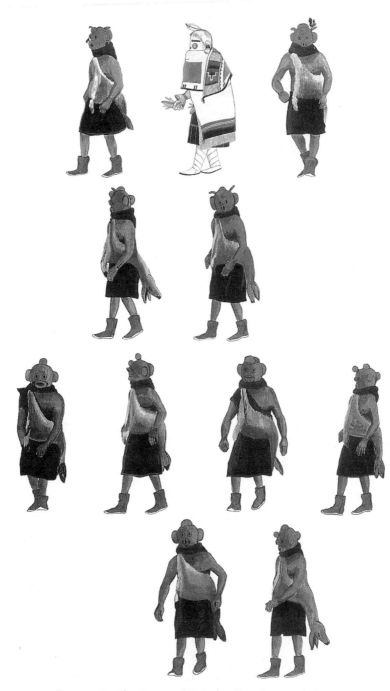

Figure 10. *The Koyemshi or Mudheads. Siwuluhsiwa,*
Siwuluhtsitsa, and their nine children

They did not return, nor did they rejoin their relatives on the other side of the river later.

Some women who were stranded on the west side of the river did not want to continue going east for fear of losing their children, but the Twin War Gods coaxed them on and they crossed safely to the far side.

After the survivors rested, they went to a plain "to the east of the two mountains and the great water between them" (a credible description of the Grand Canyon), where they camped, "mourning for their lost children" and waiting for the others who had gone south looking for a better crossing place. Those others never rejoined the group and are still referred to as the Lost Clans who went to the "Land of Everlasting Sunshine" to the south. Contemporary Zuni believe there are Indians in Mexico who are their lost relatives.[25]

Next, the story returns to the adventures of Kyaklu, the eldest son of Kawimosa, who, before the great crossing of the river, had been sent north to scout out a good route for the people. He ventured far north into the cold and became lost and blind.[26] Here the story becomes the legend of the rescue of Kyaklu by the Duck, who guided him back with the help of the Rainbow, to be reunited with his younger brother and sister, and their nine children, the Koyemshi.[27]

Again in charge as the elder brother,[28] Kyaklu instructed the Koyemshi to take him "along the trail eastward," where they found and rejoined the people still proceeding on their search. His two younger brothers, the Anahohoatchi, who had ventured south, also returned and were reunited with their relatives.

Again eastward bound, the pilgrims settled in a town identified as located on the sunrise slope of the mountain of Ka'hluelawan, the place of the Kaka and the lake of their dead. But yet another earthquake came and the Twin War Gods again urged the people to follow them eastward, seeking once more the place of the middle.

The next stop was Hanhlipinkya, the "Place of Sacred Stealing,"[29] where they built larger houses and stayed for a long time. They thought they really were at the middle place, but "the mountains trembled often." The Twin War Gods called the people together once more and instructed them in great detail, creating here the Priests of the Bow.[30]

Figure 11. *Wupatki ruins, Arizona*

Then again "the world groaned and the shells sounded warning" and the Twin War Gods led the people away from Hanhlipinkya to safety. Those who did not leave on the advice of Ahaiyuta and Matsailema (the Twin War Gods), "were choked by black fumes, or buried in the walls of their houses, which fell when presently the earth heaved with dire fumes, fire and thunder."

(Although Arizona and New Mexico have been relatively free from volcanic activity for centuries, a major eruption occurred just north of Flagstaff, Arizona, in A.D. 1064., creating Sunset Crater. The eruption covered about eight hundred square miles with black volcanic ash and may have hastened survivors farther east, as suggested in Hopi stories.[31] This major geologic event may have been one of the many earthquakes that kept them moving eastward. The Wupatki ruins [see Figure 11] now visible near Sunset Crater were built after this eruption by a population called the Sinagua. They did not stay long. By A.D. 1150, they too had moved on.)

Next came an encounter with people who lived in "great towns built in the heights (héshotayálawa)."[32] These residents owned great fields and possessions, and they had irrigation to "carry the waters, bringing new soil." These people were "of the highlands and cliffs," of the "elder nations," allied to the Akaka-kwe (The Man-soul Dance gods). A war ensued.[33] Led by a woman named K'yakweina Ok'yatsiki, the "Ancient Woman of the K'yakweina," the newcomers won the battle. Some survivors were found hidden deep in the cellars of their town, blackened by the fumes of their own war-magic. Some of the captives were adopted into the Black Corn clan and named Kwinikwakwe (Black People).

These conquered people from the cliffs in the mountains, like the earlier People of the Dew, were incorporated into the migrating group. And, for good reason: They contributed sophisticated knowledge concerning irrigation techniques. They were valued, just as were the People of the Dew, who introduced corn.

Each of these additions to the pilgrimage were, at first, "wild of tongue," suggesting they spoke a different language.

But still the A:shiwi were not at the middle: "The shell sounded warning." So the Two War Gods, Ahaiyuta and Matsailema, divided the people into "great companies, that they might fare the better" in the hopes that as they spread out they would find the middle sooner.

The separation of groups of clans associated with the North (Winter) and with the South (Summer) appeared early in the migration; the affiliation of clans further divided into seven directions (North, East, South, West, Upper, Lower, and Middle) continues today, as will be discussed in Chapter 9.

The Northern Route

Again the Winter People were sent north, accompanied by the younger brother, Matsailema, the Warriors of the Knife, and the Priests of the Bow. The People of Seed, Summer People, and Black People of Corn and their kokko (god), K'yamak'yakwe, went south. Other people of Seed and Dew were led east by Ahaiyuta and Priests of the Bow. So, through some astute leadership decisions, the A:shiwi continued the eastern journey. (Note on Map 4, based on recent research, this division into three groups is also indicated.)

The People of Winter went into the valley of the "snow-water river" (Uk'yawane, Rio Puerco del Poniente) and settled at the "mud-issuing springs" of that valley (Hekwainankwin). Shrines and mounds of their villages are still there according to Cushing, and archeologists have documented some of them. Numerous petroglyphs found in this part of the Southwest may be related to this migration, the clans, and the stopping places.[34]

This northern group also built "high among the cliffs." The specific places may include the locations now identified as Anasazi sites, such as Canyon de Chelly, Mesa Verde, and Chaco Canyon.

At a very sacred place in the Jemez mountains called "Shipapolimo" is a shrine of two stone mountain lions, one of the easternmost stopping places of the Zuni as they searched for the middle of the world (see Figure 12). Here is a description provided by Stevenson who visited the site and wrote, in 1904:

Figure 12. *Shrine of the two stone lions*

Two crouching lions, or cougars, of massive stone in bas-relief upon the solid formation of the mountain top guard the sacred spot. The heads of the animals are to the east. A stone wall some 4 feet high forms an inclosure 18 feet in diameter for the cougars. Additional stone walls, also about 4 feet in height and 14 feet in length, mark a passageway 3 feet wide from the inclosure. A monument of stones stands 12 feet before the middle of the entrance, which faces east or a little south of east.[35]

This was considered the home of the culture hero Po'shaiyanki and his followers; the lions served as guardians. Zuni continue to make pilgrimages to this shrine, one of the sacred sites on the northern migration route.

In summary, the winter clans circled north to Chaco Canyon, east toward present-day Bandelier Monument, and then turned westward, settling close to—but still east—of the middle.

The Southern Route

The summer clans, the People of Corn and the People of Seed, led by the Kwinikwakwe (Black People), headed south. They built towns along the valley of the River of Red Flowing Waters, and also left their "marks" on the rocks (petroglyphs). They went as far south as the "great valley of Shohkoniman" (La Sierra Escudilla in Arizona) beneath the Mountain of Flutes (Shohko yalana)[36] and then turned east. They continued eastward until they reached the Mountain of Space-speaking Markings (Yala Testsinapa), and then turned back westward, neared the upper valley of Zuniland (Shi-wina Teu'hlkwaina), and built the town of Speech-markings, Héshotatsina (writings), and other towns in the vicinity.[37]

The Middle Route

Finally, the People of the Middle, the Macaw clan, led by Ahaiyuta, settled at Kwakina, very near the middle. Still the "world rumbled and the shells sounded." The disturbance was not great, so they did not leave right away. But, with these warning signs, the leaders called the people together to continue to seek the "very midmost place."

Six towns (see Map 3) were built in the vicinity of present-day

Zuni and were reported by the first Spaniards who arrived in the mid-sixteenth century: Kwakina, Hawikuh, Kyanawe, Hampasawan, Kyakime, and Matsaki. The middle group thought they had found the center at Matsaki.[38] Others gathered there, too, believing it to be the midpoint of the world. But "the warnings yet still sounded," and "the gods and master-priests of the people could not rest."

Thus far, the Zuni story of their search for the middle of the world highlights basic elements of human mobility, but in unusual detail. The key features include reasons for departures, difficulties encountered and overcome, separations and reunions, meeting and incorporating new people, war and peace, new knowledge shared, and, eventually, a conclusion: the final stop.[39]

Finding the Middle

The reuniting of the clans, ultimately, at the exact center, the true middle of the world, is a dramatic story told in many ways, published in many sources. The version selected and summarized here is again from Cushing.[40]

A great council was held: men, beasts, birds, and insects of all kinds gathered. The people knew the middle was near, but where exactly was it located?

After a long deliberation, the story goes on:

The council called on the water skate, who was by some accounts the Sun Father transformed into this mythical six-legged spider. The water skate lifted himself up and extended a finger-foot in each direction, touching the waters to the North, West, South, and East, and then settled down over the middle of the Zuni valley, drawing his finger-legs over the plain, making trails to the very center. When he gradually settled down, he called out that where his heart and navel rested was the exact spot for building the town, the midmost place of the earth-mother.

And that is where the people built their next town; they called it "the Abiding place of Happy Fortune (Halonawan)." Now they were close, so very close to the middle, but they settled on the wrong side, the south side, of the river, and a great flood came. The survivors fled to the top of the nearby mountain (in some versions Corn Mountain). After a sacrifice of a young priest and priestess, the flood abated and the people descended the mountain and built a new "Town of the Middle," on the north side of the Zuni River, and called it Halona Itiwanna (Halona the Midmost).

Finally, the A:shiwi had found the true, stable, middle of the world.

In summary, Cushing's version includes fourteen earthquakes and fifteen stopping places before finding Itiwanna. At the third, fourth, eighth, and ninth stops, the pilgrims met other peoples, some of whom joined the journey. After the sixth stop, there were so many people, they separated into three groups. At one point, one group branched off and headed south, never to be heard from again. After more stops and a second separation into three groups, the others were reunited at Halona Itiwanna, the present Pueblo of Zuni. Finally, there was an end of war and wandering, and no more earthquakes.

MIGRATION MOTIFS

On their pilgrimage, the people who became the Zuni attracted other groups who were impressed with the power of the Zuni gods: "We have power with the gods above yours."[41] After generations of traveling, the great council of men and beings determined where the true middle was located. In a key passage referring to that decision, three themes dominate: six directions, the navel, and the concept of the exact middle of the earth-mother.[42]

Other motifs that persist over the years in the various narratives include the pervasive importance of finding a stable place of the world, the leadership by the Twin War Gods, the separation into three groups, the addition of new peoples encountered en route, earthquakes, stopping places, shrines, the reuniting of the clans, and the final determination of the true middle.

The farthest west contemporary versions describe for the emerging of the First People, who became Zuni from the fourth underworld, is the Mojave Desert in eastern California, but some Zuni suggest that the emergence was farther west with the Pacific Ocean and that this distance has been foreshortened over time. They no longer make religious trips west beyond the Mojave Desert, but the collective memories of the ocean continue.

The assumed place of emergence from Mother Earth is now located on the Colorado River in the Grand Canyon, Arizona. Called Chimik'yana'kya Deya, it is identified as the point of origin and visited regularly by the Galaxy Fraternity, also called the Ne'wekwe priesthood.[43]

In California, the immigrants continued to be disrupted by earthquakes, so, knowing they were not yet in the middle, they proceeded with their search farther and farther east. Stopping, resting, building, adding and mixing with other peoples, stopping again, only to have to move on after the next earthquake.

Clearly, the middle place, Itiwanna, continues to have great significance to the Zuni. Of course, many peoples of the world are convinced their place is the best place and the founding of communities is a common theme in oral narratives. What stands out about the Zuni sense of place, their place in the exact middle, are the details of the search, the annual validation, and the explanation the full narration provides for the many clans and complex ceremonies existing today. It is a powerful story, this pilgrimage from the "ocean of the sunset world": from the west to the east, with many named stops en route, rivers crossed, towns built, and people encountered and killed, or encountered and invited to join the search for the exact center of the universe.

To the Zuni, the migration is not myth; it is their history of where they came from, where they searched, and how they ultimately reunited at the middle, the true middle. Itiwanna.

JAPANESE PARALLELS

How does this long history of migration provide a link between the Japanese and the Zuni, the basic thesis of this book?

First, an obvious observation: The pilgrims came from the right direction: west to east. Second, the Zuni today have knowledge of the oceans; they were not so isolated as to have forgotten. Third, some of the places they stopped have names derived from Japanese. Fourth, certain written traditions in Japan lend credence to the purposeful intent of the journey.

The linguistic connection will be developed in Chapter 7, but here just four key names related to this chapter are introduced:

1. *Chimi,* the Zuni word for the "beginning place." In Japanese, *hajime* is the word for "beginning." Origin myths in Japan have a number of similar themes with the Zuni, including fog, mist, a cadre of deities, distinct roles for the elder and younger brothers, bridges, and rainbows.
2. *Shohko yalana,* Zunian for "Flute Mountain." In Japanese, *shakuhachi* is "flute"; *yama* is "mountain."
3. *Ta'iya,* Zuni for "Place of Planting." *Ta* is rice field in Japanese. In Zuni, *iya* or *lliya* refers to place. In America, corn *(towa),* not rice, was the sacred food. The Japanese kanji (written symbol) for rice field, ⊞, is also found in petroglyphs near Zuni.
4. *Heshoda Bitsulliya* or *Kiwihtsi Bitsulliya,* the Zuni name for Chaco Canyon, an ancestral site associated with the Sword Swallowing Society where prayer offerings are still deposited.[44] *Heshoda* means "dwelling"; *kiwihtsi* means "ceremonial center"; Bitsu is an important deity in Zuni: *Butsu* translates to "Buddha" in Japanese. Chaco Canyon, a major center of the Anasazi civilization, is referred to as the dwelling or ceremonial center of Bitsu in Zunian.

Here is the next part of my proposal: The original search for the middle began in Japan, inspired by a sect of Amida Buddhism and possibly initiated by a major earthquake. The search continued when the pilgrims reached the coast of North America. The narrative summarized in this chapter indicates they continued until they reached Itiwanna—Zuni, New Mexico. Next, the following question must be asked: Is there any indication in Japanese literature that documents interest in going east?[45]

Here is a speech attributed to the first emperor of Japan, Jimmu, reported in the early Japanese document *Nihongi. Chronicles of Japan from the Earliest Times to* A.D. *697:*

> Now I have heard from the Ancient of the Sea that in the East there is a fair land encircled on all sides by blue mountains. . . . I think that this land will undoubtedly be suitable for the extension of the Heavenly task, so that its glory should fill the universe. It is, doubtless, the center of the world.

The reference to the center of the world suggests the influence of China, the Middle Kingdom, an influence known to have been especially intense during the Nara period, A.D. 710–793. The passage goes on to refer to the condition perceived to exist in this frontier land, the central land, located somewhere to the east:

At present things are in a crude and obscure condition and the peoples' minds are unsophisticated. They roost in nests or dwell in caves. . . . Now if a great man were to establish laws, justice could not fail to flourish.

Note the theme of expansion of power and the motif of bringing law and justice to people in the east, who are presumed to need it. Next, the idea of six cardinal points appears in this early document:

Thereafter, the capital may be extended so as to embrace all six cardinal points, and the eight cords may be covered so as to form a roof. Will this not be well?[46]

The idea of a "center" and the six directions suggests concepts derived from yin-yang, themes well established by the eighth century in Japan. They also recur many times during the Zuni pilgrimage, figure importantly in the determination of Itiwanna, and continue in A:shiwi ceremonies today.

The idea of a land surrounded by "blue mountains" with people who needed to be "civilized" from their unsophisticated ways sounds like an expansionist perspective of an emperor on the move. Although this passage is usually interpreted to mean east *within* Japan,[47] the possibility must be allowed that this early emperor (and perhaps later ones) fully intended to expand east *beyond* the boundaries of the islands. Later discussion of navigation skills available in Japan will demonstrate the capability to do just that.

Much was going on in Japan during the eighth century and as the Yamato state formed and strengthened, the idea of expansion farther east was a reasonable aspiration. Perhaps someday Japanese records will reveal specific action to go east beyond Japan during the eighth century, but that predates by six centuries the theory presented here, which has the pilgrims arriving in the vicinity of Zuni by A.D. 1350.

I speculate that this speech credited to Emperor Jimmu anticipates a missionary zeal characteristic of some Buddhist sects that developed later in Japanese history. Nembutsu, one form of Pure Land Buddhism, began in the ninth century and flourished during the tenth and eleventh centuries, a time when personal charisma of individual Buddhist priests became well established.[48] One prime concern of Pure Land Buddhism was to locate the center place of the world.[49]

By the middle of the Heian period (A.D. 794–1184), an almost obsessive concern for the "Pure Land" developed, along with a fad for pilgrimages to the mountains. This was the beginning of Amida Buddhism, out of which developed yet more sects.[50] I believe the Japanese pilgrims to North America belonged to one of the many sects of Amida Buddhism.

Eventually it may be possible to identify which one. Here I venture it may have been later, in the twelfth or thirteenth century, when Japan had many Buddhists "saints." One of them, Hōnen (1133–1212) founded the Jodo sect of Pure Land Buddhism. The personal charisma of religious leadership heightened. Hōnen, who objected to formal religious leadership, was banished from Kyoto in 1207 and died in 1212. His disciples formed a religious society, and they, too, were persecuted and banished from Kyoto. Perhaps it was this sect that prepared to go east in search of the exact center of the world. They had good reason to leave, and motivation to explore elsewhere.

As noted in the narrative, certain Buddhist themes appear in the Zuni migration story. Examples include following the middle path and the use of conch shells.

PILGRIMAGE MOTIFS

Next, what about the tradition of making pilgrimages within Japan? In what ways might those traditions be congruent with the migration to Zuni, and with the Zuni sense of the sacred, their own visits to shrines, and journeys to religious locations in the mountains?

Joseph M. Kitagawa, Japanese Professor Emeritus of the Divinity School and the Department of Far Eastern Languages and Civilizations at the University of Chicago, included a chapter entitled "Three Types of Pilgrimage in Japan" in his collection of essays entitled *On Understanding Japanese Religion*. First, Kitagawa identified general characteristics of pilgrimages, such as traveling a long distance, visiting holy mountains, the physical hardship, endurance, and specific purposes for going on a pilgrimage, such as gaining merit for salvation, paying penance for annulment of sin, and praying for the deceased, healing, good fortune, easy childbirth, and general prosperity. Sometimes ascetic practices such as sexual abstinence, fasting, and dietary restrictions are included.

Kitagawa informed us that the practice of pilgrimage was probably not an important part of early Shinto, the traditional religion in Japan. Rather, he credited the introduction of Chinese civilization and Buddhism during the sixth century A.D. with merging indigenous Shinto and folk religious beliefs and the subsequent development of three kinds of pilgrimages: (1) to sacred mountains; (2) to temples and shrines based on faith in the divinities associated with them, and (3) to sacred places linked to certain holy men.

Pilgrimages to sacred mountains were guided by mountain ascetics and designed to bring favors from both Shinto and Buddhist divinities. This focus on treks to religious locations peaked during the eleventh and twelfth centuries, just prior to the time of the proposed pilgrimage to America. The Zuni search for Itiwanna clearly also includes themes of mountains and safety.

EARTHQUAKES AND HUMAN MOBILITY

Earthquakes are unpredictable, sudden, disruptive, and, I propose, a major motivator of human mobility. Earthquakes rearrange rivers, dry up wells, and cut off trade routes. Earthquakes move survivors out of one place, sometimes crowding and disrupting residents in others. Earthquakes may be linked with subsequent drought, epidemics, and famines that compound the original destruction.[51]

Anyone interested in California earthquakes will relish the detail in the Cushing account: "The heights staggered and the mountains reeled," the earth "trembled anew," the "world rumbled," the earth "groaned," and the conches sounded warning, all indicative of a tectonically active area. Also, the world's rumbling kept the people on the move, each time heading farther east. The theme of earthquakes is so pervasive, suggesting that the original migration may have been initiated by a major earthquake, perhaps in Japan, followed by a continuation of the search east out of California.

In the Zuni narrative, earthquakes kept the people moving, searching for that stable center to the east. I propose that a major earthquake in Japan initiated the pilgrimage, and a series of earthquakes in western North America kept it going. But when? Many earthquakes have been recorded in Japan.

For example, the period from A.D. 732 to 741 was a decade of disasters: Storms, earthquakes, floods, and drought were widespread. Further, crops failed, and famine and plague followed.[52]

Moving ahead six hundred years to the decade between 1340 and 1350, a whole flurry of calamities struck. In addition to the miseries of the ongoing civil war, there was a drought (1340), a great earthquake (1341), a smallpox epidemic (1342), more earthquakes (1346 and 1347), another drought (1348), then a typhoon, floods, and yet another earthquake (1349). There were so many disasters in 1349, a custom for praying for relief from natural calamities developed. Yet 1350 was marked by more severe earthquakes and typhoons.[53]

An earlier disaster, a typhoon and tidal wave that struck Hizen on northern Kyushu in 1226, may also be considered.[54] On Honshu, the Bakufu (military government associated with the Kamakura period) were trying to establish their power and were having difficulties with "turbulent monks." The historian George Sansom reported that "drought was followed by famine, famine by smallpox, and after diseases came storms, earthquakes, and floods, and such inclement and unseasonable weather that there were hard frosts in summer and even snowfalls in some places used to burning sun. To propitiate or advise the powers that regulate these climatic disaster, the professors of Yin-Yang recommended changes in the era name."[55] However, that did not help either.

Obviously, the time and specific event cannot be resolved here. We can only speculate based on limited translated information. But a major event such as an earthquake would provide a good reason for a planned departure from Japan, perhaps organized by a group of disgruntled Buddhist priests with a commitment to find a center in the mountains free from earthquakes and war.

The departure may have occurred between 1200 and 1292, a period when twenty-four major natural calamities hit Japan. The years 1257–59 deserve consideration as they involved first a succession of earthquakes in 1257, followed by storms and floods in 1258, and plague in 1259.[56]

Thus in the thirteenth century the Japanese had good reasons to search for a stable middle of the earth, to cross the ocean to the east, and to discover they had not found it after they arrived in California. So they moved on, eventually arriving at Zuni, settling there by A.D. 1350.

Many questions remain, but cannot yet be answered: When did the pilgrimage begin? What inspired it? Was it planned or accidental? Were the Japanese who came intent on civilizing Native Americans? Or were they looking for a refuge? Were the values of pilgrimages and shrines already a part of the Native American concepts, perhaps later enhanced by Buddhist inspiration? Were monks from other countries a part of the entourage that arrived? Which branch of Buddhism might it have been? Which western tribes joined the trek? Can these questions be answered in the future if we begin to ask them now?

CHAPTER THREE

LINKS
ACROSS
THE DESERT

The pilgrims from the Pacific knew where they were going: the middle of the world. The migration stories told by the Zuni suggest they were inspired by a religious commitment, and they were led by gifted priests, gods, warriors, and politicians. Unsettling earthquakes in western North America kept them going, moving east, seeking a safe place to settle.

Other people were already living in the Southwest when they arrived. What does the richly documented archeology of the area reveal about those prehistoric populations, their settlement patterns, religion, and pottery? What is known about cultural links between the Indians of California and the southwestern Pueblo groups? And about prehistoric trails and trade routes across the desert? Did the Zuni really know about the Pacific Ocean? These questions, as well as cultural change and continuity, time and distance, are pieces of the puzzle now considered.

THE ARCHEOLOGICAL RECORD AND THE MIDDLE

Studies of southwestern archeology include detailed analyses of millions of potsherds, measurements of thousands of abandoned ruins, and excavation of hundreds of sites documented by scholarly tomes, articles, and papers published over a 120-year period. Controversies surround the research, in part because there are so much data to discuss and so many alternative answers to the questions raised. What happened to the Anasazi civilization that flourished in present-day northwestern New Mexico between the tenth and twelfth centuries is one such vexing puzzle.

Although Zuni prehistory is linked to the Anasazi, especially the developments in Chaco Canyon north of the present pueblo,[1] the proposed period of Japanese influence postdates the mysterious decline of the Anasazi. Thus a brief overview of the Zuni area in the context of the larger region sharpens the focus to the late thirteenth and early fourteenth centuries, the time I believe that the Japanese pilgrims arrived.

The reconstruction of Zuni archeology does not parallel *exactly* the details of Zuni oral accounts of origin and migration outlined in the previous chapter, but the general themes and sequences agree. The addition of corn agriculture to a hunting and gathering economy, occasional warfare, and the merger of at least two cultural traditions at Zuni are parts of an oral tradition supported by archeological evidence.

The people who became the Zuni were not the first to settle in the area. Some of the clans that joined the Zuni probably had been in the vicinity for hundreds of years, receiving, modifying, and incorporating influences from previous cultures that waxed and waned over time: the Hohokam, Mogollon, and Sinagua, for example. The Mimbres people, possibly a branch of the Mogollon and located just to the south of Zuni, thrived briefly (A.D. 950–1150), and are known through their remarkable pottery designs that depict whales and eighteen different marine fish taxa, causing scholars to wonder how such precise knowledge could be gained so far inland.[2]

Something especially mysterious, and as yet unexplained, happened to the Anasazi people. By the thirteenth century, nearly all of the many Anasazi communities were completely abandoned. The population declines are variously explained as the result of drought, sickness, erosion, wars, or Athapaskan or other "enemy" invasion. Yet the Zuni area continued to be occupied and to grow in population.[3]

Migration stories include the absorption of the Black Corn clan, people rescued and adopted from a conquered town north of Zuni, possibly Anasazi people of Chaco Canyon. Perhaps some Anasazi survivors voluntarily joined the pilgrimage of the people who were seeking the center.

Oral history relates that one main branch of Zuni arrived from the west and drew in other clans that had overshot the middle when they ventured too far north and south. Based on the archeological record, a possible time for this reuniting at the true middle of the world is about A.D. 1300–50. This period, called Pueblo IV (or Post-Chacoan), seems the most likely time the Japanese pilgrims and Native Americans who joined the trek finally reached the Zuni area.

First, consider the settlement patterns. In 1990 a conference titled "Pueblo Cultures in Transition" was held at the Crow Canyon Archaeological Center in Cortez, Colorado, to review, discuss, and synthesize what happened during Pueblo III, a two-hundred-year period, A.D. 1150–1350. The 150,000 square miles of the Southwest occupied during that time were divided into twelve regions of Pueblo people variously related to the Anasazi culture. In all, information on eight hundred large sites was reviewed.[4]

In one of the twelve regions, the Zuni District (also called the Cibola Region), an area encompassing about 1,760 square miles, at least twenty-eight pueblos with more than a total of 13,000 rooms were built, and abandoned, between A.D. 1250 and 1400. Keith Kintigh, professor of anthropology at Arizona State University and a specialist on Zuni settlement patterns, reported in 1985 that this period was especially a time of "dramatic changes," "a massive upset" in the cultural systems. He wondered about "an influx of some population," and considered that "this social upheaval" and increased foreign "influences" might have contributed to rapid changes in Zuni ceramic production.[5] At the 1990 conference,

Kintigh developed his theory further, noting that the size and number of the newly built communities were impressive, and so was the short time of their occupations: twenty-five to seventy-five years. Kintigh attributed their brief duration to an absence of adequate social integration. I propose the pueblos were occupied for short times for reasons provided by the Zuni migration story: The people were in search of the middle and kept moving whenever an earthquake occurred, vacating settlements en route. For whatever reason, by 1400 the entire Cibola Region was abandoned with the exception of the area near the Zuni pueblos, where a flurry of construction occurred. In only fifty years, between 1350 and 1400, nine new Zuni communities with a total of 4,000 rooms were constructed.[6]

The consolidation of many small villages into nine large communities is credited partly to new irrigation techniques for managing riverine and spring-fed water resources. Also ceremonies, Kintigh noted, may have played a major integrative role for these Post-Chacoan societies. His colleague, E. Charles Adams, professor of anthropology at Arizona State University, suggested that the thirteenth century was the critical time for the introduction of the kachina cultures with their masked gods (the impersonators for named deities) and that major religious changes occurred first in eastern Arizona just west of Zuni.[7]

Mortuary customs changed as well during this period.[8] The Mogollon practiced cremation, and the earlier people in the Zuni area did not. After the collapse of Chaco towns, the people living in the Zuni region apparently shifted affiliations toward the west, incorporating, among other traits, cremation. At the Zuni sites of Hawikuh and Kechibawa, evidence of both burial and cremation was found. This also suggests a migration of people from the Mogollon area (Arizona) into Zuni.

I propose that a group of immigrants, including the Japanese pilgrims, came in from the Mogollon area of eastern Arizona and united with the Anasazi population that had long lived in the Zuni drainage, and the modern A:shiwi emerged from the amalgam.[9] In other words, the Zuni pueblo, like the other pueblos, may represent a selective continuity of the earlier Anasazi culture, which did not completely disappear, but shifted centers and mixed differently with other populations in each of the surviving pueblos.

At Zuni, in addition to the consolidation into large pueblo settlements, agricultural intensification, terracing, changed burial customs, and incorporation of a biologically distinctive population (discussed in Chapter 6), a most unusual ceramic technique suddenly appeared: glaze decoration on pottery. The vitrified paint is a tangible ingredient in the cultural complex that arrived in the Southwest, specifically in the Zuni area and at St. Johns just to the west, at the end of the thirteenth century; glaze is one clear marker of the beginning of Pueblo IV.[10]

To date no consensus exists concerning the source of the glazing technique. Some scholars claim it was simply an unusual, short-lived indigenous development; others question that possibility. Most simply agree with Adolph Bandelier's 1892 assessment that it is an anomaly.[11] In any event it remains part of the enigma. We know that green glaze had religious significance in Japan during the Heian period; possibly it also had religious significance during Pueblo IV in the Southwest. We will return to the glaze discussion later.

In summary, between A.D. 1250 and 1400, the archeological record indicates an abandonment of many areas in the Southwest and a consolidation of people in large pueblos at Zuni.[12] We have established a time frame, a location, a direction of arrival, and a cluster of new cultural traits that may accompany the detailed oral history of migration to Zuni. Changes were notable in social organization, religion, dwellings, consolidation of settlements, agricultural techniques, and the sudden and short-lived appearance of lead-glazed decorated pots.

In many ways, Pueblo IV may have been a propitious time for the pilgrims to arrive. The Anasazi civilization had declined dramatically, a drought had devastated the area, and famine had weakened the survivors.

THE DESERT AND THE DISTANCE

How far did the pilgrims have to travel to reach their final destination?

On present-day road systems, the distance from the Pueblo of Zuni, New Mexico, to San Francisco via Bakersfield is 962 miles, and to San Diego is 677 miles. The closest West Coast city is Los Angeles, some 664 miles away by highway. Allowing for the contours of the geography of California and Arizona, a round number of 700 miles each way is reasonable (see Map 5).

This may seem a great distance viewed from the perspective of today's automobile culture. Most contemporary Americans cannot imagine actually *walking* that far: across deserts, fording small streams, and crossing the huge Colorado River, let alone managing the risks of encountering potentially hostile Native American tribes with prior claims to the area. But if we consider the extensive trade routes already in place long before the time the pilgrims made the crossing, the distance becomes shorter and the route safer.

TRADE ROUTES TO AND FROM THE COAST

Trade from the Zuni area with people in many directions flourished for centuries before the pilgrims arrived and continued for

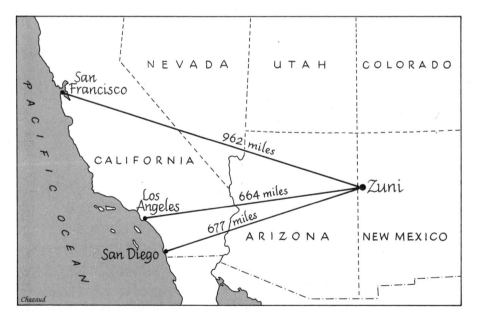

Map 5. *Coast to Zuni, highway miles.*

centuries after. As recently as the mid-nineteenth century, the Zuni obtained important items from the west coast and from Mexico, including conch shells for ceremonies, abalone shells for jewelry, and colorful macaw feathers for prayer sticks (see Map 6).

Archeological evidence reveals that extensive trade occurred among communities located between the Pacific coast and the Southwest beginning at least as early as A.D. 600, a full six centuries before the proposed thirteenth-century pilgrimage from the west coast to Zuni. Surely six hundred years was time enough to establish routes, identify partners, and learn the water hole locations along the seven-hundred-mile route. The major ancient Indian routes were later followed by European explorers and became rights-of-way for the Santa Fe Railroad and for Route 66.[13]

To summarize what is known about the trade and the routes: First, between A.D. 600 and 900, trade developed between peoples in the Gulf of California and the Mogollon area in Arizona. These trade links were expanded when the Zuni villages became part of

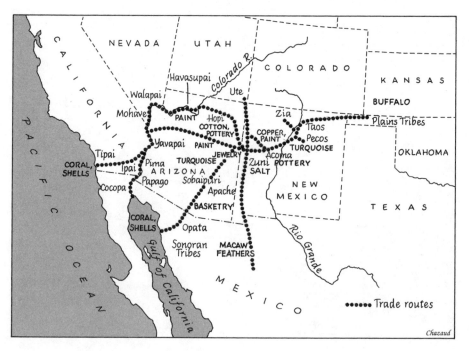

Map 6. *Zuni trade relationships.*

the great Anasazi complex at Chaco Canyon to the north and lasted about three centuries. About the time of the demise of the Chaco complex, the center of the trade network for all of the southwestern region shifted to Zuni. From that time until the Spanish arrived in the mid-sixteenth century, Zuni was a major trading place, where goods were exchanged among the Southwest communities and with peoples to the south in Mesoamerica, north and east in the Great Plains, and west to the Pacific coast. Not only did the Zuni go to these locations, but also traders from other areas came to them. (See Map 7.)

TRADE ITEMS

Among many shells found in archeological contexts in the Southwest, at least nine kinds definitely originate from the Pacific coast,

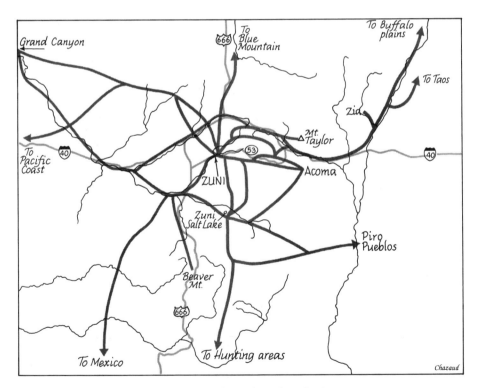

Map 7. *Zuni trails and modern highways.*

the most important being abalone. By A.D. 1000, turquoise, copper bells, and macaw birds were added to the trade inventory. By then routes extended throughout the Southwest and down into Mexico.

Turquoise was mined in various places, but a key source was in eastern California's Mojave Desert. Copper bells made by a complex lost-wax method arrived from the south; considerable discussion surrounds their exact origins. The copper was not indigenous to the Southwest or to northern Mexico, yet a total of 622 copper bells from ninety-three sites from the U.S. Southwest and Northwest Mexico have been inventoried and analyzed (see Figure 13).[14]

Trade in live parrots also occurred during prehistoric times. Red, blue, and yellow macaws originally came from South America and were traded north out of Mexico. Many macaw skeletons have been found in Anasazi sites. Is there a link between the color coding found in Zuni today and the significance of macaw feathers during Anasazi times? In modern Zuni, there is a clear association between color and directions on prayer sticks, feathers, clans, and kivas, suggesting connection with the yin-yang system (for example, yellow for North, white for East, red for South, and blue for West). The prescribed sequence of colors on prayer sticks may have made the many-colored macaws especially valuable.

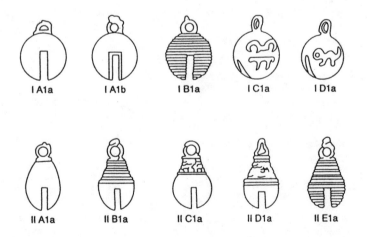

Figure 13. *Copper bell types found in the greater Southwest*

Items such as grooved stone axes of Puebloan origin have been found widely in California, and aboriginal trade routes within the boundaries of that state are numerous, some still visible in the mid-twentieth century.[15]

Established Indian trails cross the Mojave Desert; reportedly, water holes can be found every twelve miles by those knowledgeable about the routes.[16] Two major trails linked the coast of California to the Southwest by the tenth century. One connecting the Southwest and the Los Angeles area crossed the desert to Needles, then followed the Gila River north. The second came up the west coast of Mexico and then branched into the Sierras and north to the Pueblos.

A remaining question pertains to whether or not the Zuni traded items with others across great distances directly or through intermediaries. Early historic documents suggest that they had direct knowledge of the routes and traded goods on their own expeditions.[17]

The California Indian groups most often mentioned in connection with trade with the Southwest are the Tipai and Ipai, located along the southern coast of California. The most precious trade item was coral, still prized by contemporary jewelry makers at Zuni.

OCEANS TO THE WEST AND OCEANS TO THE EAST

Despite intrusion by the Spanish from the south in the sixteenth century and the Americans from the east and west in the nineteenth, the memory of the coast and oceans continues to be conserved in the Zuni stories of creation and migration. Some knowledge of trails to the west also is kept alive. References to the "ocean of the sunset world," belief in a "goddess of the ocean,"[18] and the water spider's role in locating the middle of the world (equidistant between four oceans) have kept an awareness of the oceans active in this small community tucked away on a high plateau in New Mexico, many miles from the sea.

The continuing importance of the oceans to the east and west was confirmed on visits by Zuni delegations to the Atlantic states in 1882 and 1886 and to Los Angeles in 1925. In 1882, six Zuni men accompanied Frank Cushing, who was living in Zuni at the time, to the east coast; he reported they were eager for the trip as an opportunity to bring back to Zuni some of the sacred water of the 'Ocean of Sunrise,' that is, the Atlantic (see Figure 14). As they gathered the seawater, the Zuni priests chanted songs of thanksgiving, singing, "Over the road to the middle of the world thou willst go." They also went sightseeing; made public appearances in Washington, Wellesley College, and Harvard; and visited Deer Island outside Boston Harbor where they held prayers to the "Beloved Powers of the Ocean" and held a water gathering ceremony.[19]

In 1886, Cushing again brought Zuni, three this time, with him to pay homage to the Ocean of the East. They traveled on invitation from Mary Hemenway who hosted them at her establishment called Manchester By-the-Sea in Massachusetts. Mrs. Hemenway was a philanthropist in Boston who later sponsored expeditions to the Southwest, first funding Cushing's study, and later Jesse Walter Fewkes, who commenced work with the Hopi.

This was the same year, 1886, that Matilda (Tillie) Stevenson, who was also doing ethnographic research in Zuni, took We'wha, her Zuni friend, variously referred to as "priestess" and "princess," to accompany her on the social and political rounds in Washington, D.C., including meeting President Cleveland. We'wha is now recognized as the Zuni Man-Woman, a famous American Indian berdache (a word used by French explorers also meaning homosexual, transvestite, and transsexual). He was an intelligent, knowledgeable man (Tillie later learned) who combined the work and social roles of both men and women, called by the Zuni term *llamana;* he dressed in women's clothes.[20]

Through these visits and a growing number of publications, the Zuni, as well as those studying them, were becoming well known nationally by the late nineteenth century. A modified version of a Zuni song even made its way into Puccini's opera *La Fanciulla del West* about a traveling minstrel who entertains miners in a barroom in the days of the California Gold Rush.[21]

In June 1925, twelve Zuni were invited to Los Angeles "to create atmosphere," that is, entertainment, for the Shriner's Convention. This was the first time these Zuni had been to the ocean,

Figure 14. *Zuni delegation to the East Coast, 1882.*
Portrait of six Zuni who accompanied Cushing

though their costumes included strands of olivella shell beads, coral, and bits of red shell from the spiny oyster from the Gulf of California. During their visit, Arthur Woodward went to Redondo Beach with a young Zuni translator named Warren and two of his elders: his father, Juan Ondelacy, and another Zuni, Awaleon.

In *The Masterkey,* Mr. Woodward reported the pleasure the

Zuni men had exploring the beach, picking up every scrap of shell they could find. Warren later wrote him what one old man said when they returned to Zuni after seeing the "big body of waters": "I felt it gave me a new heart, fine spirit, a new life . . . a new life because I felt that I have met the god of the rainmakers whom we have always addressed in our prayers."[22]

The bags full of old abalone shells collected by the Zuni elders were ground and mixed with sacred cornmeal for use in religious ceremonies, a custom continued today by the *uwanami,* Zuni rain priests.

These examples indicate the Zuni had knowledge about the oceans and their spiritual significance long after the time the established, direct trade routes were interrupted by Westerners.

What indications of this migration from the Pacific coast to Zuni might appear in the archeological and cultural records in California? If the pilgrimage was significant enough to be reflected in Zuni language, culture, and biology in the twentieth century, as I propose, the migrants may have left some evidence of passage between the two areas.

SOUTHWEST LINKS TO THE PACIFIC COAST

What do anthropologists say about cultural evidence of links between the Pacific coast and the Southwest? Not much. Especially not much since the late 1930s. What they have found and reported is insightful, but confusing.

Robert Heizer, a foremost scholar on California archeology, briefly mentioned that the southern California culture area was heavily influenced by the Southwest, but that was all he had to say about it in his introduction to a volume on California tribes he edited in 1978 for the *Handbook of North American Indians.*[23] In the same volume, Katherine Luomala, professor of anthropology at the University of Hawaii, who accomplished research in southern California early in her career, noted, also briefly, that the Tipai-Ipai "paintings, symbolism, clan organization, and pottery making linked these southern California and neighboring bands with the Southwestern culture area." She also reported that the Tipai-Ipai had symbolism of colors and directions, which sounds like a simplified version of yin-yang.[24] These two short references are the only mention I found on the California-Southwest cultural connection in the *California* volume of the encyclopedic *Handbook of North American Indians,* an eight-hundred-page synthesis that includes almost sixty tribes. (See Map 8 for tribal names and locations.)

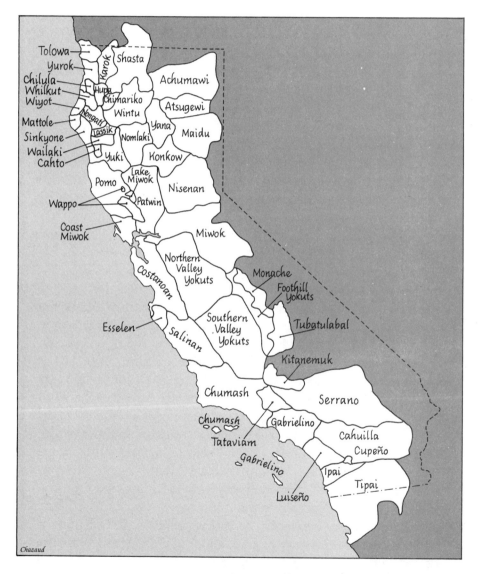

Map 8. *California tribes.*

Yet this lack of scholarly discussion does not mean there is no connection. Since the 1940s archeologists in both the Southwest and California have tended to focus on specific local sites and the development of regional methodologies. Scholarship on the Southwest is known for its detailed analysis of ceramics, which has led to sophisticated recognition of hundreds of pottery types affiliated with specific time frames for thousands of locations. The medium, mix, sources of material, shapes, and decorative styles on pottery have been analyzed extensively.[25] As a consequence, it is possible to specify when an area was occupied and abandoned by analysis of potsherds found on the surface. (Few areas in the world compare to the southwestern part of the United States with regard to the level of sophisticated pottery analysis by archeologists. One of the exceptions is the extensive research on Japanese pottery traditions over a ten-thousand-year period.)

In California, archeological research developed in a different direction, partly because pottery was rare. Basketry was far more frequently used, but baskets deteriorate over time, leaving archeologists less material with which to work. As one result, stratigraphy, the analysis and dating of layers of deposits made by human occupation, became a forte of California archeology. Stratigraphy became to California what pottery became to the Southwest: a means for dating changes over time. Shell mounds along the Pacific coast provide productive settings for dating times and changes of occupation, just as pottery does in the continental interior of the Southwest.

However, over the last sixty years little communication has occurred between the pottery hounds and the shell mound diggers. Discussions of interregional connections are rare, even at interregional meetings.[26] One significant exception is a doctoral dissertation written in 1970 by Jay Ruby, now at Temple University. His thesis, titled "Culture Contact between Aboriginal Southern California and the Southwest," presents evidence that an exchange network between the two regions began at least two thousand years ago and continued into the mid-nineteenth century.[27] Ruby interpreted the archeological record to indicate a movement of goods, but not necessarily the movement of people, between three adjacent groups through peaceful reciprocal arrangements of trading partnerships.

Here is how it may have worked: People from coastal southern California traded shells to people in the interior of southern California and in exchange received perishable goods and, occasionally, southwestern ceramics. The interior southern Californians, primarily from the Mojave Desert, traded shells east for goods, including pottery (see Figure 15).[28] Ruby's analysis is consistent with some archeologists' view that *items* move interregionally, but *people* tend not to. An alternative hypothesis is that traders would sometimes go the whole route (i.e., interregionally), as I believe the Zuni did both in prehistoric times and up to the middle of the nineteenth century.[29]

Interestingly, before regionalism settled upon the profession, the topic of coast-to-Southwest connections was hot. In 1925 Alfred Kroeber and in 1927 William Duncan Strong noted that Pueblo-like features of southern California were most common among the *coastal* peoples. Strong suggested that the Pueblo and southern California coastal areas were influenced by a spread of basic ideas, he presumed from Mexico, which affected the development of human occupation in both regions in similar ways.[30] That is, at one time they all shared common influences (from Mexico). Later, an intrusion of different people (Strong suggested Yuman and Shoshonean Indians) disrupted these links, permanently interrupting the former cultural continuum between the Southwest and coastal California.

Specific similarities between the societies of the Southwest and southern California reported in these early comparative studies in-

Figure 15. *Shells from the Pacific as trade items*

cluded semisubterranean ceremonial houses (like kivas), priests, prayers for rain, feather sticks (prayer plumes), group fetishes (sacred bundles), certain myth motifs, and sand paintings.[31]

The late 1920s was a time of lively debate about what and who came from where, including the direction. Both Strong and Kroeber suggested that the diffusion of social and ceremonial organization was primarily *from* the Southwest *to* California, but another noted anthropologist, Julian Steward, postulated an independent development of similar traits for both areas, a position consistent with the multilinear evolution concepts he developed more fully later.[32]

By the late 1930s, two women scholars entered into the fray. Florence Hawley and Elsie Parsons, both established scholars of the Southwest, supported the view that the western Pueblos, the Zuni and Hopi, had originated in the west or the south. Hawley went on to state that both scenarios, one supporting movement east to west and the other west to east, were too simple. For Hawley it seemed more reasonable to postulate at least two different places of origin for the cultures known as "Pueblo,"[33] an opinion congruent with the Zuni version and with the thesis presented here.

Another topic needing fresh reflection is whether Pueblo traders met and bartered through intermediaries or took long journeys themselves; for example, in order to obtain precious shells, did Pueblo people barter midway with other tribes such as the Upland Patayan and the Mojave Desert people, rather than make the complete round-trip to the coast?

Ruby, quoting early documents, wrote about Pueblo traditions of pilgrimages all the way to the "sky-blue-water" and that people made such a "journey of death" over a great desert.[34] Other early accounts also suggested that trading expeditions by Pueblo peoples extended all the way to the coast and into Mexico. For example, the archeologist-historian Adolf F. Bandelier, one of the earliest scholars to write about prehistoric Pueblo communities,[35] reported in 1892 that until 1859 some Pueblo people made annual trips into Sonora (Mexico), where they exchanged blankets, buffalo hides, and turquoises for shells, coral, and parrot feathers.[36]

Trails, trade, and cultural links across the desert from California to the Southwest have been modestly and inadequately explored; a medley of questions remain to be asked, including when were they established and when were they interrupted.

Looking back to the Southwest, the end of the thirteenth century may have been a propitious time for the pilgrims to arrive in the vicinity of the Zuni since the drought was ending. The new irrigation techniques, new building styles, larger settlements, a short-lived glazed pottery technique, new masked deities in the form of kachinas, and changed biological features (addressed in Chapter 6) combine to make the beginning of Pueblo IV the most likely time of arrival. Trade routes were already well established and trails to follow were marked.

Cultural similarities between the southern California coastal tribes and the Southwest tribes suggest they, too, may have received significant influences from Japan. Perhaps members of the Tipai and the Ipai tribes (now called Kumeyaay) joined the pilgrimage and provided information about the routes and the risks eastward across the desert. As the Anasazi civilization declined, surviving residents from Chaco may also have gathered with others at Itiwanna, the true center of the universe.

If Japanese priests came by ship to southern California coasts and inspired a pilgrimage across established trails to the Southwest, evidence of other Asian contact may exist along the coasts of the Americas.

CHAPTER FOUR

COASTS
AND
CURRENTS

Bits and pieces, here and there, found scattered along the coastlines of North America. An unexplained deposit of ancient Chinese coins in southeastern Alaska. Scraps of reworked iron and bamboo in a prehistoric site on the northwestern coast of Washington. Japanese-like pottery figurines excavated in southwestern Washington. Chinese porcelain sherds and iron spikes deep in shell mounds in northern California. Chinese-looking stone anchors offshore in southern California. Chinese and Japanese coins on old Native American Indian headdresses, necklaces, armor, and masks. A Japanese sword embedded in a coastal California shell mound. Are these recent intrusions or fragmented testimony of past connections across the ocean?

Trails, trade networks, shells, feathers, and other cultural ties reflect established links from the coast to the A:shiwi. The sudden and dramatic changes in the late thirteenth century in the Southwest shaped a time frame for the proposed arrival of the Japanese pilgrims. But where did the pilgrims land? Where do we begin to look? Have any items from twelfth- or thirteenth-century Japan been found, identified, analyzed, and dated?

North America's coastlines span many thousands of miles, including shores surrounding hundreds of islands—those small, scattered pieces of viable living spaces off the mainland. Likely locations for shipwrecks are numerous, but so arc safe harbors, inlets, bays, and sandy beaches for planned disembarkments. Every major city along the coast today is wisely situated near a good port of the past. But where would a twelfth- or thirteenth-century Japanese ship find a safe and friendly harbor? On which beach? What bay?

Somewhat confounding the search for a specific landing site is the fact the Zuni migration story includes reference to people gathering from all directions. The western contingent of the tribe seems to be the primary one,[1] but "west" is quite extensive from an A:shiwi perspective as well as from an oceanic one.

Southern California appears the most likely location for the landing site. Trails, trade items, and religious ideas seem to link the Zuni to that area. The wooden plank ocean-going boats, trading centers, iron, population density, and social stratification documented for late protohistoric times suggest that future searches include the Channel Islands near Santa Barbara, California, and farther south.[2] But this is only a hunch. Ultimately, the whole coastline of North America should be inspected not only for evidence of Japanese presence, but also for evidence of other early arrivals at other times from other places.

HUMAN MOBILITY: PACIFIC PATHS

The Pacific Ocean churns and flows, its tides constantly coming in and going out and its currents circulating in all directions. There are squalls and storms, cyclones and typhoons. The Pacific comprises over sixty-nine million square miles of water, covering a third of the earth's surface. The Pacific is larger than all the land surface contained on this planet, even counting Africa twice.[3]

But the ocean is not necessarily a hostile environment. The word *Pacific* means "peaceful," and at times indeed it is. Warm currents flow north past Japan, curve east around the central North Pacific, massage the islands off the shores of British Columbia, ease along the American coasts south to the equator, and then head west, to warm up again. The Black Current (Kuroshio) is one of four major currents branching around and across the North Pacific, connecting coastal waters off Japan, Canada, mainland United States, Hawaii, and the Philippine Islands (see Maps 9 and 10).

Sometimes strange things happen, like El Niño, a periodic warming of the surface of the ocean that causes changes in weather patterns and anomalous westerly winds.[4] Such events seem to affect the oceans and associated life-forms south of the equator more than north of the equator, but new scientific understandings are emerging, addressing how wind and temperature changes in and on the Pacific link with weather patterns worldwide.[5]

Ben Finney, professor of anthropology at the University of Hawaii, suggested that El Niño may have periodically assisted oceanic voyages, planned and unplanned, including the successful west-to-east migration of Polynesians. The periodic westerly

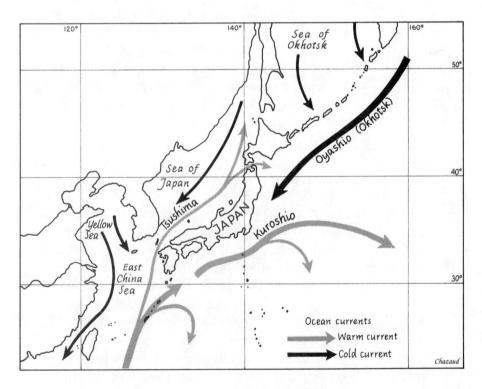

Map 9. *Ocean currents around Japan.*

wind reversals associated with El Niño events may explain how these canoe voyagers were able to migrate so far out into the Pacific. If Polynesians could reach the Hawaiian Islands using the wind changes associated with an El Niño event, "perhaps," Finney adds, "even more attention should be paid to the possibility that Hawaiians successfully followed the same strategy in the more benign North Pacific and made a landfall somewhere on the relatively close North American coast."[6]

Contemporary debris of Asian origin found along the west coast of North America suggests further thoughts of how the ocean currents provided mobility over great distances long ago. For example, Japanese glass balls used as buoys for fishing nets continue to intrigue and surprise beachcombers along sandy beaches. For some Americans "going to the beach" can mean "looking for Japanese glass balls." And finding them.

Oceans are quite amenable to the mobility of people, and have

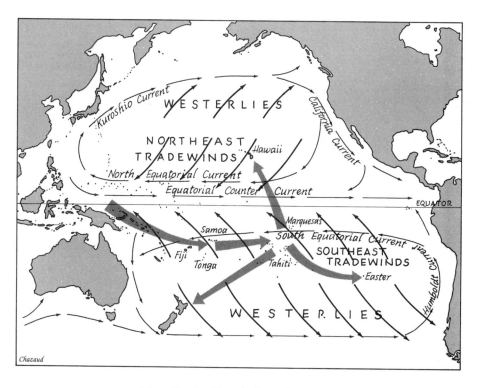

Map 10. *Pacific winds and currents.*

been so for millennia. Discoveries of early pottery in South America, predating sites in North America, encourage our reconsideration of routes of access to the New World. Thinking about Japanese pilgrims during relatively recent prehistoric times certainly leads to the logical consideration that the Bering Strait Land Bridge may be one route for the peopling of the Americas, but not the only one.[7]

Now let us turn to what the ocean streams and winds in the North Pacific gyre propel eastward, illustrating predictable water flow and wind direction.

TOYS, TENNIS SHOES, AND TURTLES

In January 1992, a forty-foot container from a vessel sailing east from Hong Kong was swept overboard in a storm near the international dateline, midway between the equator and the North Pole. An armada of twenty-nine thousand plastic toys en route from Hong Kong to Tacoma, Washington, began a long bob east across the Pacific.[8] Thousands of yellow ducks, blue turtles, green frogs, and red beavers caught the current east and by October 1992 began to surf onto beaches along the coast in southeastern Alaska (see Figure 16).

If Curtis Ebbesmeyer, a physical oceanographer with the firm of Evans-Hamilton, Inc., and his Seattle colleague, W. James Ingraham of the National Marine Fisheries Service, are right about currents, additional toys flowed around the Aleutians and headed north, catching the Transpolar Drift and are floating east toward the North Atlantic. These toys, caught in the ice temporarily, may eventually intercept the North Atlantic currents, and appear on European shores. Or, if they catch the Labrador Current flowing south, then the yellow ducks, blue turtles, green frogs, and red beavers will head down the east coast of North America and possibly show up near Boston, where the original purchase order to Hong Kong was placed by Kiddie Products, Inc.[9]

The travels of these toys are being tracked by Ebbesmeyer and Ingraham through a computer model called OSCURS, Ocean Surface Current Simulations numerical model, to enhance our knowledge about ocean currents and weather patterns; and they

Figure 16. *Toys and turtles*

challenge our imagination about human mobility on the high seas.

A similar episode occurred with a load of approximately forty thousand pairs of athletic shoes from four containers, lost overboard in the North Pacific Ocean on May 27, 1990.[10] The shoes began appearing, in excellent condition, on the coasts of Alaska, Washington, and Oregon in 1991. By late summer, 1992, some sixteen hundred shoes had been retrieved. Whole families beachcombed and outfitted themselves with matching pairs of fine quality. By late 1992, a few shoes began to show up in Hawaii. Because of the location of the original spill, the OSCURS model predicts some may end up in Japan.[11]

Live turtles that originate in Japan swim to America. According to B. W. Bowen of the University of Florida and colleagues, Baja California turtles carry the same mitochrondrial DNA genetic markers as those in Japan. Not only are the American loggerheads *(Caretta caretta)* related to Japanese turtles, but also they are hatched on Japanese shores, swim the ten thousand kilometers along the warm Black Current across the North Pacific as babies, feast on crabs, and grow up along the coast of Baja California.

They then swim back across the Pacific on the warm westbound equatorial currents, to breed and hatch the next generation of ocean-going Japanese-American turtles.[12]

If toy ducks, synthetic shoes, and baby turtles can make it, why not people? Given the great length of time *Homo sapiens* has lived on both sides of the Pacific, the possibility of a Japanese-Zuni connection appears reasonable to consider.

COASTAL ENVIRONMENTS

An anthropologist once argued with me that even if a few Japanese did reach the coast of North America alive, the local Native Americans would have killed them promptly. Perhaps sometimes that did happen. Certain tribes, such as those along the northwest coast, were indeed fierce and defensive of their territory, as reported in written records from the nineteenth century. But at other times, it is at least possible that encounters were peaceful and even productive.

In the last chapter, we traced the trade routes that crisscrossed the Southwest to the coast and to Mexico, providing access for goods and people across land. Oceans and their coasts provided similar access to novel items, people, and ideas. Coastal Indians would surely have had a keen interest in any new arrivals—about their language, clothing, technology, ideas—perhaps leading to a peaceful exchange and occasional adoption of the newcomers.

Native Americans have their own stories of voyages abroad and returning. The extent of Native American coastal travel has yet to be studied deeply but some discussion about the use of sails and plank-sided boats has appeared in scholarly literature in recent years.[13] One result of the cultural revival of the *Hokule'a,* an ancient Polynesian voyaging canoe, and its 1995 visit to Alaska is the retelling of stories by Indians along the northwest coast of their own successful trips abroad.[14]

COASTS AND SEAS AS BUFFER ZONES

In some ways, the oceans may have been even more amenable to prehistoric human mobility and more conducive to cultural contact compared to limited and constricted land avenues. Potential land routes may be traced more easily, but they were difficult to traverse, especially without the horse.

Further, tribes living in the interior of a land mass were often surrounded by other tribes, sometimes hostile. Boundaries were fought over, defended, merged, and changed, from all directions. Over the long human history, earth's land spaces have become increasingly filled up with people—mountains and valleys, nooks and crannies, niche by niche, continent by continent. This constantly shifting population has been pushing boundaries here and there, restlessly, aggressively over the millennia. People living in the interior of a land mass seem potentially vulnerable to attack from all directions. On the other hand, tribes located along a coast would have had the water as a buffer against attack on at least one side, more if they lived on a peninsula. Tribes on islands may have been the most secure of all, especially if surrounded by rich ocean resources, and with planned escape routes around any bend.

Not only were coasts relatively safe on at least one side, but also attack by boat concentrated a potential enemy into small containers, making them more easily defeated than a dispersed force on land. Survivors of a disabled or shipwrecked vessel may have been too debilitated to fight. The local people would quickly have assessed their vulnerable condition and may have chosen to kill them outright, or alternatively, perhaps partly out of curiosity and out of compassion, nursed the strangers back to health.

Japan's many islands provided their populations considerable control over who, when, and what influences were allowed on shore, and under what circumstances.[15] The periodic edicts cutting off contact with China during the Heian period, the successful rebuff of the attempted Mongol invasion during 1274 and 1281, and the long period of isolation during the Tokugawa period (1600–1868) clearly illustrate the power coasts and islands gave Japan. I think the North American coastal Indians probably had similar prerogatives. The Chumash Indians of the Channel Islands off southern California are one example. Their navigational skills provided power, social stratification, and economic clout not available to their inland relatives.[16]

Among the Indians of the northwest coast, slaves were highly valued until the late nineteenth century, so a live body arriving on their shores would not necessarily have been disposed of before an assessment was made. A few words, a few genes, and a few new ideas may have been introduced and integrated into the local population with the survival of even a single Korean, Chinese, Japanese, Polynesian, Micronesian, Melanesian, or Southeast Asian.[17] The length of the Asian and Pacific island coastlines, the size of the populations, the sophistication of the boats, and the great time depth of known human occupation—at least forty thousand years for Australia and two thousand years for Polynesia—provided ample time and setting for migration farther east. Indeed, the probability of occasional contact between the Old and New World seems stronger than that of no contact at all.

But, during most of the twentieth century, evidence of pre-Columbian Asian influence in North, Central, or South America has been generally dismissed as not worth researching by most scholars. The idea of the peopling of the Americas solely via the Bering Strait Land Bridge (Beringia) is so embedded that little discussion of alternate routes has occurred. Despite the distance from Beringia, many scholars seem to cling to the idea of a walking migration from Siberia, through North America, squeezed through the Ithmus of Panama and arriving, finally, in South America.

However, indicative of a growing interest in coastal areas, the 1998 volume of the journal *Arctic Anthropology* provides twenty-five articles by American, Japanese, and Russian scholars addressing the North Pacific–Bering Sea maritime societies. The organizers of the 1993 symposium state in their introduction that boat construction, seamanship, and the hunting of large and dangerous sea mammals far from shore "must rank among the impressive cultural achievements of cultural evolution," but they remain cautious and conservative about maritime routes for the peopling of the New World. Rigorous regional research has been done and reported, providing a firm base for future discussions on the coastal hypothesis for the peopling of the Americas.[18]

I believe a strong case can be made that navigation along the coasts of Asia had been ongoing over many millennia and that shipwrecks along North America almost certainly occurred, perhaps even frequently, as I discuss more fully later. Shipwrecks resulted in dead bodies, certainly, but sometimes live ones. To assume that all ships arriving on the west coast of America brought only dead sailors underestimates the human creative ability and will to stay alive. To assume that all survivors would be killed by local tribes is too narrow a conclusion. That some Japanese, and others, made shore safely seems to me quite probable. Some may have even planned to come.

The last organized discussion by archeologists on the topic of transoceanic influences in the Americas was in 1968, at a symposium held in Santa Fe, New Mexico, during the national meetings of the Society for American Archaeology. The theme, "pre-Columbian contact between the hemispheres and within the New World," resulted in a volume entitled *Man across the Sea. Problems of Pre-Columbian Contacts.*[19] The twenty-four papers provided valuable commentaries on the status of research at that time, but so many problems and so many highly charged controversies arose that archeologists have not held a similar conference since then.[20]

Because so little subsequent attention has been given to the topic, I draw on a few findings, especially botanical evidence, that reveal the academic milieu and the arguments.

Plant species considered for possible pre-Columbian distribution included the coconut, bottle gourd, sweet potato, corn, and cotton. Generally, authors of the papers in *Man across the Sea* seemed to waffle about on their topics; none stated categorically that any of these plants were definitely distributed across the seas one way or another before European contact. Further, the discussants concluded that if these plants did come from abroad, they probably floated without human assistance, and in truth, it really did not matter much either way.

Coconuts can float on their own; there is no conclusive evidence that their pre-Columbian distribution was aided by people coming across the Pacific. Bottle gourds, indigenous to tropical Africa, also could be "natural," rather than the result of human-assisted distribution. They too, floated, this time to the west, and presumably were successfully planted by beachcombing people native to South American shores, people who somehow knew exactly what to do with them by about 3000 B.C.[21]

The origins and distribution of the sweet potato and corn generated much debate in Santa Fe. Apparently sweet potato seed capsules also float in water, but the distribution of corn needs human assistance; therein lay a peculiar puzzle. Maize (corn) is a pre-Columbian, New World vegetable, domesticated in Mesoamerica. It was assumed to have been discovered by the Spanish and introduced to Europe in the sixteenth century. No one, as far as I know, has proved that corn can float to India, yet corn appears on sculptures there by the eleventh to thirteenth centuries.[22]

Herbert G. Baker, director of the Botanical Garden at the University of California, Berkeley, concluded, in his commentary to Section III of *Man across the Sea* on transoceanic contacts, that if they did occur, the question remains, Were they significant culturally?[23]

Generally, the arguments turn on the human capacity for innovation; any similarities between the Old and New Worlds during prehistoric times are testimony, many scholars believe, to the remarkable scope of human creativity: innovation, then, and not diffusion. These are important perspectives, but perhaps it is time to reconsider them, to reassess the evidence, and to recognize a need to develop new analytical tools for understanding a broad range of possible explanations, including the diffusion of ideas and people over surprising distances. Much new science has emerged since the 1968 Santa Fe conference. How might it apply to the many unresolved questions concerning human mobility across the seas?

PUZZLING DEPOSITS

Sometimes archeologists find the most unusual items in the strangest places. That is part of the challenge of the discipline. What does this small piece of information, this artifact, mean? How does it fit? Or sometimes just "what the hell is this doing here?"

A number of items found along the west coast of North America have generated that question.

Little by little, piece by piece, mile by mile, I think the evidence of trans-Pacific migration is accumulating and becoming more compelling. What were once believed to be uninhabitable coastal areas of northwestern North America during the last glacial period now clearly held pockets of living spaces called *refugiums,* where animals—and perhaps people—stopped, lived, and moved on. Ancient bear bones discovered in a cave in southeastern Alaska suggest that the coastal areas supported life much earlier than previously thought possible. Perhaps humans did not have to wait for the glaciers to melt; it is at least possible that prehistoric peoples traveled along the coasts in water craft, stopping here and there on the edges of land—the refugiums—and also along the edges of glaciers.

Glaciers can seem merely terrifying masses of dangerously shifting ice, major obstacles to human terrestrial travel, but for knowledgeable glaciologists, massive miles of ice at certain times of year are quite safe and interesting environments to explore. Early human travelers in small boats could have found rich marine resources all along the front faces of glaciers where they abutted the coasts, during the long glacial periods of the Pleistocene and also during the interglacial periods. People in small boats did not have to wait for the ice to melt to explore and populate the New World.

Cumulative information about the coasts and the currents strongly increases the probability that Asian navigators arrived on the west coast of America many times over the millennia. None of the bits and pieces discussed in the next section is conclusive on its own. A coin here and a sherd there can be explained away as a fluke. But the *combination* of cultural remnants along the coasts, added to the growing knowledge of currents, El Niños, and boats, generates reasonable speculation about the larger picture.

The theory of Japanese influence at Zuni does not propose a specific place where they landed or identify the Native Americans they encountered. However, the Chumash, Ipai, and Tipai of southern California are likely candidates. Further, given the amount of trade between Japan, Korea, and China on the western Pacific, can the origins of the curious items discovered in North America be determined?

Where is evidence that Japanese arrived? The Chinese porcelain identified as Ming probably from the Wan-li era (1573–1610) and found along Point Reyes just north of San Francisco, for example, could have traveled as cargo on a Japanese trading ship, rather than on Sir Francis Drake's ship *Golden Hind* in 1579 or Cermeno's ship *San Agustin* in 1595, the traditional explanations.[24] Also, Chinese coins could have been the currency in Japan at the time of a Japanese shipwreck or planned pilgrimage. The evidence of Asian material items is piecemeal, but the series of coastal discoveries we now turn to challenges us to think creatively about alternative explanations. If not by Asian ships, how did these items get to where they were found?

METAL IN AMERICA

Ancient coins occasionally crop up across America, including Chinese coins dating back to the fifth century B.C. along the west coast.[25] They are found in sites of former human occupation, on Native American ethnological items such as headgear and necklaces, and carefully stitched on armor. Given what we know about Pacific currents and the antiquity of Asian navigational skills, the presence of these coins should neither surprise nor puzzle us.

Chinese coins were first minted twenty-six hundred years ago. Margie Akin, who specializes in them, reported that literally billions have been distributed widely since then. For example, during just a few years in the Sung dynasty (A.D. 1004–7) the rate of coin production was 1.8 billion annually; later, during the 1070s, the production rate rose to over 5 billion annually. In one much-later year, A.D. 1527, China turned out 45 billion coins.[26]

Traditionally, all Chinese coins found in America are assumed to be post-European introductions, regardless of the date stamped on them. Yet, logically a coin could travel quite some distance anytime after it was minted. Old coins could join new ones in different uses. Akin found that Chinese coins were used for trading, gambling, decoration, medicine, and protection.

A magnificent Tlingit armor coat (see Figure 17) on exhibit at the Field Museum in Chicago provides an example.[27] Hundreds of Chinese coins cover the hard, tanned, old caribou skin, making the coat both an elegant piece of art and a formidable deterrent in close combat. A total of 222 coins cover just the right side; no count has been made of the whole coat. However, Akin studied

Figure 17. *Tlingit armor with Chinese coins*

this piece and estimated the total number of coins to be between 800 and 1,000. From the photographs she was able to identify 324. Further, she was able to report the mint names on 9. One coin is Japanese from the 1626–1769 period and the others are Chinese dating between 1644 and 1820, which suggests the coins identified could have been imported as early as 1796, when the youngest were minted (Jai Qing 1796–1820).[28]

If one-third were identified, what about the other two-thirds? Did all the coins arrive simultaneously, or were they accumulated over time from numerous sources? Chinese coins, regardless of age, tend to be associated with studies of *historical* archeology of Chinese immigrants, and thousands have been recorded in those contexts, yet a few seem always to remain unidentified, leaving open questions of their age, their origins, and the circumstances of their distribution.

CHINESE COINS IN JAPAN

This discussion is related to the Japanese-Zuni theory in two ways. One, it provides another kind of evidence to consider of Asian contact during prehistoric times. Second, more importantly for the Zuni enigma, Chinese coins might have arrived via Japan.

After a flurry of exchanges between China and Japan in the seventh to ninth centuries, a period of three hundred years followed, between 894 and about 1192, when supposedly no "official" contact took place between China and Japan. When the Japanese economy picked up after a civil war in 1221, the demand for luxury goods increased, putting pressure on Japan's limited currency, especially coins of small denominations. The resulting export of copper coins from China to Japan allowed a rapid increase in domestic trade.[29]

But the situation was complicated. Japan needed coins because it had stopped minting its own for a long period after the Tentoku era (957–961). No trade with China was supposed to occur and, by edict, coins were kept in short supply. Goods, not coins, were supposed to be used in exchanges.[30] (See Figure 18 for examples of Japanese coins minted in the eighth to tenth centuries.)

But despite official constraints, Japanese trade in Chinese coins increased. So, it seems logical to consider the possibility that old Chinese coins found in America could have been either old Chinese coins direct from China or Chinese coins cycled first through Japan.[31]

Sometimes the age of these coins and the context of their discovery raise questions of possible ancient origins. The October 2,

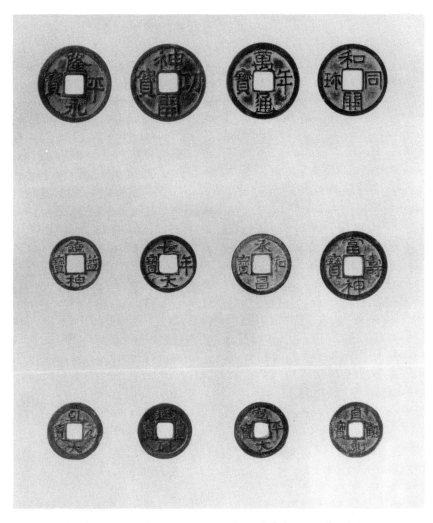

Figure 18. *Ancient Japanese coins, eighth to tenth century*

1911, issue of the *Alaska Sourdough,* a newspaper published in Douglas just across the channel from Juneau, the capital of Alaska, reported that Tlingit Indians had turned up a coin minted more than two thousand years ago, among many others, in a pottery jar near the village of Wrangell. One particular coin, being made of copper, stood out. It had a square hole in the center and was larger than a silver dollar. This coin was so old that some Chinese at the time thought it spoke of their ancient migration to the Americas.

Chinese coins show up on Shaman's masks[32] (see Figure 19)

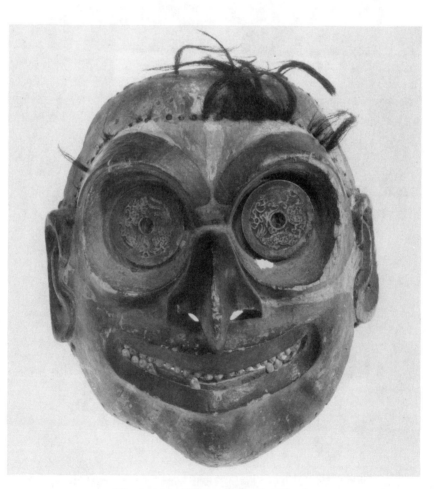

Figure 19. *Shaman's mask. Tlingit*

often enough to raise the question of possible prehistoric trade or other forms of contact. William Fitzhugh of the Arctic Studies Center of the Smithsonian Institution noted the parallels between America's northwest coast and Asia. Rather cautiously, he allowed that Asian influence may be the result of trade, flotsam, and disabled Japanese vessels and their crews arriving on the western coast of North America.[33]

FROM IRON TO ANCHORS

A variety of other Asian materials have cropped up along American coasts, most of it dismissed without sophisticated testing.[34]

The presence of prehistoric iron came to light at Ozette, a site on the Makah Indian Reservation on the northwest tip of the Olympic Peninsula in Washington. Ozette, a sort of American Pompeii, encompassed five long houses buried there by a sudden mudslide more than five hundred years ago. Thousands of its artifacts have been excavated; some are on display in the Makah Cultural and Research Center at Neah Bay. Among them are iron chisels (see Figure 20) used by whale hunters in ocean-going sailing canoes. Pieces of tropical bamboo also turned up in the mud-covered houses.[35]

Moving down the coast, clusters of Asian-related artifacts have been found in several areas: about sixty miles up the Columbia River on a small tributary in southwestern Washington and in shell mounds along the coasts of both northern and southern California. Pottery, baked clay figurines, iron, porcelain, and stone anchors are among the items found.

Pottery

Alison Stenger, an archeologist at the Institute for Archaeological Studies in Portland, Oregon, excavated and analyzed some two hundred pieces of pottery from a tributary near the Columbia River. The ceramic figurines date to a precontact period (A.D. 1250–1550) and appear to incorporate Japanese manufacturing techniques, including formal kiln firing.[36] Nothing like them has been found among the Indians now living in the area; they do not have a tradition of pottery making.

Figure 20. *Iron tools: Ozette site*

Several hundred fragments of Chinese porcelain dating to the fifteenth and sixteenth centuries were found in the vicinity of Drake's Bay, Marin County, just north of San Francisco. Currently the sherds are considered remnants of gifts to local Indians by Sir Francis Drake on the *Golden Hind* in 1579, or attributed to the wreck of the Spanish ship *San Agustin,* which was returning from the Philippines to Acapulco in 1595. An alternative source for some materials could be a Chinese ship with Chinese goods or a Japanese ship with Chinese goods. As we will see in the next chapter, commerce was active in the western Pacific hundreds of years before the Spanish arrived on America's coasts. Europeans came late to the Pacific compared to the Chinese, Koreans, and Japanese. Many Asian ships were transporting Chinese pottery along the Asian coasts during the previous thousand years; it seems possible that some of them may have drifted or explored eastward. I propose that Ming sherds sometimes associated with iron spikes in prehistoric and early historic sites in Marin County may originate from Chinese or Japanese trade or shipwrecks (see Figures 21 and 22). Numerous porcelain sherds have also shown up in excavation of Pecos, New Mexico.

Iron

Iron was a highly valued trade item in North America before our earliest written records. When Europeans first reached the west coast, they reported iron already present and in great demand. This fact is well established in the northwest coast area, but less certain for areas to the south. As the Spanish moved up the coast and the Russians moved down it in the late eighteenth century, however, both encountered Native Americans with iron and a great desire to obtain more.[37]

Northern California saw a flurry of archeological activity in Marin County during 1940 and 1941 under the direction of the anthropology department and the Lowie Museum at the University of California, Berkeley. Richard Beardsley, a graduate student at the time (he later became a specialist on Japanese culture), reported the recovery of sixty-nine Chinese porcelain fragments, thirty-eight bent iron spikes, and numerous human figures of baked clay in two principal and four minor sites around Drake's Bay. These artifacts were found from the surface to thirty-six inches deep.[38]

On July 16, 1941, at the height of an unusually busy summer field session, E. W. Gifford (then curator of the Anthropological Museum at the University of California, Berkeley) sent six iron spikes and three dirt samples from the Estero site, Drake's Bay, to Professor Colin Fink at Columbia University, for analysis. On October 17, 1941, Gifford received a letter from Fink stating, "There is no doubt in our mind that the spikes are of ancient origin."[39]

How "ancient" was that iron? Can those spikes be relocated? The photos can (see Figure 23). What about all that other iron so carefully labeled from Ron Olson's excavations on Santa Rosa Island during the 1920s (discussed in the next section)? Perhaps it is time to date selected iron pieces recovered from the shell mounds all along the coasts, using modern techniques. They may be Asian treasures from a prehistoric time.

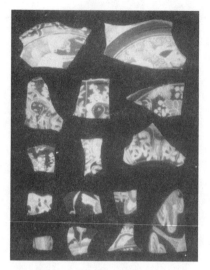

Figure 21. *Porcelain sherds from northern California coast*

Figure 22. *Porcelain sherds found at Drake's Bay, California*

Figure 23. *Iron spikes from Marin County, California*

The Tricky Gophers in California

When something is out of context, archaeologists sometimes say with the shrug, "The gophers must have put it there." And they are indeed pesky fellows, those gophers, disturbing stratigraphy everywhere. However, I think gophers may be too handy an explanation for archeologists who have to deal with things that are not where they are supposed to be. Here is an example:

While doing research in the Phoebe Hearst Museum at Berkeley on the porcelain pieces found along Reyes Point in Marin County, north of San Francisco, I came across a magnificent Japanese spearhead that had been found in a shell mound in Tamales Bay, just north of Reyes Point.

While helping me check the acquisition number and correspondence on that piece, Principal Museum Anthropologist Frank Norris opened other drawers that held remnants of iron from other places. In reading the descriptions of those fragile pieces, I learned that one iron fragment had been found thirty-eight inches below the surface in a shell mound on Santa Rosa Island, excavated in 1928 by Ronald Olson. Olson also encountered many other pieces of iron, including a knife fragment at a depth of three feet, six inches; even so, no reference to any iron appears in Olson's 1930 publication called *Chumash Prehistory*.[40]

In the museum's handwritten record book, there is only this comment for one specific piece of iron found thirty-eight inches deep in an undisturbed shell mound on Santa Rosa Island: "A gopher must have put it there."

In truth, those were early days for large theories, and Olson was an open scholar. Although he found iron in present-day Chumash Indian territory and assigned it, as was expected, to a *historic* intrusion (all iron is still automatically assigned to a historic period), he concluded his twenty-one-page report with a refreshing consideration of "Possible Oceanic Affiliations." Of course, not claiming definite evidence, he cautiously noted that late innovations, such as the circular shell hook, the perforated stone (a faint reminder of the club heads of Oceania), and by inference, the plank canoe, resembled Oceanic culture, which he called "relatively recent," without precise temporal definition.[41]

In 1975, divers off the coast of southern California found at various depths large stones with holes drilled through them (see Figure 24). More than twenty have been retrieved, some weighing as much as one thousand pounds. We don't know what they are. Some believe that they were Chinese anchors from large ships arriving during prehistoric times; others dismiss them, suggesting that they date to nineteenth-century Chinese fishermen. A possible quarry source in southern China has been identified.[42]

Among other items from sites in California is a cast bronze statuette that may be a knife handle, found eighteen inches deep in pit K, Smuggler's Cove, Santa Cruz, in 1928.[43]

The Japanese spearhead in Figure 25, identified as coming from the Magari Yari class, was found in a coastal shell mound in Marin County, just north of San Francisco, and assigned to the Final Pacific Period (1500–1769). Again, the explanation provided is that it probably came on a shipwrecked Manila galleon.[44]

Thus far, nowhere have any such obviously Japanese and Chinese items been credited as definitely prehistoric, regardless of how deeply they were buried in a shell mound. The Western perspective is consistent: An old Asian item found in America is

Figure 24. *Stone anchors, southern California*

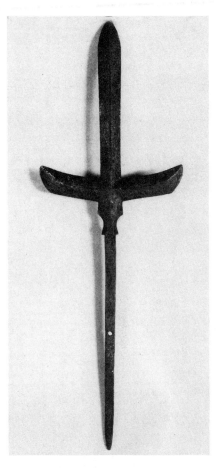

Figure 25. *Japanese spearhead excavated in a shellmound in Marin County, California*

assumed to have come during historic times, with the Spanish, the Russians, or the British, or in the exceptional case of the Ozette steel, possibly via a late prehistoric Japanese shipwreck.

What does this mean for the Zuni-Japanese connection? As yet, I cannot identify a landing place nor have I found a specific Japanese item in North America dated to the twelfth to thirteenth centuries. Does this mean no contact occurred at that time? Or that we have misidentified what has already been found?

I believe that some of the iron from the Santa Rosa Island and Marin County sites, when tested, will be found to be of early Japanese origin, that the technology for making and firing pottery figurines as found in northern California and Washington is Japanese, and that the pieces of Chinese porcelain found in California, and also Pecos, New Mexico, arrived via Chinese and Japanese ships. Further, I believe some of the early Chinese coins predate the European presence in North America, and that some of the hundreds of copper and bronze bells found may have come with pilgrims on a religious journey. It is time to look seriously and critically, using modern technologies, for past connections across the oceans. The evidence just might be there—in museum collections waiting for analysis, or in next season's archeological dig.

CHAPTER FIVE

SHIPS AND SHOALS

O n August 14, 1962, the *San Francisco Chronicle* reported that a young Japanese man had sailed alone in a nineteen-foot sloop from Osaka to San Francisco. It took him seventy-three days, from May 12 to July 24, and he endured five storms. It was an amazing transoceanic trip.

On June 28, 1980, a crew of six Japanese sailing a catamaran from Japan landed in San Francisco. They had been at sea fifty-three days in the forty-three-foot double canoe, *Yasei-go III*, built according to a design found on stone paintings believed to be five thousand years old. The voyage was sponsored by the Ancient Pacific Cultures Research Project in Tokyo and subsidized by Haruki Kadokawa, president of Kadokawa Publishing Company. The *Yasei-go III* had followed the North Pacific route along the Japan Current, the Kuroshio. Equipped with only sails, a rudder, and a centerboard, and propelled by winds and the current, the boat logged up to 170 miles a day, traveled 4,842 nautical miles, and arrived in San Francisco seven days ahead of schedule (see Map 11).[1]

In San Francisco, the crew complained only about the crowded quarters and that the boat sometimes got wet. The *Yasei-go III* continued south to Lima, Peru, and Valparaíso, Chile, weathering two hurricanes along Central America. The trip proved it is possible to cross the Pacific from Japan to North and South America in a catamaran.[2]

Courageous people continue to go great distances on small boats for pleasure and for adventure, even pedaling across the Atlantic in a self-powered boat. Rowing across the Atlantic is so common now that one man did it in 1995 just to raise money for volunteer ocean-rescue teams. It took him 103 days and about 500,000 oar strokes.[3]

Most of us modern landlubbers are intrigued but intimidated by the oceans. We cannot read the stars, assess the winds, or hoist a sail. The scientific knowledge possessed by a Micronesian sailor or a Polynesian navigator is not part of our intellectual tool kit.[4]

The navigational knowledge of people of the Pacific Rim goes back at least several thousand years, though little of it is understood by Westerners whose orientation historically is focused on Europe, the Atlantic, and the relatively small boats that began serious oceanic exploration in the late fifteenth century. By that time, Chinese, Korean, and Japanese ships had been on the high seas for at least a millennium, and all the major Polynesian islands had been inhabited.

Since much of early human activity occurred along coasts, quite likely more of our ancestors lived along the extensive coastal zones than lived inland. Agriculture is a relatively recent innovation, dating back only some twelve thousand years, and for a long time existed only in a few locations. The cultivation of crops eventually allowed a shift away from coastal and riverine areas and encouraged an increase of inland populations. But for much of human history, the seas, the coasts, the tidal waters, and the oceans were the most dependable sources of subsistence.[5]

It makes sense that much more prehistoric evidence awaits discovery along the millions of miles of coastlines on earth. Shifting sea levels surely conceal many ancient sites. Being in an interglacial period, as now, when sea levels are high, means that many early human occupation sites along the ocean coasts have been inundated. Sometimes, however, earthquakes uplift an area, as happened on Anangula Island in the Aleutians, thus protecting

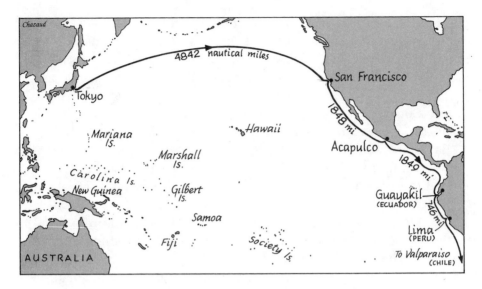

Map 11. *Route of the* Yasei-go III.

a five-thousand-year-old site. The Great Alaska Earthquake of 1964 uplifted a part of Montague Island in Prince William Sound twenty-three feet, exposing rock, beach, and a prehistoric site. The geologic history of Middleton Island, also in Prince William Sound, reveals six elevated marine terraces formed during earthquakes. The oldest and highest terrace was uplifted ten meters about 5,100 years ago and the youngest was uplifted 3.5 meters out of the intertidal zone during the 1964 earthquake. Twenty-two additional prehistoric sites were found through investigation of the older terraces along the central Gulf of Alaska coasts, further documenting a continuous 7,000-year archeological sequence in that region. Further south, along the Queen Charlotte Islands, exciting discoveries continue to be made, including human artifacts in ancient submerged locations.[6]

Also, in Japan, changing sea levels have modified the coastlines many times over the millennia. The same is true all around the Pacific "Ring of Fire"[7]; tectonic activity periodically altered the contours of coasts, sometimes inundating settlements and other times lifting them out of danger.[8]

BOATS, RAFTS, AND SMALL CANOES

Stephen Jett, professor of geography at the University of California, Davis, summarized the major findings by experts on the history and distribution of sailing craft in his comprehensive chapter "Diffusion Versus Independent Development" in *Man across the Sea*.[9] From this well-documented summary, we learn that canoes, small boats, and log rafts are safe and also fast; that Asians had sophisticated boats and large ships earlier than Europeans did; and that sea-going sailing rafts were in use off China's coasts before the fifth century B.C., and perhaps more than two millennia earlier.

The designs of log sailing rafts in Asia and in aboriginal America appear to be so similar that Edwin Doran, an expert on sailing craft, believes they must be related (see Figure 26). And since they are found on both sides of the Pacific, sailing rafts may have been the means of some of the earliest trans-Pacific voyages.[10]

A flurry of interest in oceanic travel was generated by Thor Heyerdahl, a maverick Norwegian adventurer, and his 1947 *Kon-Tiki* voyage, which focused on South American crossings to Polynesia on balsa rafts. In the 1970s, Heyerdahl shifted his interest and experiments to crossing the Atlantic on reed boats from Morocco to South America. His most serious and scholarly work, "American Indians in the Pacific: The Theory behind the Kon-Tiki Expedition," published in 1952, was attacked vehemently by many reviewers who objected to the idea of possible American origins of Polynesians and probably also to the success of his *Kon-Tiki* book and his subsequent fame. However, the feasibility of such a voyage was clearly proved to those less skeptical, those who were perhaps more knowledgeable of and less afraid of oceans.[11]

The distribution of balsa rafts, log dugouts, log rafts, and multiplank canoes along the west coast of southern California suggests links to Asia. Long before the sixteenth century, the Chumash Indians of the Santa Barbara area were quite accustomed to fishing in sea-going plank canoes in deep waters (see Figure 27). As noted earlier, the Island Chumash dominated an extensive shell trade and developed a complex, stratified society partly because boat ownership conveyed economic and political power.[12]

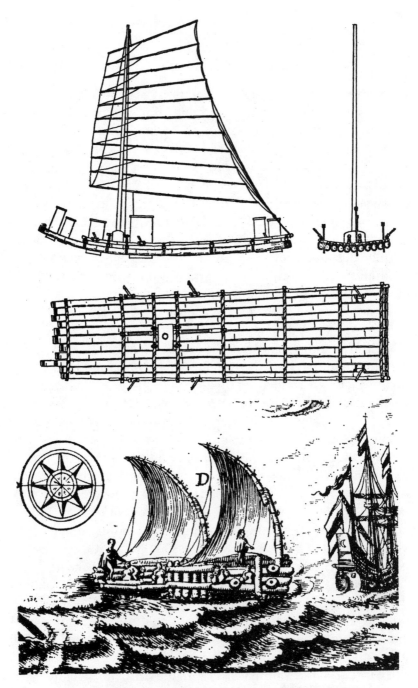

Figure 26. *Sailing raft designs. Top: Raft of Formosa.*
Bottom: Raft of Ecuador

To gain perspective on the relatively late but prehistoric contact of Japanese in the American Southwest (i.e., between the twelfth and thirteenth centuries), we need to acknowledge the great time depth for known oceanic travel elsewhere. For at least 40,000 years, *Homo sapiens* has had the same basic physical structure and intellectual capacities as now. If individuals and small teams of people in small boats and rafts can cross the oceans now without modern power, why could similar journeys not have been made repeatedly millennia ago?

E. James Dixon, with the Denver Museum of Natural History, raised significant questions in his book *Quest for the Origins of the First Americans*.[13] He and others have been puzzled that the earliest evidence of Paleo-Indian people in *North* America is not old enough to account for the earliest evidence of human occupation in *South* America. If the first inhabitants of the Western Hemisphere walked across Beringia from Asia, how could this be? The earliest sites should be in North America; they have not been found there yet.

Knut R. Fladmark, professor in the Department of Archaeology at Simon Fraser University in British Columbia, suggested the northwest coast might have been a means of access to North America via watercraft; there were some ice-free areas along British Columbia by 11,000 B.C. Fladmark further suggested that people in simple watercraft could negotiate the entire west coast of North and South America in ten years, which is much faster than walking the distance over the Ithmus of Panama. Fladmark posited that people did not have to wait around for the glaciers to melt in the continental interior to meander south by land; they could have moved quite rapidly along the coasts (see Map 12).[14]

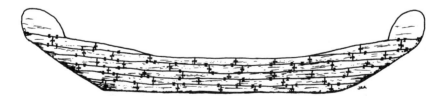

Figure 27. *Chumash seagoing plank canoe*

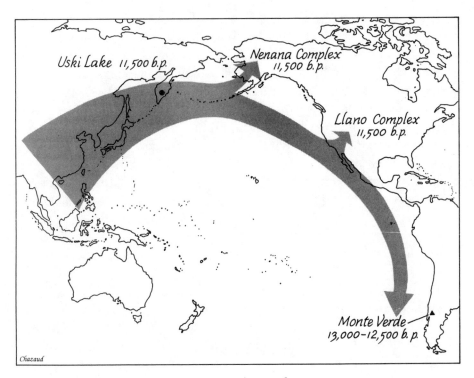

Map 12. *Proposed coastal routes.*

But the coastal route theory is not popular. Trekking the continents after the Pleistocene glacial period persists as the most accepted explanation for the exclusive avenue to the Americas.

Let us rethink this position:

The debate about the dating of the Monte Verde site, an early inland human occupation location in Chile, South America, is finally agreed upon: 12,500 B.P. (Before Present).[15]

An even earlier human presence in South America is suggested by traces of another occupation, located only seventy meters away. These appear to date to thirty-three thousand years ago. David J. Meltzer of Southern Methodist University reported this information in 1997 but he, like others, clings to the idea that people must have passed through North American heading south, somehow beginning the trek before twenty thousand years ago because the interior and coastal routes south from Alaska were presumed impassable during the long glacial period between twenty thousand and thirteen thousand years ago.[16]

Why is there this obsession with a north-to-south route by land? Couldn't people have come across the South Pacific, established themselves along the coast of South America, and then moved north? Might there not have been several routes, and numerous times when people arrived—from many directions?

Dixon also puzzled over the fact that Austronesia, which includes New Guinea and Australia, was occupied by modern humans at least by forty thousand years ago; significant water negotiation was necessary to get there. He and a few others are beginning to think that the Americas were, perhaps, populated from the south.[17] The possibility of an early south-to-north route requires serious thinking about possible marine routes to the Americas.

In addition, we should grant that some of the early people into the New World died out, or were taken over by later migrants, thus leaving no clear indications of their continuity.[18]

As suggested in Chapter 4, did periodic El Niños, with their anomalous westerly winds, hasten voyages eastward to many landings, adding new ideas and new people to the New World? Once on the high seas, catching any one of the established currents and assisted by winds from the west, the huge continents of the Americas might be quite difficult to miss.

JAPANESE SHIPBUILDING

The next question is, If significant Japanese contact occurred on the west coast of North America, followed by a migration of people to the Zuni area, what is known about Japanese mastery of navigation and about the relative size of their boats in the thirteenth century? I am not proposing a small canoe with a single messianic Buddhist leader traveling alone; I suggest we consider a ship with at least fifty to one hundred persons committed to finding the safe middle of the world in the east. Did the Japanese have the navigational knowledge to embark on such a planned, one-way trip?

Here is some background:

Japan has been peopled at least thirty thousand years and

probably much longer. The earliest arrivals could have walked across land at two points: from the peninsula now known as Korea to Kyushu and from Siberia to Hokkaido, the northernmost island. Then about twenty thousand years ago, land access to the Asian continent was cut off by rising water from the melting of massive glaciers, marking the end of the Pleistocene period and creating the cluster of the Japanese islands (see Map 13), and also separating North America from Siberia. The distance across the Sea of Japan to China now is more than 800 kilometers (500 miles) and the shortest distance between Japan and Korea is 200 kilometers (125 miles).[19]

Even after the Japan islands became separated by water, new populations continued to arrive across the intervening seas, obviously by boat or raft. The earliest ceramics known in the world mark the beginning of the Jomon (meaning "cord-marked") period, twelve thousand years ago.[20] Subsequently, other distinctive populations arrived representing, for example, the Yayoi period (300 B.C.–A.D. 300) followed next by the Yamato influences, all of which arrived across water. Although there is no clear evidence that the first occupants of Japan were frequent or willfully ocean-going people, the extensive coasts of the island cluster and the long-established importance of fishing to the economy imply ocean-going skills. Recent archeological evidence at the Shimo-Takabora site on the western coast of the volcanic island of Oshima, about fifty kilometers south of Tokyo, indicates that by eighty-five hundred years ago a variety of fish, including tuna as well as sea turtle and dolphin, were being caught. To obtain these resources fishermen had to venture quite far offshore, where they were vulnerable to periodic storms and, perhaps, also the wind shifts initiated by El Niño events begun south of the equator.

One of the major controversies in anthropology in the twentieth century was provoked by Emilio Estrada, of Museo Victor Emilio Estrada in Ecuador, and the Smithsonian team of Betty Meggers and Clifford Evans. Their documentation of remarkable similarities between Japanese Jomon pottery and the ceramic complex excavated at Valdivia, Ecuador, generated a roar of disbelief in the 1960s. Yet sixteen of the decorative techniques identified as diagnostic of Valdivia A have been identified in Jomon samples: twelve of them at the Sobata, Ataka, Izumi, and other sites on Kyushu. This was early, very early—3000–1500 B.C.—but

Map 13. *Japan and the Far East.*

consistent with the fishing capabilities and ceramic production in Japan at that time.[21]

Boat motifs featured in several Japanese tombs date to about the first century A.D.[22] Also, clay models from tombs of the Kofun period (circa A.D. 300) display fairly sophisticated knowledge about boats (see Figure 28).

During much of Japan's history, transport by land was far more difficult than transport by sea. Many sheltered channels and safe anchorages exist all around the islands, which, combined with the mountainous character of 70% of the land area, encouraged a flourishing marine-based transportation system.[23]

The earliest Japanese chronicles mention that shipbuilding and navigation skills progressed rapidly during the reign of Empress Suiko (A.D. 593–628) when the Japanese court sent frequent missions to the Chinese courts of Sui and Tang. Between A.D. 630 and 894, fifteen official embassies journeyed to China by boat. This was a period when Japan incorporated and modified Chinese items and ideas, such as writing, architecture, Taoism, and Buddhism. A suspension of official envoys occurred in A.D. 894, but informal exchanges continued via limited trade and increased pirate activity to meet the demand for luxury items. Even when trade with China was forbidden, shipping between the many Japanese provinces thrived. Indeed, the decrease in envoys to China led to an increase in shipping on the Japanese coast to collect annual tribute and rents. Sea routes connected nineteen Japanese provinces.

By the eleventh century A.D., extensive sailing capabilities had developed in Japan. Numerous Japanese-built ships continued to traverse the unpredictable and frequently turbulent waters between Japan, Korea, and China during the twelfth century.[24] A vigorous exchange of goods and ideas continued during the thirteenth and fourteenth centuries.

After Kublai Khan became emperor of China and established his capital at Peking in 1264, he sent envoys to Japan demanding

Figure 28. *Model of a Japanese Haniwa clay boat. Length 35 inches*

that the Japanese, then under Hōjō leadership, submit to his rule or be invaded. When the Japanese refused, the Mongols made two major attacks on Japan, in 1274 and 1281, with large numbers of troops (variously reported as fifteen thousand Mongol and Chinese and seven thousand Korean sailors) and as many as three hundred large vessels and four to five hundred small craft.[25] Both invasions were unsuccessful, turned away by Kamakura's samurai forces, storms, and a "divine wind" or *kamikaze* that broke up the attacking fleets.[26] During those troubled times of invasions and threats, many a boatload of Buddhist monks traveled to and from Japan, to and from China, and to and from India. Then why not to North America?

PIRATES

Another area of Japanese success in navigation is the number of ship-borne plunderers called *Wakō*. A considerable nuisance at times, they also were sometimes employed by the courts to operate like protective navies along the Kyushu coast.[27] Wakō activity increased after 894, when official commerce with China was supposed to cease. By the sixteenth century, they had reached the Straits of Malacca, three thousand miles south.[28]

Koreans also participated in coastal raids; pirates from northern Korea attacked Japan in 1019.[29] But mostly, Japanese pirates harrassed the Korean coast. In fact, the Wakō caused such a commotion that in 1026 rumors of a possible Korean-Japanese war spread in Kyoto, then capital of Japan. The following year, the Korean government sent a protest mission to Japan and ninety pirates from Tsushima, a center of Japanese pirate activity, were executed in front of the Korean envoy. Further, the Japanese authorities sent a letter of apology to Koryo, the Korean capital at the time, and requested that formal trade relations be established, which they hoped would direct Wakō activity into legitimate commerce.[30]

If there was this amount of pirate activity along the Asian coasts including China and Korea, perhaps peoples other than Japanese also sailed to the Americas. The Koreans had better boats and built them earlier. The Japanese adapted refined shipbuilding skills from the Koreans, who in turn had acquired technical knowledge developed even earlier from the Chinese (see Figure 29).[31]

In any case, by the thirteenth century, Japanese ships were strong, well designed, and able to mount between thirty-five and seventy-five oars, and, clearly, to sail thousands of miles abroad, as demonstrated by the pirate ships to the South China seas and beyond.[32]

SHIPWRECKS

The number of Japanese shipwrecks on the coast of China offers additional evidence of the frequency of Japanese-initiated voyages to the mainland. Here are documented examples: Six Japanese ships were wrecked off on the Chinese coast during a twenty-six-year period between 1176 and 1202. At least one of those ships was large enough to hold one hundred men. Another carried seventy-three.[33] If six ships of this size were lost during so

Figure 29. *Japanese ship: Kyushu*

short a period, how many made the passage successfully? And if the Japanese could navigate the notably difficult passage between Japan and China, could they not also have sailed safely to the east, either by intent or by mishap?[34]

Additional information is available for the fourteenth century, when Ashikaga Yoshimitsu, a successful, aristocratic shogun, commissioned large ships for overseas trade. These vessels were made of planks linked together with iron brackets and caulked with rushes. They came in three sizes: large vessels carrying 300 men, medium ships for 100 to 200 men, and smaller ones for 40 to 80 men. Korean sources report an average of 100 men per Japanese ship. The Wakō flotillas ranged from twenty to a hundred ships, from 2,000 to 10,000 men. One unusually large Japanese fleet of 350 ships attacked the Korean city of Happ'o in 1374, killing a reported 5,000 Korean troops. Although some of these ships were unwieldy, with flat bottoms, and had to be rowed when moving against the wind, many Wakō bought better-designed vessels with double hulls and sharp prows from Fukien and Chekiang provinces in China.[35]

For additional perspective, though this postdates the time of the proposed pilgrimage to North America, consider the intentional voyages that some Japanese made to Mexico in the early 1600s, a time of active participation by the Japanese government in exploring trade opportunities with the Portuguese, Spanish, and Dutch. (For an example of ships of that period see Figure 30.) By 1602, Japan already had a colony of fifteen thousand people on Luzon in the Philippines, and did not want to miss out on trading opportunities opened up by the Spanish in the New World. In 1610, twenty-three Japanese merchants and two Japanese noblemen, Tanaka Shōsake and Shuya Ryusai, sailed for Mexico City with Vivero, a retiring governor of the Philippines who had been shipwrecked on Japanese shores in 1609. The Japanese on that first embassy returned the following year, 1611.

Next, in 1613, Shogun Iyeyasu sent an embassy of 180 Japanese including 60 Samurai first to New Spain (Mexico), where some were baptized and perhaps remained. Others continued, on a Spanish ship, first to Spain and then to Rome where they met the Pope on November 3, 1615, returning to Japan by 1620. For a while then, in the early seventeenth century, the Japanese were active on the high seas, exploring market opportunities abroad.[36]

Figure 30. *Japanese ship, early seventeenth century. Painting of a "Licensed Vessel" from Nagasaki, 1622*

JAPANESE SHIPWRECKS IN AMERICA

Prehistoric times in North America (i.e., before written records) overlap times of written history in Japan where writing had been introduced from China in the seventh century A.D. The documentation on which this discussion relies is limited to sources available in English, set down after Europeans began to arrive along the North American west coast. It clearly indicates a Japanese presence all along the coasts as soon as records became available.

Starting at the far end of the central North Pacific, in the Aleutian Islands, and moving east and down the Pacific coastline, a number of wrecked and disabled Japanese ships were reported by European explorers and traders beginning in the late eighteenth century. Russians discovered Japanese stranded on the Aleutian island of Unalaska in 1794.[37] In 1837, Ronald McDonald of the Hudson's Bay Company found a ship from Japan at the mouth of the Columbia River.

The most complete compilation of early historic Japanese shipwrecks in North America was made by Charles Wolcott Brooks, who worked for the government of Japan at the port of San Francisco from 1853 until 1875. His report, first published by the California Academy of Sciences in 1876, provides details on sixty ships, the survivors, cargo, and often other circumstances encountered between 1613 and 1876.[38]

The population of Japan stood at some thirty-three million in 1874. A total of 22,670 sailing vessels of Japanese style were registered for coastal trade. Their size ranged from 8 to 383 tons, and the number of crew members averaged from eight to twelve men.[39]

An important event in Japanese history, one that influenced ships and trade, was the imperial decree of 1635, which stipulated that any Japanese who left their country for whatever reason, even to study, and thus were exposed to foreign influences could not return. This applied to fishermen blown off course.

Another edict, under Shogun Iyemitsu in 1639, commanded the destruction of all boats built using a foreign model. Only the junk of Japanese design could be used, with no improvements allowed. These mandates weakened Japan's sea-going abilities, making its ships more vulnerable to shipwreck than the earlier and more-sophisticated vessels that had been modeled after Chinese, Korean, and sometimes Portuguese and Spanish ships.[40]

The Japanese junk specifications required open sterns and large square rudders that made them unfit for ocean navigation, which was the whole idea: Get off course, catch a storm, lose a rudder, and there was no way to return home. The Isolation Period worked. Very few Japanese exposed to any foreign influences returned during the Tokugawa (Edo) period, and no foreigner was invited to visit, effectively cutting Japan off for almost 250 years until 1868.[41]

Brooks's analysis of the sixty disabled Japanese craft documented between 1613 and 1876 included where some were found, for example, eight on the Aleutian Islands; six off the coast of Kamchatka; two each in other Alaskan, Oregonian, and Hawaiian, and Brooks islands; and one each off San Diego, Acapulco, Nootka Sound, and San Bonito, Queen Charlotte, Cedros, Providence, Baker's, Stapleton, Ocean, and Ladrone islands. In twenty-three wrecks, the number of persons on board was known to total 293, or an average of almost 13 people to a junk (from 3 to 35 in individual boats). Sometimes the survivors were identified: 222 persons were saved in thirty-three wrecks, or an average of about 7 persons in each disaster documented. The 122 known deaths on eleven ships averaged 11 deaths to each wreck. The average drifting time for fifteen vessels was a little over seven months.

Brooks also noted an increase in the number of shipwrecks reported during the nineteenth century, a time when more ships of many nationalities were on the high seas, making the likelihood of wrecks being identified far greater. In the seventeenth century, only a few Spanish galleons were plying the Pacific and European traffic had just begun.

Given the number of disabled Japanese vessels recorded on the North American west coast during historic times, how many might have made land on eastern Pacific shores during prehistoric times? Surely the Japanese ships did not suddenly start arriving only after someone was there to write about them.

George Quimby, Professor Emeritus at the Burke Memorial Washington State Museum of the University of Washington, attempted to figure how many. Quimby became interested in the amount of iron found on the northwest coast, and estimated the number of prehistoric shipwrecks, based on the number documented during historic times. Using the data in Brooks's 1876 report, Quimby noted that six Japanese vessels reached the northwest coast shores during the fifty-one-year period between 1782 and 1833. (The number was actually seven, counting one with three survivors found shortly before reaching shore.) Based on this record, Quimby stated, "One can hypothesize that 14 or 15 wrecked vessels per century reached Northwest Coast shores." Quimby applied that figure to the twelve and a half centuries between A.D. 500, when tools of iron became standard on ships, and A.D. 1750. He projected there could have been 187 wrecked junks between A.D. 500 to 1750, which at the rate of three adze blades and three chisel blades per junk would have totaled 1,122 iron blades available. A more radical estimate of one wreck per year, he suggests, would have made seventy-five hundred iron blades available to Indians on the northwest coast of North America.[42]

Quimby based his estimates on two assumptions: Ships were, first, inadvertently swept off course and subsequently wrecked. He does not discuss those that might have arrived safely. Perhaps our Western mode of thinking tends to assume that the Japanese would not come to North America on purpose; if they came, it was by accident—a storm, a shipwreck.

In an article on Japanese drift records, Fumio Kakubayashi, a Japanese scholar in the Department of Modern Languages at Massey University in New Zealand, responded to a hypothesis posed by Andrew Sharp in 1963 about motives for migration.[43] According to Kakubayashi, there are hundreds of pre-modern Japanese records on drifting. His research indicates that Japanese boats drifted in almost all directions, depending on the time of year or the current they caught, accidently or otherwise. There are records of Japanese ending up in Hawaii, North America, Micronesia, Southeast Asia, and Kamchatka.[44]

Kakubayashi noted that official envoys were sent to China during the Sui (A.D. 589–618) and Tang dynasties (A.D. 618–907) and stated the ships were fairly large by then; the distance between coastal China and Japan was only about five hundred miles. Still, "the trip was very dangerous." Sometimes the ships were caught in storms and drifted as far as Southeast Asia, two to three thousand miles south. During the Tokugawa (Edo) period (1600–1868), Japanese ships were reported in Annam (Vietnam), and in Mindanao and Luzon in the Philippines.

Kakubayashi apparently found no Japanese records of two-way "accidental" trips until the Tokugawa period, when occasionally drifters were rescued and returned to Japan by Europeans, Americans, Chinese, or Southeast Asians. His discussion of the causes of migration expands on the reasons given by Sharp, who emphasized the role of accident, unintentional one-way trips. Kakubayashi argued that departures from Japan need not have been by accident or by exile; some migrations might have been initiated on purpose because of trade, natural disasters, quarrels, warfare, and population pressure at home.

RELIGION AND MOBILITY

Especially significant for the theme of this book is Kakubayashi's statement that "one direct impetus which motivated people to navigate the ocean for an unknown destination could have been religious belief."[45] The American archeologist Gordon Ekholm also pondered religious motives, particularly some Buddhist sects' predilection for proselytizing.[46] The incentive supplied by religion, while rarely discussed, is especially relevant to the theory of the Japanese-Zuni connection.

Kyotsu Hori reported that more than 120 Buddhist monks of Chinese and Japanese origin crossed the sea between China and Japan during the hundred-year period preceding the Mongol invasions (A.D. 1274 and 1281). Much religious activity took place during the twelfth century. Some of the Chinese monks who came to Japan exchanged letters with their friends and masters in China. One shogun, Sanetomo, was planning a pilgrimage to a holy mountain in China and had a ship constructed for the trip to the mainland. Even during the hectic times of the first Mongol crisis, a shogunal regent, Tokimune, sent two monks to study with a Chinese Zen master, and a few years later (1278) he sent the same two monks back to China to invite their Zen master, Mugaku Sogen, to come to Japan as head of the Engaku Temple at Kamakura.[47]

Religion is a powerful motivator and Japan was the center of a great deal of religious activity during the twelfth and thirteenth centuries. Clearly, substantial Japanese ships were available and could provide a means to venture east in search of the middle place of the universe.

CHAPTER SIX

TEETH AND BONES, BLOOD AND DISEASE

ertain branches of biological anthropology and medical science provide important information about past populations by studying selected aspects of the human anatomy: a tooth here, a fossil bone there, frequency of specific blood types, evidence of past diseases, and vulnerability to present ones.

So, what about biological evidence of this proposed migration and the merging of two populations? The Zuni are known to be different from other Native Americans. Might their distinctive physical characteristics be the result of admixture with Japanese?

Ultimately, I believe DNA studies will support my premise that Japanese pilgrims arrived in the Zuni area in the late thirteenth century. The Human Genome Project eventually may be able to identify which specific populations came to North America and merged with which populations of Native Americans. But these potentially conclusive studies have not been accomplished yet. And if they are to be done, I believe it should be at the request of the Zuni Tribe.

Perhaps the mixed heritages of human genes will someday be read like x-rays of bones and sonograms of soft tissues, but there is good reason to present data now in hand on the biological questions pertinent to the theory under discussion.[1]

If the Japanese and the Zuni shared an ancestor in the far distant past, would the descendant population carry a genetic record? I believe it would because our bodies are bundles of genetic material with critical clues to biological history. Before proceeding further though, I present a little genetic terminology to assist in assessing biology's role in solving the Zuni-Japanese enigma.

Molecules called *nucleotides (bases)* are made of proteins, which are represented by four letters: A, C, G, T. These four letters are combined in millions of different ways and strung along threads called *DNA (deoxyribonucleic acid)*. DNA holds the information necessary to tell the genes what to do. As many as three billion nucleotides are strung together inside gametes, which are cells with special genes that have the capacity to split into reproductive blueprints located on the twenty-three pairs of chromosomes found within each human cell. Somehow all the proteins, molecules, and genes are programmed to provide critical information in each chromosome, hopefully at the right time and in the appropriate sequence without any serious errors. These processes contribute to our birth and keep us alive for an amazingly long time.

In order to reflect past changes, rearrangements of proteins have to mark a molecule, be "read" by RNA (ribonucleic acid), be translated to DNA, and endure the selective pressures against changes detrimental to the survival of the organism.

To support my theory, tiny rearrangements of proteins-molecules-genes must be identified in the key populations: Zuni and Japanese. If the variations are so minute that they do not show up in the phenotype or the genotype of the Zuni or the Japanese, then we are not likely to see any significant differences in bones, teeth, blood, or incidence of disease.

Fortunately, dental morphology was analyzed in the 1970s; prehistoric skeletal remains were analyzed in the 1930s and 1940s; a major study on blood alleles was performed by physical anthropologists in the 1970s; and the "Zuni disease" was revealed in the 1980s.

DENTAL MORPHOLOGY

Teeth are remarkably resilient records of our prehistoric pasts. Without intervention, we cannot alter the wrinkles on cusps or modify the number of roots of our molars. We are born with them.

To support the Japanese-Zuni connection, Zuni teeth should be different from other Native American teeth and similar to Japanese teeth in some specific features. And they are.

The cusp of Carabelli is one of many dental characteristics that varies in frequency among different human populations; it is an extra cusp on the upper first molar (and sometimes on the second). As far as we know, there is no advantage to having or not having this particular bump on a tooth (see Figure 31). It is just one of those peculiar genetic features that appears in human populations in different forms and frequencies.

Caucasians are much more likely to have a cusp of Carabelli than are Asians. Native Americans are more likely to have it than are Japanese. The Zuni incidence of the cusp is about the same as the Japanese: relatively rare.

Here are some figures. In 72 Japanese families studied in 1958 by Tadashi Tsuji, the extra cusp on the upper first molar appeared on 67 (39.64%) of 169 male teeth and on 53 (31.18%) of 170 female teeth examined.[2] The frequency of Carabelli's cusp on 339 teeth of Japanese children, ages 9 to 11 years, was 35.4%.

A study reported in 1987 by Christy G. Turner, II, an American dental morphology specialist and professor of anthropology at Ari-

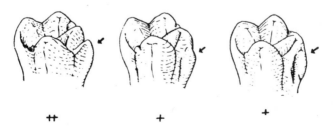

Figure 31. *Three types of Carabelli's cusp*

zona State University, indicated that 143 (31.2%) of 458 recent Japanese teeth (in contrast to prehistoric Jomon teeth) examined had this feature.[3]

In New Mexico, the incidence of Carabelli's cusp in 517 Zuni teeth was 36.2%, reported in 1972 by a team of researchers who looked at many biological features in Southwest Indians. This Zuni frequency appears in sharp contrast to that for other Native Americans. For example, over half (53.3%) of the nearby Pima Indians in Arizona have the extra cusp; Native Americans in general average a 60.2% frequency for the feature.[4]

Why is the frequency of this wrinkle different in Zuni teeth (36% in contrast to 60%)? And why is it so similar to the Japanese incidence of the feature (36% in Zuni and 31%–35% in Japanese)?

Next, almost all North Asians and Native Americans have shovel-shaped incisors; almost nobody else does. The Zuni incidence differs from that in other Native Americans in a way that I believe reflects Japanese admixture. Like the Japanese, most Zuni have the extra enamel ridge around the inside of the front incisor teeth (see Figure 32). Generally *all* full-blooded American Indians have this extra strengthening of the front teeth (Caucasians almost never do and Africans, very rarely).

A study of Japanese living in Valparaíso, Chile, reported that 87.3% of the incisors examined were shovel-shaped.[5] A comparable study in Japan reported 94.6% of subjects (686/725) having this shoveling feature.[6] The Zuni incidence is also high (94.4%), but lower than that in other American Indians, which is usually 100% in unmixed populations. There is a clear similarity between the Japanese (94.6%) and Zuni incidence (94.4%).

The number of cusps on the second molar on the lower jaw also varies among human populations (see Figure 33). Both Indians and Eskimos tend to have a relatively high incidence of the five-cusp pattern (60.4% and 57.4%, respectively).[7] The incidence among Asian populations is much lower. Turner's examination of 352 Japanese lower second molars revealed that only 46 (13.1%) had the five-cusp feature. In the Zuni study, 183 (34.9%) of 523 individuals had this pattern.[8] The Zuni are intermediate, having a lower incidence than American Indians (60%), but a higher incidence than the Japanese (13%).

These three features are not the only ways that Zuni dentition

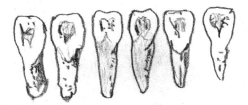

Figure 32. *Shovel-shaped incisors*

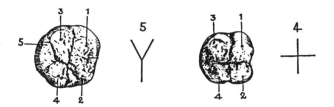

Figure 33. *Second lower molar cusp patterns*

differs from other Native American teeth. In another study, Richard Scott and colleagues inspected and measured hundreds of teeth and diagrammed the relative distance, or closeness, of the frequency of ten crown features for five major American Indian populations in the Southwest United States. The Zuni cluster was consistently set apart, not only from the Navaho and Apache, but also from other populations nearby: the Papago, Pima, and Maricopa.[9]

Finally, in another study, James Spuhler found that Zuni dental features, though clearly distinctive in many ways, seem to fit slightly more closely with California Indians than with their nearby Indian neighbors in the Southwest. This is in the right direction for the migration theory presented here.[10]

Since Turner and his students arrived at some general and important conclusions relevant to my theory, let us consider his thesis about Asian teeth.[11]

Turner's global survey reveals significant differences between the southern and northern Asian populations, which he labeled Sundadonts and Sinodonts. The Sundadont (South Asian) pattern is less variable and older than that of the North Asian Sinodonts.[12] Overall, the contemporary Japanese dental pattern is more similar to the teeth of people from southern China. However, Turner suggested that the teeth of Jomon people were more like North Chinese Sinodonts. Later admixture occurred in Japan when the Yayoi people (Sundadonts) arrived from the south with slightly different dental genes, and also a rice agricultural tradition that added more carbohydrates to the diet, promoting, Turner suggested, a general deterioration and gradually smaller teeth.

Turner further proposed a three-part reconstruction of the history of Japanese populations on the basis of teeth: (1) The ancestors of the Ainu were derived from a southern Sundadont population. (2) They mixed to some extent with immigrants of Jomon people who were Sinodonts from the north. (3) A third major population, the Yayoi, from the south introduced different clusters of teeth features along with rice-crop technology.

Can similar kinds of changes over time be identified in the Southwest? Could it not be that Zuni teeth, like Japanese teeth, have genetic histories that reflect admixture with different populations arriving from different directions? Just as hominid structural skeletons have become weaker, thinner, and more fragile over time, teeth have tended to become smaller and fewer in number.[13] Further, there is a trend toward fewer cusps on the crowns, and Japanese and Zuni teeth reflect that trend, more than do other Native American groups.

Turner's dental studies encounter the same difficulties with genetics as do studies of the rest of the human anatomy: Why and how did particular clusters of traits come about? What possible difference does more or fewer cusps or roots make in evolutionary terms? How are the drift of gene clusters over time and space and the founder effect (the differential frequence of alleles in fragmented populations) factored in? What happens with admixture? Which features are "tougher," more dominant, and more likely to appear in mixed populations?

We might also ask how contemporary teeth compare with ancient ones. To answer that question, Turner further refined the method of measurement of dental variations by introducing "expression counts," which measure the continuous variation of a crown or root trait, thus increasing the likelihood of recognizing its presence in archeological populations represented only by a few individuals.[14]

I have shown that three modern dental features—cusp of Carabelli, shovel-shaped incisors, and the number of cusps on the lower second molar—place Zuni dentition clearly separate from that of other Native Americans in ways that might be explained by admixture with Japanese.

Why else might Zuni teeth be so different from the teeth in other Native Americans? And so similar to Japanese? How many Japanese possessing a lower incidence of the cusp of Carabelli, shovel-shaped incisors, and five cusps on the lower second molar in the late thirteenth century would it take to lower a Native American population's incidence of these features reported seven hundred years later? Has anyone looked at the teeth from the prehistoric sites and found them also different in these ways?

RECONNECT THOSE BONES

Next, what do the bones from the Zuni area of Southwest America reveal about thirteenth-century populations? Do the remnants of burials excavated at the famous Hawikuh village site and other ruins in the Zuni vicinity indicate continuity of one population over time, or two or more separate populations merging? If the new population that came was large enough and different enough to be identified in the skeletal remains, then the burials for that critical period should reflect two populations (see Figure 34).

And they do, but there is little agreement about how much.

Frank H. H. Roberts and Carl Seltzer[15] came to this conclusion about the Zuni bones they analyzed in the 1920s and 1940s. The Zuni skeletons from Pueblo IV sites, beginning in the late thirteenth century, suggest the arrival of a new population characterized by rounder, smaller crania and shorter leg bones. Further, the period after their arrival was marked by many changes in the local culture, as documented in the archeological record. Here is a summary of the discussion of the skeletal remains for that period.

Figure 34. *Excavation at Hawikuh site, 1921*

Frank Roberts of the Bureau of American Ethnology directed the excavation of the Village of Great Kivas, located just northeast of present-day Zuni. He also excavated the Kiatuthlanna site, just west of Zuni in eastern Arizona. He found both long heads (clear continuity of the previous population) and also distinctly Mongoloid broad heads—evidence for the arrival of a new element in the population, "clearly demonstrated by the physical remains of the people." Further, he reported that the advent of this "alien group" was followed by a period of transition and instability.[16]

Carl Seltzer studied thirty-five crania found in burials at the Old Hawikuh Zuni site and he agreed with Roberts that the physical features of the group he studied are "in many respects highly distinctive in character" and that the group of Old Hawikuh is represented by small heads, "illustrated by the size of the cranial capacity and cranial module, and the presence of a short skull length and narrow skull width."

However, Seltzer differed with Roberts about the significance of the changes and the amount of outside genetic influence reflected in the skeletal modifications observed. He suggested the modifications were the result of absorption of new blood through intermittent small contacts with other groups, intermarriage, and so on, but not any "enormous influx of new blood" nor a "whole-sale arrival of new peoples."[17]

Roberts reported sharper indications of two populations and included more skeletal features in his analysis. As far as I know, the question of skeletal evidence of two different peoples at the onset of Pueblo IV remains unresolved. Perhaps the migration stories of the Pueblo peoples will keep the question alive: How are the variations to be explained? And, what measurements are the most significant?

These two scholars were working with different skeletal remains excavated in the 1920s and 1930s. What might a contemporary team of physical anthropologists trained in the latest technology find if they were to review the skeletal material from Pueblo IV sites on the Zuni Reservation? And, what might be learned if they compared them with Japanese skeletons from the same or slightly earlier period? Exploring and testing the evidence of this one small Japanese-Zuni migration may provide larger insight to what has happened periodically throughout human history. But new methods and new models must be generated to test for biological messages of past mixes embedded in bones.

Certainly data for future comparative studies abound in the Southwest and in Japan. The Japanese have an impressive amount of archeological materials, including bones, teeth, pottery, and settlements. Over five thousand Paleolithic sites have been identified predating Jomon (twelve thousand years ago), hundreds of these have been excavated. In addition, thousands of reports and articles have been published, mostly in Japanese, about sites postdating the Paleolithic period.[18]

Japanese crania are known to be broad and small. I believe the changes observed in Pueblo IV skeletons are consistent with the introduction of Japanese immigrants.

In summary, at least two early studies of Zuni remains reveal distinctive changes in skeletal measurements suggesting new additions to the gene pool about the thirteenth century. And, Japanese skulls and skeletons have characteristics consistent with those changes: broader and smaller crania and shorter stature.

However, by themselves such bones from the excavations near Zuni do not necessarily confirm my theory. Many other kinds of information must be considered.[19] For example, were the short skeletons in late thirteenth-century burials the result of nutritional stress? This was a tough and lean time (1275–1300) of drought. Perhaps the genes shaping the skeletons came from the same pool as earlier, but manifested a shorter stature because of famine. Nutritional deprivation may modify overall height, but how is the changed *shape* of the skull from a long head to a rounder head explained? Cradle boards used to support infants can mold skulls, but the crania selected for measurement do not reflect cradle board use. Some of the skulls are significantly smaller and rounder than those of the earlier general population of the area.

The long-head, tall-stature genes of the previous population were not lost. They remain reflected in the bones in archeological sites and also occasionally in the contemporary population at Zuni. I concur with Roberts's and Seltzer's speculation that some mixture of distinct populations must have occurred. One population did not completely wipe out and displace another. Rather, a new population with a different distribution of some structural genes (i.e., shorter stature, smaller and broader skulls, a low incidence of the cusp of Carabelli, shovel-shaped incisors, and five-cusp patterns on the lower molars) arrived and intermarried with a local Native American Indian group.

Gene mixing obviously is not a new or rare event. The process has kept our species one large, interbreeding population for at least 200,000 years. *Homo sapiens* is an interesting, genetically diverse species—not a bunch of broken branches, but a unified pool of richly heterogeneous, interwoven links. These links are indicative of a lot of lively sexual activity in the past, sex not inhibited by differences, but perhaps enhanced by them, protecting the species from unhealthy homogeneity and from traveling down some blind biological alley that would permanently divide the gene pool.[20]

In 1962, another physical anthropologist, Marshall T. Newman, reported changes in body size and head forms among American Indians. He found a general trend in the Southwest toward mesocephaly, that is, a shift from long toward broader skulls, which he considered a "general evolutionary trend." He also noted that in both the Pueblo area of the Southwest and the Lower Sacramento Valley of California, stature decreased by two to six centimeters over several millennia.[21] Might the changes noted at Hawikuh be the result of California Indians coming east? They would have come from the right direction, consistent with Zuni oral traditions. And perhaps the California Indians included Japanese immigrants.

Another report suggesting a possible link between California and Zuni was published in 1979 by the late James Spuhler of the University of New Mexico. He found a cluster of genes at Zuni that appear closer to the California Indians than to other Southwest Indians.[22]

The La Jollan Burials

The only comparison of Native American skeletons with Japanese skeletons I know of was by Spencer L. Rogers of the San Diego Museum of Man. Rogers's study of prehistoric Indian skeletons from the southern California coastal area in the vicinity of La Jolla (and south along Baja California) revealed a population with remarkable resemblances to prehistoric skeletons from the Mitsu site on Kyushu Island in southern Japan.[23] In fact, the similarities between the La Jolla and Mitsu skeletons appear closer than the similarities between the La Jolla crania (see Tables 2 and 3) and other Native American Indian crania. Further, the La Jolla bones are different from other Native American Indian skeletons and similar to a Japanese sample from a time preceding the proposed admixture of Japanese in New Mexico.[24]

Here are further details about these bones.

Rogers compared the small sample of La Jolla skeletons to a number of other populations, including a large Japanese sample dating to the Yayoi period, about 300 B.C.–A.D. 300, on the southern Japanese island of Kyushu. The date of the La Jolla burials is not precise, but is estimated to be at least two thousand years ago, which places the bones right in the middle of the Yayoi period.

Like teeth, bones undergo stress during life, and analysis after death can be problematic. Always the question must be asked, How much of the measured variation, or the lack of variation, resulted from observer error? Rogers compared the La Jolla skulls with seven other populations studied by six different observers. How might the results be different if only one researcher analyzed all the samples using the same measures? Would the results

TABLE 2

COMPARISON OF LA JOLLAN MEAN CRANIAL MEASUREMENTS WITH SERIES FROM OUTSIDE CALIFORNIA

	Old Zuni[1]	La Jollan	Great Basin[2]	Ventana Cave[3] (undeformed)	Ventana Cave[3] (mean)	Pecos[4]	Paa-ko[5]	Modern Papago[3]	Mitsu, Japan[6]
Cranial length	175.76	190	182	177	161	164	164	178	185
Cranial breadth	133.4	145	137	137	147	145	142	135	146
Basion-bregma height	133.53	139	133	120	138	140	135	132	137
Cranial capacity	1302.6	1528	1457	1120	1358	1368	1344	1265	1502
Cranial module	147.6	158	151	145	149	148	147	148	156
Bizygomatic diameter	134.45	132	139	137	137	139	132	134	142
Basion-nasion length	99.48	103	105	100	96	102	95	99	103
Basion-prosthion length	98	106	102	93	99	98	93	95	101
Nasion-prosthion height	73.34	70	72	—	72	73	69	—	75
CRANIAL INDEX	75.91	76.2	76.1	77.4	91.5	88.9	86.3	75.8	78.4
LENGTH-HEIGHT INDEX	76.1	73.1	73.1	67.8	86.4	85.8	82.4	74.0	74.1
BREADTH-HEIGHT INDEX	100.23	96.1	96.8	87.6	94.2	96.9	95.0	97.9	94.9
MEAN ORBITAL INDEX		83.9	89.4	92.3	85.3	87.8	89.4	90.6	82.4
NASAL INDEX	49.53	47.5	49.3	42.3	48.3	51.0	51.7	49.1	51.4
COEFFICIENT OF DIVERGENCE		0	0.02015	0.06203	0.04617	0.04359	0.03868	0.03770	0.01706

Source: Rogers, 1963, Table 6. [1]Hawikuh, mean, 35 males. (Not part of Rogers's study.) Seltzer, 1944:11, 26. [2]Kennedy, 1959. [3]Haury, 1950 (Measurements by Gabel). [4]Hooton, 1930. [5]Rogers, S. L., 1954. [6]Ushijima, 1954.

TABLE 3

COMPARISON OF LA JOLLAN MEAN CRANIAL MEASUREMENTS WITH THOSE OF OTHER CALIFORNIA CRANIA

	(♂) La Jollan	(♂) Santa Barbara Co.[1] (mainland)	(♂) Santa Cruz and Santa Rosa Islands[1]	(♂) San Francisco Bay and vicinity[1]	(✳) Sacramento Valley (early)[2]	(✳) Sacramento Valley (late)[2]	(♂) Stanford Skull[3]
Cranial length	190	179	180	183	190	182	185
Cranial breadth	145	138	140	139	144	146	140
Basion-bregma height	139	132	129	136	146	143	136
Cranial capacity	1528	1390	1349	1372	1589	1576	1460
Cranial module	158	150	150	153	160	157	154
Bizygomatic diameter	132	135	135	137	143	143	—
Basion-nasion length	103	—	98	100	107	104	103
Basion-prosthion length	106	—	98	100	104	102	—
Nasion-prosthion height	70	70	70	71	76	75	—
CRANIAL INDEX	76.2	77.1	77.9	76.0	75.8	80.7	75.7
LENGTH-HEIGHT INDEX	73.1	73.4	71.7	74.8	76.8	78.8	73.5
BREADTH-HEIGHT INDEX	96.1	105.0	108.5	102.1	101.2	98.1	97.1
MEAN ORBITAL INDEX	83.9	89.6	91.9	90.2	89.9 (L)	90.7 (L)	—
NASAL INDEX	47.5	48.4	47.1	48.9	50.0	48.9	—
COEFFICIENT OF DIVERGENCE	0	0.02657	0.03165	0.02390	0.02383	0.02402	0.01086

Source: Rogers, 1963, Table 5. [1]Hrdlicka, 1927. [2]Newman, 1957. [3]Heizer and McCown, 1950.

(✳) Males and females unsegregated.
(L) Calculated from left orbit only.

indicate more similarity with the Japanese or less? Are the results primarily an artifact of who studied and measured the bones? Or, are the similarities between La Jolla and the Mitsu Japanese population essentially accurate?[25]

Sixty-six burials from sites along the coast of southern California and northern Baja California have yielded nineteen skulls complete enough and in good enough condition for analysis (see Figures 35 and 36). All burials were presumed to be pre-Yuman, that is before A.D. 1000, because the Yuman-speaking people practiced cremation, which obviously limits the material available for bone analysis now.[26]

The cultural context of the bones reveals a shellfish-using and sea-fishing people who lived along this rather remote and uninviting coastal area between 5,400 and 1,500 years ago. By about A.D. 500 the intrusion of a northern group, a Shoshonean population, separated the Yuman from the Chumash peoples. No explanation of what happened to the La Jolla people is yet available.

One more note: The La Jolla skeletons were found in the same coastal vicinity as the loggerhead turtles mentioned in Chapter 4. If Japanese-American turtles found the currents and the coastal environment amenable to their mobility, perhaps people did too.

BLOOD AND OTHER BODY PARTS

Like cusps and crania, minute components of blood reveal important facts about human origins. They reveal, for example, how closely we are related to all other forms of life. Most of the same combinations of ingredients that comprise human bodies also comprise all other living creatures. We do not vary much from the rest of the animate world; we are simply sophisticated extensions as semidomesticated bipedal apes.

Analysis of blood alleles, which are alternative forms of genes at the same locus within a chromosome, informs us of how basically common we are. Not only do we share most of our DNA with other species of animals, we hardly differ at all from human population to human population. When small variations do occur, they may imply long-forgotten linkages, or separations, between groups. Like a shift in a phoneme, a small sound in a word, a

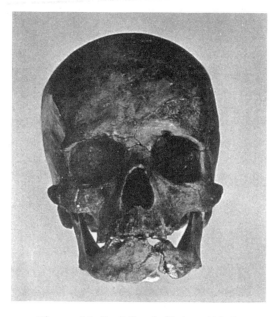

Figure 35. *La Jolla skull, (no. 19243)*

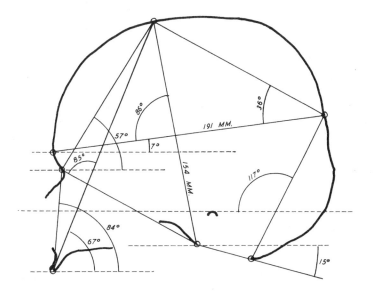

Figure 36. *La Jolla skull (no. 19243) measurement points*

tiny shift in a blood feature frequency may help identify past events.

Three clusters of data comprise this next discussion: (1) blood type distribution, (2) a kidney disease, and (3) data from blood-matching studies developed for organ transplants.

Blood Alleles

In the 1970s, two major studies that incorporated blood analysis were published: one on the Indians of southwestern United States, including the Zuni, and the other on the Japanese. The Southwest study clearly documented that Zuni blood allele frequencies differ from those in other Native American Indians. The Japanese publication provided comparative data beyond the boundaries of the North American continent.

Of course, Japanese and Native American Indians share some remote common ancestor (as we all do from a time in the distant past). But recent admixture of Japanese with Zuni is suggested by the ABO blood type distribution. In general, the allele for type B is totally absent among American Indians, present in a high percentage (20%–40%) of East Asian populations, and present in relatively low percentage (0%–15%) among Caucasian groups.[27]

By 1975 at least thirty studies on the ABO series were reported in Japan and included in a report by Watanabe, Kondo, and Matsunagi.[28] The lowest incidence of allele B was 10.6% and the highest, 32.4%. In the largest sample, 77,623 people in Tokyo, 22.1% were type B. (In contrast, a French sample of 10,433 persons had a 7.99% incidence of type B.)

The 1958 study by Brown and colleagues of a sample of 1,234 Navaho, Apache, Pima, Hopi, Tewa, Yuman, and Maricopa Indians of the Southwest found only 2 with type B.[29] Like almost all other Native Americans, these Indians were type O, as expected.

However, in a later study, Workman and colleagues discovered that 71 Zuni (10.7%) in a sample of 662 were type B.[30] This fact surprised and puzzled the researchers at the time, and the issue has not been resolved.

This team of physical anthropologists considered the possibility of the presence of type B in a pre-Spanish population. They stated it is "not impossible," but since that scenario had "no support in any other study of southwestern or Mexican Indian tribes,"[31] they did not pursue it either. Yet they found that type B was old and not of Spanish origin because the individuals with type B had no other Caucasian features.

Earlier in the same article the authors inferred the amalgamation of at least two presumably "indigenous" southwestern Indian groups at Zuni during the Regressive Pueblo period, A.D. 1200–1350, and noted that this fusion continues to be reflected by "visits to shrines in the west." But they did not connect the possibility that type B was introduced at that time. They remained puzzled by the high presence of type B in the Zuni.[32]

All the other data here suggest that the introduction of type B could have been from a Japanese population, which today has about a 22% to 32% frequency of the allele. Certainly that seems more likely than its introduction from a Spanish population, which has a much lower frequency of type B. Furthermore, nothing in the blood studies of the type B individuals in Zuni indicates any Caucasian admixture, whereas dental morphology and skeletal changes presented earlier also suggest Japanese admixture.[33]

The Zuni Disease

The biological evidence does not stop with teeth, bones, and blood. In 1990, forty-four Zuni were on dialysis; in 1995, sixty were, and in 1996, seventy-five Zuni were in kidney failure and receiving dialysis treatment in the public health hospital at Blacktop, the suburb of the Pueblo of Zuni. Like other Indians, Zuni have an increasing incidence of diabetes, but the Zuni also have an exceptionally high incidence of mesangiopathic glomerulonephritis, which is chronic renal failure ultimately leading to end-stage renal disease (ESRD) and death. The Zuni incidence is 14 times greater than that in Caucasian Americans, 6.2 times greater than that in black Americans, 6.3 times greater than the incidence in Ramah Navaho, and 3.7 times greater than the rate in their near neighbors, the Hopi.[34] This disease is reported to be also "extremely common in some Oriental populations, the best described prevalence being in Japan and Singapore."[35]

Since the Japanese also have an unusually high propensity for this particular kidney deterioration, we must consider a genetically based (and shared) vulnerability to this disease.

Histocompatibility

One result of the high frequency of diabetes and glomerulonephritis is that lymphocyte (blood) studies must be performed
to match kidneys for transplantation. In order for a transplant to
suceed, detailed information about the blood of both donor and re-
cipient must be available. Therefore, histocompatibility studies,
called HLA studies, must be done. And they have been done on
many populations, including the Zuni.

In 1971, blood samples were obtained from 158 Zuni belonging
to fifty-three families. The histocompatibility study was published
in 1973, with the formidable title of "Analysis of the HL-A, Erythrocyte and Gamma Globulin Antigen Systems in the Zuni Indians of New Mexico."[36]

This detailed information about Zuni blood features was assumed to represent a "typical" North American Indian sample
when the Zuni HLA data were compared with HLA data of three

Figure 37. *Rowena Him, Zuni artist*

South American Indian groups: the Waorani of Ecuador and the Kaingang and Guarani of Brazil. In 1992, the esteemed British science journal *Nature* published two studies about unusual HLA-B alleles identified, and both drew on the Zuni data.[37] One of the surprising discoveries from comparing Zuni HLA data with other HLA systems is that the Zuni have a highly specific feature called the B*3501 subtype, identical to the Japanese.[38]

Teeth, bones, and blood are things we associate with murder mysteries, not migration. Forensics, not history. Although all humans share most of their biology, when tiny variations do occur, whether in a cusp, a cranial shape, or a blood allele, something new can be learned about our species. In this chapter, the combined evidence of dental morphology, prehistoric skeletal remains, blood analysis, a kidney disease, and histocompatibility studies strongly suggests that the Zuni population includes an addition of Japanese.

The Zuni people did not become Japanese because of this admixture. They continue to be a vital, resilient Native American Indian population (see Figure 37). The Zuni merely incorporated new genetic material, as well as linguistic and cultural material, from a Japanese population relatively late in North American prehistory: the late thirteenth century A.D.

CHAPTER SEVEN

WORDS
AND
WANDERERS

*"I always wondered why I spoke
Japanese so easily."*

—Zuni veteran of World War II

This Zuni veteran, a councilman, had just heard about my theory and he had not seemed particularly surprised. He had been a prisoner of the Japanese for nearly three years during World War II and independently had noted some remarkable similarities between his language and Japanese: the consonant-vowel (CV) pattern, the grammatical structure, and an occasional, vaguely familiar word such as *yama* for mountain (the Zuni term is *yala*). He also knew that his language was not spoken by any other population in the world. Now he was intrigued. What possible connections could there be?

I propose that the similarities between Japanese and Zunian derive from two sources: an ancient and shared protolanguage that shaped the two languages' common phonemic and grammatical structures and a relatively late, thirteenth-century borrowing by Zunian of specific Japanese words in selected categories.

Scholars in comparative linguistics have yet to agree on a criterion for proof of linguistic relationships, especially between languages that have no known historical connection. Even so, I hope my evidence is sufficiently compelling that the linguists known as "splitters," who spotlight details of differences, and "lumpers," who focus on broad similarities, will be challenged to address this part of the larger enigma.[1] If Zunian is not related to Japanese, to what language is it related? How many alternative explanations might there be? How many linguistic features and specific word correspondences does it take to prove Zunian and Japanese are related?

LANGUAGE AND IDENTITY

Speakers of both Zunian and Japanese strongly link their identity with their language. Both grow up believing their language is unique, distinct from all the world's languages. An important part of "being Zuni" (see Figure 38) and of "being Japanese" (see Figure 39) is speaking a special language.

If the genetic admixture of the Pacific pilgrims is reflected in the biology of the Zuni population, perhaps clusters of words and concepts also were introduced, and perhaps from across an ocean.

The mobility of *Homo sapiens* is one theme in this discussion. I believe that the Pacific was a liquid highway providing a rather convenient route to North America, an alternative to the northern hurdle of a tundra trek across the continents.

But if Japanese speakers came to Zuni with a package of new cultural concepts and merged with the indigenous population, what would the blend of an "Amerind" language and Japanese sound like? Comparisons of Japanese and Zunian lexicon in this chapter and the next two include nouns, verbs, kinship terms, and religious terminology.

HUMAN LANGUAGES

Before beginning the comparison, let us review some basic facts about human languages.

At least five thousand languages are spoken today. How many others have been lost in the past? Or mixed and merged in layers of hybrids, confusing reconstruction of their origins?

Figure 38. *Two Zuni boys at sheep camp*

Figure 39. *Japanese students on a holiday in Kyoto*

Second, humans are uniquely dependent on the ability to speak. Although rather frail animals and not very good at any single physical feat, we babble exceptionally well. Speech is our biological specialty, our species-specific source of survival. No matter what language we speak, we must talk to be human or be around others who can. A debate continues concerning when in the prehistoric past we began to talk, but without doubt a series of critical physiological changes occurred when we came down from the trees. We hominids had to learn to walk upright, carrying food and kids along, gripping them with opposable thumbs, a physical remnant of digital strength we fortunately retained from our past in the trees.

In the process of standing upright, our pelvic region changed to allow the hind end and rear legs to bear the weight of the whole body. Those changes appear linked to a longer gestation and bigger-headed babies, which end up being dependent much longer than are the offspring of other primates.

Fragile, thin, but expanding crania allowed for the greater internal neurological complexity needed to accommodate the extra learning that was necessary by helpless babies who took so long to mature. To accommodate to upright stature, the cranium shifted on the neck in such a way that the larynx was freed from the surrounding structures, allowing an increasingly wider range of sounds—tiny, discrete sound bites called *phonemes*. The greater the number of sounds, the more sound combinations were possible; indeed, modern humans can make so many sounds that no single language begins to utilize the total range possible. Once the physiological structures were in place, we didn't stop talking. Or walking. Our species literally took off.

By fifty thousand years ago human bodies and brains were as modern as they may ever be (unless we permit major meddling with our genetic makeup, as we are beginning to do with plants and other animals). Once modern, *Homo sapiens* began to fill up the planet rather successfully in a relatively short time. Dispersal and fragmentation of populations promoted diversification of speech.

Some ancient languages survive with small pockets of speakers, such as the hundreds recorded in New Guinea; a few others (such as Chinese, Japanese, Hindi, Swahili, Spanish, and English) continue to expand with millions of speakers.

According to Johanna Nichols, professor of linguistics at the University of California, Berkeley, contemporary languages are clustered in about three hundred different stocks: fifty are located in North America, twelve in Mesoamerica, and eighty or more in South America. Zunian is one of the fifty stocks in North America. Zunian has about 8,000 speakers and Japanese has more than 140 million.

PHONEMES AND MORPHEMES, GRAMMAR AND SYNTAX

Phonemes are to languages what DNA fragments are to genes: small potentially meaningful units of analysis, the tiny building blocks, the discrete sounds of language. Japanese and Zuni speakers utilize only twenty-one phonemes. Seventeen of them are the same.

Morphemes are words or parts of words that have specific meaning. Morphemes are composed of phonemes, only one step up in complexity. Single phonemes often have no meaning; they need to be combined with one another to convey meaning. All morphemes have enough content to convey identifiable sense. They are the building blocks of whole words, sometimes standing alone as a single phoneme "word," such as /a/, but usually attached to at least one other sound to provide a small unit of meaning, such as /me/ (composed of two phonemes, /m/ and /e/).

Combining phonemes into sounds that have meaning, morphemes, is a universal characteristic of language. Both Zunian and Japanese build words by combining twenty-one sounds into syllables usually of CV sequences. (For example: *wannaka,* old Zunian for "middle," and *mannaka,* Japanese for "middle"). Modern Japanese has sixty-two syllables, a simplification of Old Japanese that had eighty-eight. The Zunian total has not been determined.

Learning how words combine can be a deadly exercise for an adult trying to learn a new language. Minute sounds tucked in here and there make a monumental difference in conveying what is meant. Some languages attach meaningful sounds (prefixes) at the beginning of a root word, such as /un-/ in English; others tack sounds, such as /-ed/, onto the end of a word (suffixes). Still others change the interior of a word (infixing), keeping the sounds on either side unchanged, such as changing /come/ to /came/ in English. This vowel change /o/ to /a/ is an example of a single-sound, a phoneme, change in the middle of a word, modifying the meaning from present to the past tense. Some languages use all three methods, as does English. But Zunian and Japanese depend primarily on suffixes to modify the meaning of root words.[2] Neither Zunian nor Japanese modify the internal structure of their root words.

The rules for arranging words into larger segments for complete statements provide the language syntax: where the adverbs show up relative to the verbs, the location of adjectives relative to nouns, and the proper sequence of subject, verb, and object in a sentence. Zunian and Japanese arrange words in the same order: subject, object, verb. English and Chinese, in contrast, arrange sentence parts in the order: subject, verb, object. English uses prepositions, particles that precede nouns, such as "go *by* car"; Zunian and Japanese connect parts of the sentence with particles in postpositions, following a root word, such as "densha *de* ikimasu" in Japanese, "car by go."

HISTORICAL LINGUISTICS

Three threads run through the reconstruction of the historical links among languages: the incidence of chance similarities, the basic genetic relationships, and the borrowing of words. All three weave within my analysis of Zunian and Japanese. Some of the parallels I found are probably coincidence, the result of both languages utilizing a limited number of similar phonemes. Others are less easily attributed to chance.

Archeology employs carbon 14, tree rings, and potassium argon to date past events; biology is developing a molecular clock to estimate the timing of mutational events in genetic systems. Likewise, linguistics has methods for calculating when languages separated. Of course, various dating methods, whether analyzing potsherds, mitochrondrial DNA, or vocabulary lists, have limitations and associated controversies, but they still provide a useful framework for adding time depth to understanding the distribution of artifacts, genes, and languages.

The principle behind lexicostatistics is that languages have a fairly uniform rate of vocabulary retention—about 85% over a thousand-year period. Or, put another way, lexicostatistics assumes that languages have a steady rate of lexical change over time, losing about 15% of shared vocabulary during a thousand-year period. The list of key, basic words and the formula for calculating gradual loss and linkages were developed in the early 1950s by the linguist Morris Swadesh.[3]

His idea was to reconstruct a protolanguage for the languages being compared and to determine how long it would have taken for the observed changes to occur. His method employs a basic set of words considered least likely to be replaced by borrowing, common terms such as *man* and *woman.* The approach seems to work well with languages known to be related, such as the Indo-European languages, but it also has some serious limitations.

Swadesh reviewed the basic one-hundred-word list of Zunian and Japanese that I sent him in 1966. He did not think there was a case for a close relationship but he did find three good word pairs and six fair ones that suggested to him the two languages had separated about eleven thousand years ago. This calculation is in keeping with the then-current views of the peopling of North America through gradual migration, by land.[4]

When Swadesh reviewed a two-hundred-word list and other word pairs I also provided, he found more than twenty "reasonably strong" pairs and less than thirty in the "fair category." "A comparison which allowed for semantic change," he added, "would certainly increase this number."

Interestingly, Swadesh noted that word diffusion also needed to be considered, and he identified some apparent loan words on my extended list, words he judged as possibly borrowed by Zunian (Zunian first, then Japanese): *Bitsitsi, Butsu* (Buddha); *kokko-lhana, kogo-shi* (god); *shiwani, shinkwan* (priest), and *kwe, kwai* (society, a word stemming from Chinese). Note these four loan words refer to the religious system; these, and others, are discussed in Chapter 9.[5]

Johanna Nichols, noting the temporal limitation of reconstructions based solely on vocabulary lists, suggested a method for identifying linguistic relationships further back in time by focusing on structural features: the way words are put together and statements are made. As the reliability of lexical analysis weakens, the importance of tracking continuity of structural features kicks in. For example, Nichols sees a gradient of language links across the world from west to east and she maps the movement of people as they expanded across the world during the past fifty thousand years by tracing a dozen features that she believes are "stable."

COASTAL COLONIZATION
OF NORTH AMERICA

Especially relevant to my theory, Nichols finds linguistic evidence of four strata of colonization of North America, that is, four different populations arriving from the Old World with multiple coastal contacts. Three key features in her analysis of Pacific Rim languages are lack of gender, adding suffixes rather than prefixes to change root words, and the use of postpositions rather than prepositions for linking parts of sentences. (For an example of the latter feature: Japanese for "go to the store" is *mise ni ikimasu,* "store to go"; /ni/ is the postposition that links the subject, store, with the verb. In English the preposition /to/ links the verb to the object by preceding it—not "store *to,*" but *"to* the store.") These three features contrast with Indo-European[6] and are present in both Japanese and Zuni.

William Jacobsen of the University of Nebraska developed further the idea of Pacific coastal colonization of western North America.[7] He identified forty-five of the sixty-six Native American language families as having a "coastal center of gravity." Jacobsen recognized he is not the first to notice this linguistic concentration along the western side of North America. In 1891, John Wesley Powell, the first director of the Bureau of Ethnology, observed that thirty-two on his list of fifty-eight Native American stock were located along the Pacific coast; further, forty-one were located west of the Rockies. In all, about two-thirds of all the languages in Native North America, representing all six of Sapir's 1929 superstocks, have a Pacific coast presence.[8]

Jacobsen believed this concentration of diversity of languages on the western side of the continent indicates early migrations via the Pacific coast, followed by fanning inland and eastward across the continent.

Zunian may be one of those languages with a coastal origin followed by an inland migration. Stanley Newman applied the lexicostatistical method to Zuni and two California Indian languages, Yokuts and Miwok, that he had worked with before studying Zunian. His analysis suggests a California Penutian base for Zunian dating back seven thousand years ago, a connection and a date "suggestive" but not found acceptable by other linguists.[9] However, this finding is consistent with the direction of Zuni migration stories, though much earlier than I am proposing. It may also reflect that the indigenous antecedents to Zunian were to the west. Perhaps speakers of languages like Miwok and Yokuts, and other Penutian speakers (including Mayan), also moved east from Japan, a speculation of course.

Jacobsen, like Nichols, believed the western concentration of language families in North America supports the idea that they originally came from populations that migrated via the Pacific coastlines, not through the interior of the continent. Further, Jacobsen, like Nichols, assumed a north-to-south migration.[10]

Recent developments in linguistics and archeology suggest an encouraging trend: looking at the coastal distributions of languages and of peoples. If these ideas are combined with an effort to work toward a new synthesis in North America, perhaps along the line suggested by Colin Renfrew in Europe, then things are looking up for a fresh approach to the study of the peopling of North America.[11]

Studies of mitochondrial DNA (the fragment of DNA that is passed on only through females) by Torroni and colleagues, like Nichols's theory of four coastal migrations, suggest four separate biological lineages present in North America.[12] Perhaps these separate studies will provide a larger perspective through productive interdisciplinary discussion.

CHANCE SIMILARITIES

The Zunian-Japanese theory must address the problem of chance resemblances. If any two languages have words that sound similar, historical linguists can argue it is because all languages must have some chance resemblances. Unless I can demonstrate greater frequency than they judge attributable to chance, linguists will deny the existence of a Zuni-Japanese link. However, I have yet to locate a linguist who will state what percentage of a total word list must be identical to crest the boundary between accident and historical relationship. Further, how are loan words that are borrowed differentiated from cognates that are not, especially in two languages that may have been linked two or more times in the past?[13]

Donald A. Ringe, Jr., with the Department of Linguistics at the University of Pennsylvania, developed a statistical method to test whether words in two languages are similar by chance.[14] He stated that every comparison of any pair of languages can be expected to exhibit a "non-negligible number of fortuitous similarities." His computer analysis is impressive (he proved that English is not related to Turkish or Navaho), but he did not define what is "non-negligible." The question remains, How many words are "fortuitously" identical? And how many similarly sounding words with the same meaning does it take to make a case worth investigating further?

In comparing vocabularies, Ringe warned that the individual sounds in any language do not appear equally often. Some phonemes such as /k/ are used heavily and others such as /q/ in English and /b/ in Zunian and Japanese rarely occur. Some phonemes may appear at the beginning of a word, but not in the middle. Other sounds pop up in the middle, but never at the end.

Next, there is the problem of synonyms: How similar in meaning must a word be to be judged a cognate, that is, sharing a common ancestor? How much flexibility and proximity are acceptable? For example, can *cheek* be paired with *jaw* and with *chin,* or should comparisons be focused on exact word for exact referent?[15]

How many words will be the same or appear similar depends on many factors, including the total number of phonemes available for both languages. Some languages utilize a large range of separate, unique sounds, whereas others manage with fewer discrete phonemes, but apply them in a great variety of combinations. With a total of only twenty-one phonemes, both Japanese and Zunian are at the low end of the total number of phonemes employed. In contrast, Navaho uses forty-six. How many sounds overlap and how many differ also affect the probability of chance morphemic similarities. Because Japanese and Zunian share many sounds, a high incidence of chance similarity of words might be expected, providing a test case for Ringe's method.

The use of different orthographies by variously trained linguists also adds to or detracts from the "chance" element endemic to linguistic comparisons. Again, neither Ringe with his sophisticated computer model, nor others, indicated how many exact correspondences are required to establish a genetic relationship between two or more languages. There is also another variable: knowing that two languages are related and investigating how closely linked, versus not knowing whether they are related and wondering if they might be. Are there different standards of criteria for "proving" as yet unknown linkages?

In short, the problems in historical linguistics can be discouraging, especially when initiating a comparison between two languages with no previously suspected relationship. So, where does this lead? To paralytic limbo? Or to a rather remarkable challenge?

ZUNIAN: AN ORPHAN ON THE CONTINENT

Zunian is one of many languages in the Southwest (see Map 14), but one with no known affiliation with any other language not only on the continent, but also in the world.[16]

In a 1929 classification of North American Indian languages, the American linguist Edward Sapir placed Zuni with the large phylum Aztec-Tanoan, but followed that tentative identification with a question mark, an uncertainty of relationships that continues to be debated.[17] In 1937, two other well-known American linguists, Benjamin Whorf and George L. Trager, commented that "the general structure of Zuni resembles that of Tanoan, but no details of coincidence in morphemes can be cited."[18]

In 1953, Joseph Greenberg, a Stanford University scholar known for his early and accurate general classification of African language families (and his more recent and controversial classification of New World Indian languages), considered Sapir's inclusion of Zuni with Aztec-Tanoan one of the most doubtful points of Sapir's sixfold classification.[19] If it is not Tanoan and not Aztec, what family does Zuni resemble?

Although Zunian has defied close affiliation to surrounding languages in the Southwest (see Map 15), it has been tentatively listed as a separate language under a large, comprehensive Macro-Penutian phylum.[20] Swadesh included Zunian with Macro-Quechuan. Perhaps

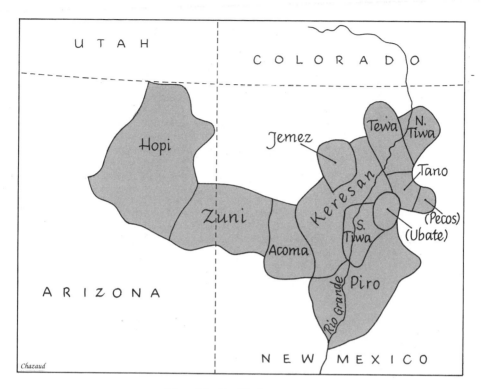

Map 14. *Pueblo languages.*

most interesting is Newman's 1964 weak demonstration of a possible remote genetic relationship between Zuni and California Penutian, especially Miwok and Yokuts.[21] More recently, Greenberg placed Zuni, without a question mark, as one of nine subgroups of Penutian, a major Amerind subgroup.[22] (Penutian is one of eleven subgroups in Amerind, the linguistic stock that includes almost all New World languages in Greenberg's classification system.)

However, the Californian Penutian link for Zuni is not strong and has been questioned.[23] Newman's lexicostatistical analysis suggests that the separation of Zuni from California Penutian occurred about seven thousand years ago. My inspection of the 288 Penutian etymologies presented by Greenberg in his book *Languages in America* revealed that Zunian counterparts appear in only 14 words (5% of the total of 288 Penutian etymologies) and the relationship of those 14 seems far more remote than my analy-

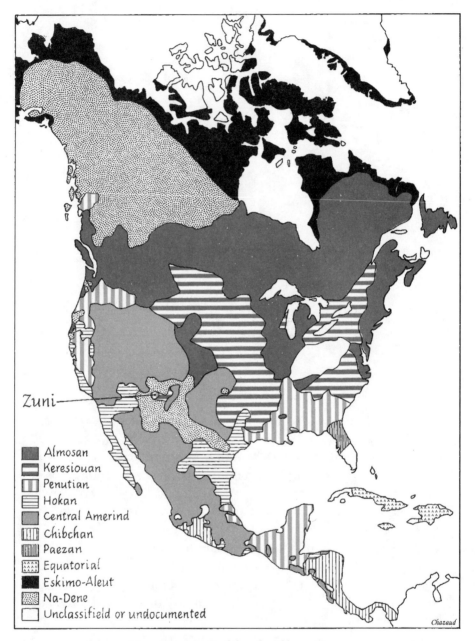

Zuni—

Almosan
Keresiouan
Penutian
Hokan
Central Amerind
Chibchan
Paezan
Equatorial
Eskimo-Aleut
Na-Dene
Unclassifield or undocumented

Chazaud

Map 15. *Amerind family of languages.*

sis of Zunian with Japanese. The words I compared not only look similar, but also have exactly the same meanings. I did not have to fish around for synonyms, a fact that may be indicative of recent borrowing rather than distant genetic links.[24]

In summary, the linguistic relationship of Zunian to other New World languages remains unresolved. It seems to be an orphan on the continent.

JAPANESE: ISOLATED ON THE ISLANDS

Like the currents that swirl around the islands of Japan from many directions, different languages and their speakers also came and circulated around the islands from many directions. Linguists continue reconstructing the sources and the directions of those influences, but no consensus has been reached despite vigorous research and discussion.

Attempts have been made to compare Japanese with Ainu, Aleutian, Eskimo, Hyperborean, Altaic, Ural-Altaic, Dravidian, Korean, Chinese, Tibetan, Burmese, Austro-asiatic, Austronesian, Persian, Greek, Irish, and other Indo-European languages,[25] yet Japanese remains a separate and isolated language. In 1990, Professor Masayoshi Shibatani of Kobe University stated in *The Languages of Japan*, "Japanese is the only major world language whose genetic affiliation to other languages or language families has not been conclusively proven."[26]

Professor James Matisoff of the University of California, Berkeley agreed, noting that Japanese is "arguably the world's most culturally important language whose genetic affiliations are still controversial." He lists six theories of potential relationships: Japanese-Dravidian, Japanese-Tibeto-Burman, Japanese-Ainu-Korean-Chinese, Japanese-Korean-Altaic, Japanese-Austronesian, and finally (and by far the most embracing), Japanese as part of nine subgroups of Eurasiatic that include Eskimo-Aleut and Indo-European. No agreement on any of these theories has been reached.[27]

In addition to questions on the origins of the basic language, numerous dialects exist within and between the islands, and these continue to be studied and mapped on various criteria, including accent differences identifying speakers in twenty-one different cities.[28] (See Map 16 for geographic division of Japanese dialects.)

The features of Japanese that suggest a southern origin include the way words are shaped by syllables of sequences of a consonant and vowel (CV), for example, *mannaka,* meaning "middle." This CV pattern is common in Austronesian languages such

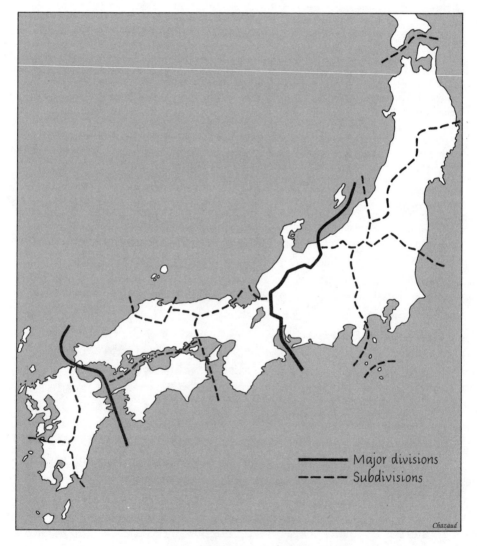

Map 16. *Japanese dialects.*

as Polynesian and Indonesian.[29] However, modern Polynesian, like Hawaiian, tends to drop the consonants; in contrast, modern Japanese tends to drop vowels in certain positions, confounding understanding of what the protolanguage might have been thousands of years ago.

Other peoples with other languages related to a very different family of languages called Altaic apparently came to Japan from the north and the west, possibly linking Japanese to languages in faraway places like Turkey and Dravidian in southern India. A number of isolated words in Japanese appear to be cognate to Korean, a known Altaic language, but not enough words to convince everyone that Japanese is, like Korean, Altaic.[30]

Altaic languages tend to have "closed syllables" that end in consonants, which is not like Japanese or similar to Polynesian or other Austronesian languages that leave syllables "open," ending with vowels. Words in Altaic are formed by a series of consonant-vowel-consonant (CVC) combinations and include many consonant clusters without vowels to separate them.

According to Professor Shibatani, Japanese is beginning to look like an amalgam of both Austronesian and Altaic elements. The Austronesian characteristics include the typical bisyllabicity (CVCV), some prefixes (rare), a simple vowel system, open syllables, an uncomplicated consonant system, and a characteristic shared with Polynesian of losing the /p/ sound; /p/ shifts to the /h/ sound in both languages.[31]

Japanese, like Zunian, remains a linguistic orphan. Unidentified. A mystery.

PROBLEMS WITH THE COMPARATIVE METHOD

Generations of scholars have been working on the comparative analysis of the Japanese language, but lexical comparisons have not answered the numerous questions raised. Which influence came from which direction at what time in Japanese prehistory? In what ways did the adoption of Chinese words modify the original Japanese language? What language did the immigrants associated with the Yayoi period bring? Recently, Shibatani of Kobe University reported a trend away from the comparative

method dealing with discrete words (the same kind of disillusion-
ment with the results that Nichols reported), toward an increased
attention to grammatical comparison and reconstruction.[32]

But how languages have responded to different linguistic influences during prehistory, and also during historical times, remains
a legitimate issue. Is Japanese a "mixed language," a hybrid? Is one
major substratum an Altaic structure confounded by a later layer of
Austronesian words? Or is Austronesian the substratum with Altaic
a superstratum? Was an Austronesian language spoken in Japan
during the long Jomon period (12,000 B.P–250 B.C.) and later modified by Altaic speakers associated with rice cultivation, bronze, and
burial mounds during the Yayoi period (300 B.C.–A.D. 300)?

Both Shibatani in Japan and Nichols in the United States noted
that the comparative method may work well for Indo-European,
but not as well in other situations, especially where language relationships are not already known to exist. Indo-European has the
advantage of many historical links in known directions with documented periods of separation. Hindi is Indo-European; Spanish,
Italian, English, and German are known by comparative linguistics
to be related to each other with established links in time. Perhaps
different rules apply to Altaic. To Tibeto-Chinese. To Austronesian.
To Penutian. Why should all human languages respond to change
like Indo-European? Perhaps in Altaic and Japanese, Penutian and
Zunian, the phonemic and structural changes march to a different
tune, and at different rates, under different conditions.

At the height of use of the comparative method in the 1950s
and 1960s, phonemes and morphemes were envisioned as floating
around the world, like verbal flotsam and jetsam, and like potsherds of the Southwest seemed to lead independent lives of their
own, changing by hidden laws assumed to exist but yet so elu-
sive.[33] Little wonder scholars like Shibatani and Nichols search for
alternative methods of analysis.

THE COMPARISON: ZUNIAN AND JAPANESE

Now for some specific comparisons. Let us step into the war
zone of historical linguistics and consider what a comparison of
the two orphans, Zunian and Japanese, might reveal.

Method

This is the way I began my research on the Zuni enigma in 1960.

Using Stanley Newman's Zuni dictionary,[34] supplemented by words from Ruth Bunzel's grammar[35] and texts,[36] a few words from Matilda Stevenson's tome,[37] and words from three of Frank Cushing's works,[38] I compiled a list of 882 Zuni words, recording each on a three-by-five-inch slip of paper. No Japanese term with the same meaning was found for 78 of these words and therefore they were eliminated.[39] Known borrowing from other languages, such as Spanish and English, led to the removal of 179 more slips. This left 625 Zunian words available for comparison. Each of these words was compared with a Japanese word with equivalent meaning, in most instances the first word listed in the Japanese dictionary. A number of words appeared similar even without considering possible sound shifts. When sound shifts, such as the Japanese /m/ to the Zunian /w/ and Japanese /n/ to Zunian /l/, were identified, many more words appeared to be cognates or loan words.

One problem inherent in this kind of comparison is the absence of the same phonetic transcriptions for both languages. The words compared are from sources that reflect different time periods, different systems of transcriptions, and even different degrees of accuracy. One must constantly ask, Is this particular correspondence an accident of differing orthographies? Linguists use different systems for recording sounds, and nonlinguists are quite innovative in the symbols used to write what they think they hear.

Specifically, I tried to reconcile the differences between Newman's work in 1954 and Bunzel's 1937 material, not to mention the earlier accounts by Stevenson, published in 1904, and Cushing, published in 1889, 1892, and 1920.[40] This was particularly perplexing because Bunzel's account includes more "ancient" words than does Newman's *Zuni Dictionary*. Newman reported he was unable to elicit the religious language, which both he and Bunzel reported to be a separate language. And it is Zuni religious language that is of greatest significance for this study.[41]

These problems of vocabulary lists highlight the question, How much change might have occurred in the Zuni language over the last 40 to 60 or 120 years? We know the Pueblo has experienced a great increase in population, and people today commiserate about the deterioration of their language, though in fact it is one of the most viable of Native American languages.[42]

The problems with Japanese also are great. A long period of Chinese contact resulted in a tremendous borrowing of Chinese words. Without engaging experts on these languages, it is impossible to distinguish the words of native Japanese origin from those of Chinese origin. This seeming naivete was ultimately a benefit, however, because the presence of Chinese in Japanese words strongly suggests that the Japanese influence on Zunian occurred after Chinese influence on Japanese. In addition, differences between modern Japanese and the ancient native language must be considered.

Another potential complication is the fact that Zunian remains an unwritten language whereas Japanese has been written since the eighth century A.D. How does this affect the rates of change and, consequently, the comparisons?[43]

Finally, these two languages have been exposed to different linguistic and cultural influences through their particular histories: Japanese with Chinese, Korean, and now the Western languages— Portuguese, Dutch, French, German, and English; Zunian with at least Keresan, Aztec-Tanoan, Athapaskan, Spanish, and English. The open structure of both languages makes addition of foreign words relatively easy.

In summary, endemic to the study are five persisting problems created by differences:

1. Differences in orthography. Transcription methods have changed over the past century for Zuni, and over the past twelve centuries for Japanese.
2. Differences between the old language and the modern. Japanese has some record of the ancient language before the significant influence of Chinese words, but we do not have equivalent early sources for Zunian.
3. Differences between the written and the unwritten.
4. Differences between a large society with millions of speakers and a small society with only a few thousand.
5. Differences between exposure to different histories and associated influences during historic times.

Despite these difficulties, there are some basic similarities.

Phonemes

Both Zuni and Japanese use few phonemes to construct their words and most of them are the same. Both languages have the same five basic vowels: a, e, i, o, and u.[44] Old Japanese may have included eight vowels, but there are no basic differences in the number of vowel sounds in these two languages today.[45]

Japanese utilizes sixteen consonants. Zunian also uses sixteen; twelve of them are the same as in Japanese: ch, h, k, m, n, p, s, sh, t, w, y, and z. In addition, Japanese has b, d, and g. According to Newman, these three phonemes do not occur in Zunian, but according to Bunzel, they do occur, though she added, "they are barely distinguishable from the unaspirated p, t, and k."[46] The only Japanese consonants definitely not found in Zunian are r and f. The Japanese /r/ is the open /r/, close to /l/ in pronunciation, and /r/ seems to occur, as we shall soon see, in a similar phonemic environment as the Zuni /l/ and /n/, in the middle of words, not at the beginning. The /f/ sound was used in Old Japanese (Nara period 710–793), but has been documented to have changed first to /p/ and finally to /h/ in modern spoken Japanese.[47]

Two phonemes used in Zunian that definitely do not appear in Japanese are /l/ and /lh/, called the barred l.

Finally, students of both languages have addressed whether or not the glottal stop (a barely discernable gap between audible sounds), a tiny sort of hiccup—as when we pronounce *bottle* as "bo-tuhl"—is meaningful or not. It is, in both languages.[48]

Overall, Zunian seems to have far more phonemic commonalities with Japanese than with any language in North America; Aztec-Tanoan languages spoken by the Pima and the Shoshoni, for example, have many more phonemes. Pomo has forty-three, thirty-eight consonants and five vowels. And Navaho has sixty, fourteen vowels and forty-six consonants!

Because they are phonemically very similar, more words that sound alike might also, quite by accident, have the same meaning than would be the case if the two languages had a very different repertoire of sounds. However, if Japanese and Zunian are related, we should find not only some word similarities by accident, but also some by historical linkages. Since there is no agreed-upon formula for determining which word similarity derives from accident and which from historical linkage, I simply must find a lot of words with very similar sounds and identical meaning.[49]

Earlier chapters introduced a few words I believe are related; the list in Table 4 presents more in selected categories. Additional words are introduced in the next two chapters, on kinship and religion.

GRAMMAR AND SYNTAX

Structural features of a language are less numerous than phonemes and words, and being so basic, they are more difficult to modify over time. Hence, if two languages are identical in certain structural ways, then their historical relationships may be stronger.

The specific structural elements shared by Zunian and Japanese include the following:

1. Constructing words by combining a consonant with a vowel, generally avoiding consonant clusters. This is called the *CV pattern*. Both are "agglutinative"; that is, morphemes are glued onto the front and back of words called *stems* or *roots*.
2. Using few prefixes, no infixes, and many suffixes.
3. A subject-object-verb word order and a tendency to leave the subject unexpressed.[50]
4. Using particles to link words together—postpositions, not prepositions.

There are some differences in the specific arrangement of some parts of a sentence. In Japanese, the modifying word may either precede the stem modified or appear after, connected by a particle. In Zunian, the adjective usually follows the noun, but this is not always the case. When two nouns comprise one stem, the modifying element may come first: *pila shiwani*, "bow priest" (*pila* means "bow," *shiwani*, "priest").[51] Another example, which appeared in the Zuni migration story, is *Shohko yala*, "Flute Mountain" (in Japanese, *shakuhachi yama*; see Figure 40).

Nouns, adjectives, adverbs, and verbs have similar characteristics. A root or stem may function by itself as a noun, or with inflection as an adjective, adverb, or verb. The noun may be uninflected

TABLE 4
SELECTED WORD COMPARISON[52]

ENGLISH	ZUNI	JAPANESE
Environment		
river	kawina	kawa
summit, top	kazzowa	kashira
to cross over	yato	yoko
to arrive, reach	techi	tochaku
originate, begin	chimi-ka	hajimi
sand	so	suna.
road	ona	orai
woods	ta	takigi (wood, fuel)
leaf	ha	ha
crow	kalashi	karasu
sparrow	suzua	suzume
mountain	yala	yama
badger	tonashi	tanuki
Verbs		
to become hot	kalhi	karai
to feel cold	izuma	samui[53]
to become angry	ikati	ikari
to become tall	tashi	takashi
to be mean, to attack	samu	seme (ru)
to wake up	okwi	oki (ru)
to say	ikwa	ika
Nouns		
dish	sale	sara
back	si	se
spherical object	mo	mo
Adjectives and Adverbs		
ancient	ino:te	inishie
old	lhashshi	mukashi
wide	kapa	hapa (width)
within	akka	dakara
be inside of	uchi	uchi

Figure 40. *Flute from the Southwest region*

and its relation to the rest of the sentence determined by particles, by the inflection of other words, or by juxtaposition. Stems are neutral in mode, tense, number, and gender. All but gender may be added through affixes, primarily suffixes, in a certain order.

Both Zunian and Japanese depend primarily on suffixes to change or add meanings to root words. Some prefixing is used, and it occurs more frequently in Zunian than in Japanese. Zunian indicates indirect objects, pronouns, and some plurals by prefixing stem words. Japanese, on the other hand, has few regular prefixes other than the honorific prefix /o-/ or /on-/. However, it has been proposed that prefixing was more common in Old Japanese and represents a remnant of Austronesian origin. For example, the prefix /ma-/ is added to enhance the intensity of the root word.

A distinct difference between the two languages occurs in the mode and frequency of pluralizing. Number is not expressed in Japanese except for specific reasons, so most plural root forms have special meanings.[54] However, many separate number words and separate endings are added to categories of nouns. In contrast, the singular, dual, and plural are expressed in Zunian through suffixes, prefixes, and plural stems. Ruth Bunzel referred to number as "fundamental" to the language.[55] Again, Japanese may have had more plural root forms in the past, becoming lost as the language became simplified over time. Certainly there are many suffix endings in Japanese for indicating numbers, but nouns can usually stand alone without reference to number.

One especially interesting plural suffix in Zunian is *-atchi*, meaning "two." Recall in the migration story, the two brothers: Anahohoatchi. The suffix *-atchi* in Japanese is also a plural form that means more than one, but is not limited to two (for example, "I" is *watakushi;* "we" is *watakushitachi*).

Neither Japanese nor Zunian make a big deal out of tense, that is, when something occurred. They both have a present and a past form, but the future is often not expressed. The suffix for the singular past tense in Zunian is a small morpheme, /-ka/; in Japanese, /ta/ denotes both singular and plural past tense.

The negative is indicated by suffixes in Japanese; in Zunian, it is indicated through suffixes and a particle, *kwa,* which introduces the negative clause. The sounds for /n/ (-nu, -ni) are characteristic for the expression of the idea of "not" in Japanese.[56] In Zunian, the negative suffix is /-m/ (-ma, -me).[57]

Both languages have two pitches, normal and higher, and the higher pitch and a slight accent are most commonly placed on the first syllable.[58] Finally, both Japanese and Zunian include age and sex dialects,[59] which are discussed in the next chapter.

In summary, general differences in syntax and morphology are noted. Zunian has greater development of root words allocating number, and prefixes are more common, varied, and morphologically significant. Also, there are some differences in the specific arrangement of attributive aspects within a statement.

Among the similarities are the following: Both languages are agglutinative and synthetic, and share the same general syntax. Stems may function alone as nouns and with suffixes as verbs, adverbs, or adjectives. Suffixes also add mode, tense, and number to otherwise neutral root forms. Gender is not expressed and conjunctions are rare. Postpositions and particles relate the parts of the statement. Both languages have two pitches; the higher pitch and greater stress tend to occur in the first syllable of a word. Finally, both languages include significant age and sex dialects.

These general linguistic features may occur in other languages around the Pacific Rim, but not, to my knowledge, in such remarkable combination. I propose that the Japanese language, like Japanese genes, was introduced into Zuni by men on a religious pilgrimage, who also brought new religious concepts, new organizations, and gender-specific words.

This leads, rather logically, to the next chapter on family, fraternities, kinship, and kachinas.

CHAPTER EIGHT

KINSHIP AND KACHINAS: CULTURAL CONSEQUENCES OF SOCIAL MERGERS

Just as genes and language mixed and merged when the two groups came into intensive contact, so the overall cultural patterns of the people who became the Zuni had to respond creatively to the pilgrims. What indications of a blending of traditions could survive to be identified today, after seven hundred years? Cultures are sometimes perceived as soft and malleable. What cultural data persist to support this theory? How firm or flimsy is the evidence?

In this chapter four categories of Zuni culture that reveal aspects of the social merger are presented: certain kinship patterns and terminology, clan organization and names, the persistence of separate dialects for men and women, and a specific ritualized method for frightening children into proper behavior.

KINSHIP CONFUSION

Part of the Zuni enigma is the fact that anthropologists have not yet figured out the kinship system; it is full of anomalies. Why?

Human populations have been moving around and about the planet for a long time, periodically running into differently organized groups. What happens to separate societies when they find themselves not only adjacent to each other, but also integrating with each other?[1] Is the Zuni pueblo an example?

First some background: Kinship systems and social organizations provide the intellectual guts for a branch of cultural anthropology called *social anthropology,* which studies the way societies name, arrange, and educate their members.[2] Our interest in other people's kinship systems may stem from the relative poverty of our own. How, we Westerners ponder, do people in small villages and tribes keep track of so many named relatives? How do they maintain their balance in face of so many expectations from kin, for services, time, goods, and in the modern day, money and jobs? The Zuni, for example, have sixteen different kinship terms for blood relatives and ten of those same terms also designate certain ceremonial relatives. How do they apply those special words appropriately at the right time in the proper circumstance?[3]

The Zuni people are unusually rich in relatives. They have, in fact, so many relatives in so many different categories, all in the same town, that they have confused the anthropologists. The key to this academic confusion may be the way the kinship system is linked with everything Zuni: not just numerous named blood relatives organized in fourteen matrilineal, exogamous[4] clans, but also special relationships with "relatives" in religion, including eight curing societies, sixteen priesthoods, and six kiva groups, each with many associated responsibilities and ceremonies that occur year-round. Further, the political system is also tied to the religious leaders, the rain priests, kiva officials, and the sun chief, and for them, too, there are special terms.[5]

Perhaps Zuni social organization is so complex and puzzling because it has adopted some Japanese ways.

KIN AND CLANS

The sixteen basic kinship terms delineate Zuni biological kin, and ten of the same words extend to relatives by marriage, and further, to clan members and to ceremonial "relatives." So what is the uncertainty about?

Obviously the Zuni understand it. As the Zuni anthropologist Edmund Ladd pointed out, "Standing at the center of his universe, which is determined at birth, the individual is keenly aware of his relationships . . . he is never confused among blood kin, clan kin, and ceremonial or religious relationships. . . . He is aware of the broad outlines of the total system that includes the entire village."[6]

Smart Zuni. Does this mean dumb anthropologists? Not necessarily. Frank Cushing, Alfred Kroeber, Fred Eggan, Robin Fox, Matilda Stevenson, David Schneider, John Roberts, Stanley Newman, Ruth Bunzel, Ruth Benedict, and Elsie Parsons were astute scholars, but they never considered the possibility that the Zuni system was at one time a clear-cut, typical Native American matrilineal system, before the thirteenth century. But it is not so simple or typical now, possibly because a population of male Japanese pilgrims with a patrilineal background arrived with a religious mission, and the two populations merged their kinship systems. The addition of a patrilineal influence upon a matrilineal base resulted in something quite different and unique in North America.

Before proceeding, let us consider what is meant by a "kinship system" and how that relates to the larger "social organization."

A society's social organization provides organized ways of thinking about human relationships, ordering them, and naming them; it has to do with how our species manages its face-to-face and people-to-people relations. Kinship systems address how a society perpetuates itself through prescribed marriage patterns, and then with the long-term investment of civilizing the babies born from these arrangements. Aspects of the social organization of a culture are reflected through kin terms that connote those systems.

Here is an example: What do you call your mother's brother's son? Is he called "cousin" or "brother" or something completely different, possibly indicating he is a potential mate? Do you call your mother's sister's daughter a different term? Or the same? Is she "like a sister" or is she "like a cousin"? And what difference does it make?

What people call themselves in relation to biological kin and to kin by marriage varies in remarkable ways. Sometimes the reason for the names and the relationships can be analyzed; sometimes they make no sense at all. Regardless, anthropologists still try to tease out a kinship "system" that will explain something about the whole society. Sometimes it works fairly well.

In small tribal societies, knowledge of kinship relationships is important because it provides a key for identifying who can marry whom, and who is completely off-limits. When biological kinship terms are crisscrossed, as they are in Zuni, by clan, by fraternity, by medicine society, and by kachina society, the system becomes impressively complex.

David Schneider and John Roberts presented their analysis of Zuni kin terms in 1956.[7] Three distinctive aspects of the Zuni kinship system emerged. First, the Zuni system is neither pure lineage nor pure generational, but rather, "modified Crow."

The traditional Native American Crow system is strongly matrilineal, tracing descent only through the mother's side. This system, reported by Robert H. Lowie in 1935, stemmed from a study of three bands of Crow Indians who live on the Great Plains in northern Wyoming and Montana.[8] Of course, the matrilineal clan system is much more widespread than just on the Great Plains, but the original study by Lowie of its social functions provided a basis for study of other groups and the allocation of the term *Crow system* to other tribes with similar kinship and clan features. The Zuni seem to have innovated a "modified" Crow system, sharing a strong matrilineal base, but with puzzling irregularities, including one set of terms used by men and a different set by women.

Second, Schneider and Roberts reported that alternate terms are used for significant kinsmen and these terms appear to have role significance; they make a difference in how people behave. In other words, more than one set of terms can be given for the same person, but they are used differently according to circumstance.

Third, there is a "high incidence of apparent irregularities or 'wrong' usages"; that is, "wrong" in the sense that they would not be "expected" in a system that was either consistently lineal or consistently generational. Schneider and Roberts believed these facts are all interrelated and this led them to consider this question: "Is the Zuni system in process of change from a lineage to a generational type?"[9]

Quite likely the system is in a process of change, and has been at least since the late thirteenth century. Recall that Zuni oral traditions of migration indicate a mixing of two or more groups; the changes identified in the archeological record and skeletal remains confirm that something significant happened; and the biology of the population today suggests admixture. So, if a new group moved into the area and got established, would the kinship system and social organization of the original occupants shift away from a lineal system toward a generational system?

The original Zuni "lineal" system may indeed be a typical Crow arrangement of people with named clans that traced descent through the mother's line, and it may have changed to accommodate the Pacific pilgrims who brought a powerfully organized male-dominated religious system with them.

Consider the fact that the economic base of Zuni society is still centered in the matrilineal household, which controls land usage. A woman's identity is closely affiliated with her mother's household and clan for life. But this is not quite so true for Zuni men. A man's more significant identity is through his father's side with kiva groups, medicine societies, and kachina societies, which cut across household clan affiliation. This thick fabric of organizational complexity does not seem to apply to women.

Nowadays a modern Zuni male identifies clan relationship on both sides, not just one. With a clear-cut lineage system, only one side—either mother or father but not both—is recognized. But in Zuni, a man first names the mother's clan, then adds the clan of his father, such as "I am also child of Eagle." Both are significant in pueblo life. The father's side provides the religious ties a Zuni man needs for his full identity (see Figure 41).

Here is an example: A Zuni scholar, Willard Zunie, is a teacher in continuing education in the Gallup and Zuni branch of the University of New Mexico. Part of his identity is shaped by his degrees, work experience, and memberships in educational associations. But, Mr. Zunie adds to his resume the following: "I belong to

Figure 41. *Zuni artist Randy Nahohai and son Joshua*

the Frog clan and am a child of the Parrot clan. I am initiated into a Kiva Group that represents the West (color-blue). Also, I am a member of the Shalako fraternity. Thus, I have two sets of . . . parents—one set for Kiva initiation, and the other for sponsoring me at their 'Shalako' house, and—of course—brothers and sisters from these families." Mr Zunie is rich in relatives—and associated responsibilities.[10]

Is this kind of complexity reflective of a creative social response to a new patrilineal system, introduced by the Japanese pilgrims, thus creating a modified Crow system?

Now what of specific kinship terms? If a social merging of systems occurred, it should be reflected in the words referring to members of the society.

ZUNIAN AND JAPANESE KINSHIP TERMINOLOGY

Several key Zuni kinship words indicate a genetic linguistic relationship to Japanese or, alternatively, are borrowed words from the merging of two populations. I am not sure which is the stronger explanation because basic words such as *man* and *woman* that appear on the Swadesh one-hundred-word list are presumably relatively immune to borrowing. That is, if two languages are related to a shared language in the past, their connection should be revealed through "basic" words—words that would not ordinarily be "borrowed" later from a different, unrelated language.

Some of the first words to come to my attention in checking Zuni texts were words on that basic word list. For example, the Zunian stem for "woman" is *oka. Oka* also refers to "woman" in Japanese. The Zuni word for "wife" is based on the same stem: *okassiki*;[11] *okasama* or *okāsan* is "mother" in Japanese.

The Zunian word for "man/male" is *otse.* An ancient Japanese word for "man" is *osu.*[12] In modern Japanese *osu* means "male animal." A modern Zuni word for "husband" (and in earlier documents, "father") is *oyemshi.* In Japanese one common word now is *ototsan,* and an alternative term is *oya* (father or parent). Are words for "man" and "woman," "husband" and "father," the kind that might be borrowed by a Native American group if they merged with Japanese? Or might these terms stem from a remote shared ancestral protolanguage? If Japanese males arrived without Japanese females, would these basic words likely be adopted by the merged population?

In both nations, the very large one, Japan, and the much smaller one, Zuni, kinship terminology extends far beyond blood relationship and tends to be generational. This means a single term might be applied to a number of relatives of the same generation.

The classificatory system of the Zuni is well known.[13] All the rain priests are called "father" and everyone calls the governor's wife "mother." These terms are generalized far past biology and applied horizontally by generation.

Edmund Ladd provided an example of these tenets. When a young man joins a kiva, he acquires a new set of older and younger "brothers" in his own generation. The kiva leaders are called "father" and the older men, "grandfather." His sponsors are "father" and "mother," and they call him "cale" (child).[14] Through these terms, the young initiate recognizes changed relationships in age, rank, and social distance, applying biological kin words to nonbiological relationships.

In Japan, the *oyabun-kobun,* the father-child, or "boss," relationships and attitudes of kin and authority, are also generalized far beyond the family into many professional relationships in such areas as industry, government, theater, and education.[15]

In 1988 Linda Watts presented a paper at a meeting of the Anthropological Association in Phoenix, Arizona, titled "Relational Terminology and Household-Group Role Structure at Zuni." In addition to summarizing the literature that addresses the confusion about Zuni kinship, she added new information and analysis.[16]

First, Watts confirmed what others had reported earlier; the Zuni continue to use "fictive" kin words for nonbiological relationships, and she demonstrated that the principle of seniority is generalized to include a ranked arrangement of clans, priesthoods, and kiva groups.

Four Zuni terms may be related to Japanese:

1. Parents, or other seniors, including ceremonial officers, sacred personages, and civil authorities on the village level: *a:lashhina:we* (Japanese: *mukashi,* "old").
2. All senior males in a household, regardless of biological relationships: *ottsina:we* (Japanese male: *osu*).
3. All senior women of a household group: *okkyana:we* (Japanese mother: *oka*).
4. All young male adults: *zawaki* (Japanese youth: *wakai*).

Finally, Watts identified three principles that account for the dynamic features of social interaction at every level of Zuni social structure: ranking according to relative seniority, social distance, and ceremonial sponsorship. Anyone who knows Japanese may sigh and comment, "How Japanese." Social consciousness and sensitivity to fine lines of ranking by age, sex, and position are also highly developed in Japan where it was already in place by the eleventh century.

AGE AND RANK

Age distinctions *within* generations also occur in both Zuni and Japan.[17] In Zuni the older brother is *papa;* the younger brother, *suwe,* to a male speaker. A differentiation of older and younger brother is also reflected in women's terms: *papa* for the elder and *hani* to the younger. Likewise separate terms apply to older and younger sister: *kawu* and *ikina* for the male speakers, and *kawu* and *hani* for female speakers. Note this is a total of five terms for siblings. In Japan, four different terms are used to designate older and younger brothers, and older and younger sisters. The elder brother, *ani,* has well-established seniority. In contemporary Zuni, women refer to the younger brother and younger sister as *hani;* men do not use that term (see Figure 42).

The age factor plays a significant role in mythology and in ritual directional orientation. Frequent reference is made, for example, to "elder brother of the north" and to "younger brother of the south."

Finally, in Zunian, "young man" is *zawaki.* In Japanese, "youth" is *wakai.* Recall from Chapter 7 that Zunian utilizes more prefixes than does contemporary Japanese, but that Old Japanese included more prefixes than found now in the modern language. I suggest the /za-/ prefix was retained in Zunian but lost in Japanese.

Figure 42. *A Zuni younger brother and older sister*

In summary, some terms strongly suggest linkage between Japanese and Zunian. Since both languages and the social organizations affiliated with them have been changing over the last seven hundred years in different directions and probably at varying rates in different categories, specific resolution of individual words may not be feasible. It is the combination of many words in numerous categories that lends credence to this theory.

Zuni ceremonial life includes deities also grouped in terms of kinship. For example, the roles of the elder brother and the younger brother are differentiated in the migration story; the sons of Kawimosa are clearly identified as the elder son and the younger sons.

Likewise, as noted, Japanese differentiate between older and younger brothers and older and younger sisters. Further, one set of kinship terms is used when talking about one's own relatives; another set, when referring to someone else's relatives.

Edmund Ladd explained that how a Zuni selects a kin term "depends on how close the speaker wishes to bring the person into the circle of kin—blood or clan."[18] Rank, age, and status stratification are also features in Japan; they continue in elaborate forms today. The Japanese system establishes relative distance, or closeness, by selecting certain words, suffixes, and even different verbs, verb endings, and pronouns according to relative status, age, and sex of the persons speaking with each other. The honorific speech in Japan is called *keigo*.[19]

The last chapter briefly mentioned three linguistic features shared by Zunian and Japanese: distinctive age, sex, and status dialects. Both languages have some terms that are used only by men and others only by women, and both languages have special terminology that reflect levels of respect, age, and status.

GENDERLECTS

Sex-specific dialects seem to be one shared characteristic of four major Pueblo languages in the Southwest. In Zuni, Bunzel found "there is considerable difference in the speech of men and women" but gives only a few examples. Newman reported distinctly separate sacred and slang words, and noted that Zuni sacred terms were used in prayers, myths, songs, and traditional sayings within the setting of the kiva. Further, he referred to a "kiva language," which is spoken exclusively by men. Another linguist, Paul Kroskrity, found distinct male and female speech in three other Pueblo language families: Uto-Aztecan, Kiowa-Tanoan, and Keresan.[20]

The Japanese employ whole sets of respectful terms appropriate for a woman to use when speaking to women and a different set to apply when speaking to men, and when speaking to someone of higher status, lower status, and approximately the same status.[21] Thus, both Japanese and Zuni have clearly differentiated "genderlects." Certain terms, word phrases, and verb endings are used by one sex and not by the other.[22]

Here is a personal example of the men's language observed in Zuni on May 5, 1995:

Robert Lewis, distinguished Zuni governor of four terms, was listening carefully, attentively, to the head of the Bow Priesthood. After their traditional, ritual "breath" greeting, their conversation had begun. Both were sitting on the edge of their chairs in the Lewis's home talking in Zunian about hay and ranching.

I sat quietly and listened, noting immediately that the Zuni language spoken by these Zuni men sounded quite different from the Zuni language spoken by women. Although I had read about the dialect variation between Zuni men and women, what I had heard was mostly women talking to women in the four-generation household where I stayed.

A slight pause occurred in the conversation, and the Governor said, "Hai." And the priest continued. I listened politely, not understanding a word.

The Governor said, "Hai" again. This second time I caught it again and listened even more intently. The Bow Priest continued.

A slight pause. "Hai," said the Governor, a third time.

And I knew. Without a doubt. The sound, the intonation, and the timing of the Zunian *hai* is identical to Japanese *hai*.

Hai in Japanese is said by the person listening, and responding. My Japanese teacher used the same expression frequently when talking with her assistant, and when listening, validating, my hesitant efforts to speak Japanese. "Hai," she said, meaning,

"Yes, I understand, I hear you, I am listening, please continue." The Japanese *sound* for *hai* is identical with the Zuni *sound* for *hai*. The accent occurs on the first syllable on a slightly higher pitch than the second syllable. Recall that both Zuni and Japanese have two pitches, upper and lower, and both have a tendency to place the emphasis on the first syllable: HA-ee.

But, I wondered after hearing it three different times in the conversation, does the Zuni *hai* actually *mean* the same as the Japanese *hai?*

The gentlemen concluded their conversation; the visitor, backing out the door, bowed slightly, and left.

The door had barely closed and I blurted out: "When you say 'hai,' does that mean 'yes'?"

"It does," Mr. Lewis replied. "But it also means, 'I am listening, I hear you. I understand. Go on.' "

Puzzled that I had not heard women use the expression, I asked, "Do Zuni women use 'hai' "?

"No. They don't. Only the men when talking with men."

A classic example of the men's language.

Why do both Japanese men and Japanese women use *hai,* with the same meaning, but only Zuni men say "hai" when speaking with other Zuni men? Is this fact one more indication that it was Japanese men who came, unaccompanied by Japanese women?

It makes good sense: The women kept their Native American clans and language, selectively adding Japanese words. The new migrants, mostly males, kept their original Japanese language, and added, selectively, Native American words. If the two major languages were grammatically and phonetically similar to start with because they share a basic, though ancient heritage, then the creative merging of the two languages would have been easier, and more probable, than if Japanese and Zunian had been as different from each other as, for example, Chinese from German.

The possible social and linguistic mixture between Japanese-speaking males and Native American Penutian-speaking females may complicate solving the riddle of the Zunian language and kinship terminology, but this theory provides a provocative lead.[23] *Hai.*

TWINS AND BROTHERS

The Twin War Gods of Zuni play important roles in the story of their migration to the middle of the world, as noted in Chapter 2. The concept of twin brothers, and clearly separate identities for the older brother and the younger brother, also appears in the earliest Japanese literature. Here is a synopsis of the story from *Nihongi*, dated A.D. 720[24]:

Two brothers were the twin offspring of the August Grandchild, named Ama-tsu-hiko-hiko-ho-no-ninigi no Mikoto, and Ka-ashi-tsu-hime, who was the daughter of the Great Mountain Deity, O-yama-tsu-mi Kami. The elder brother's name was Ho-no-susori no Mikoto, and he had by nature a sea-gift. The younger brother, Hiko-hoho-demi no Mikoto, had by nature a mountain-gift. They exchanged gifts; the elder brother tried out and then returned the younger brother's bow and arrows, but the younger brother lost his elder brother's fishhook. In the search to retrieve the fishhook, the younger brother, Hiko-hoho-demi, met the Sea-God's daughter, named Toyo-tama-hime. Hiko-hoho-demi retrieved the hook, and married Toyo-tama-hime, who turns out to be his elder brother's daughter. (Note that part of the elder brother's name is *Hono* and part of the younger brother's name is *hoho* and the Zuni pair of twin brothers is called "Anahohoatchi." The *-atchi* suffix connotes more than one person in both languages. *Him* is a Zuni family name; *hime* means princess in Japanese.)

The Zuni kinship system, social organization, and certain elements in mythology reflect evidence suggesting a merging of systems; specifically, they may be the result of Japanese religious and patrilineal influence on an older, matrilineal Native American Indian base.

ZUNI CLANS AND JAPANESE UJI

Another level of analysis must include clans and *uji*. Zuni matrilineal clans are associated with six directions in their religious system. Sixteen clans were reported in 1880; fourteen continue to provide the household and land base for all Zuni people.

Matrilineal clans were mentioned but not named in the Japanese book *Kojiki*, written in A.D. 712. Apparently they were displaced by patrilineal "clans" called *uji*, which became the key organizational force during the Yamato period (A.D. 300–645). The *uji* concept was possibly introduced to Japan by an Altaic-speaking pastoral tribe that arrived about the fourth century. *Uji* had all the characteristics of traditional clans: social, economic, political unity with a religious solidarity centering around a *uji-gami*, the deity of the clan. It is possible that the *uji* replaced matrilineal clans of the previous Yayoi period, then became an integral part of the development of the Japanese state and empire. Here is a brief summary.

About the fourth century, one *uji* began to gain military power, and established its mythological claim to genealogical descent from Amaterasu, a female sun deity. The chieftains of this imperial *uji* were then in a position to confer titles to other *uji* chieftains, grant sacred seed at the spring festivals, establish sacred sites, and regulate rituals for various *kami*, which are named Shinto deities. The early Yamato kingdom was unified by the imperial *uji* into a loosely knit confederation of semi-autonomous clans. This principle of unity of religion and administration established during the Yamato period continued through the imperial family to the end of World War II.[25]

Historians of Japan apply the concept of "clan" somewhat differently than do anthropologists. Japanese "clans" *(uji)* are not the totemic descent groups named after plants and animals such as found in many peoples around the Pacific and in Native America (and Zuni), although there may have been a time before the fourth century when they were also so named in Japan.

Until A.D. 645, the year of the Taika land reform, the *uji* were the most important groups in Japanese society, united in a loose federation of units bound by both territory and kinship. Each *uji* had a chieftain and a deity *(ujigami)*. What seems to have happened was a consolidation of power under the chieftain of the Yamato *uji*, which led to the formation of a state in the sixth century.

The historian G. Cameron Hurst provided an analysis of kinship in the early Heian period[26] and there are commonalities with the way the Zuni arrange their families. Hurst, and others, interchange the word *uji* with *clans,* and he notes each "clan" was divided into a number of lineages. He uses the example of the four branches of the Fujiwara "clan" and diagrams them very much as an anthropologist would: clan-lineage-sublineage-household, each with a name.

Although the Yamato "chieftain" was a ruler, his responsibility was more religious than political. After the Taika coup d'etat of 645, the Yamato *uji* sought to further centralize the state, and made considerable headway in doing so. The Yamato *uji* became the imperial house and placed other *uji* under their control. They had successfully reassigned lands under public control to form a state bureaucracy. The emperor emerged from the Fujiwara *uji* as a public figure, with much prestige and political authority as a descendant of the Sun Goddess.

This development was an attempt to respond to and emulate Chinese structure, but it did not eliminate the old *uji* system. The chieftain of the local *uji* continued religious leadership through control of clan temples and shrines. Even at the height of Chinese influence, the local *uji* never lost its power. By the end of the Heian period, the local *uji* were strengthened, and independent again.[27]

Japanese *uji* during the Heian period seem very similar to today's Zuni clans: strong sources of continuity, well grounded with a religious base. The new, superimposed ranking system that developed in Japan simply rearranged people who were already ranked in lineages. The Japanese system moved into, first, a state and then an empire. Were the Zuni priesthoods and centralized towns also moving in that direction when the Spanish arrived in 1539?

Next consider Zuni clan names. Here are four that may have derived from Japanese words: The Crane clan of the north, *kalakta (kwe)* is one.[28] "Crane" in Japanese is *karancho.* The /l/ to /r/ correspondence in the medial position is also found in the terms for "crow"—*kwalasi* in Zuni and *karasu* in Japanese. The Zuni Crow clan is also associated with the north. In Zuni, "badger" is *tonashi,* associated with the south; in Japanese, badger is *tanuki.* Badgers seem to play similar roles in folklore.[29] Finally, the word for "deer," also associated with a clan in Zuni, is *showita.* The Japanese word is *shika.* These two words share three phonemes (i.e., three mini-

mal sounds): /sh/, /i/, and /a/. The /t/ and /k/ sounds are similar in location and sound.[30] The deer figures as an important
religious animal in ancient Shinto, in Buddhism, and in contemporary Zuni religion.

These four Zuni clan names may well be based on Japanese
loan words that came with the pilgrims from the west.[31]

NAMAHAGE AND KOJIN; UWANAGA AND KACHINA

All human cultures try to civilize their children into respectable members of their society, sharing its values and behaving appropriately. How this task is accomplished varies greatly
across the world's myriad of societies.

The Namahage ceremony in northeastern Japan and the
Uwanaga ceremony at Zuni include a series of remarkable similarities that may share a common ancestry. Both ceremonies function to terrify children into good behavior by ritual visits from
horrible masked monsters who threaten to kill and eat them.

The Namahage ceremony in Japan was formerly quite widespread, but in recent years it has been practiced in only a few
small communities in Northeast Honshu. In her book *Namahage:
A Festival in the Northeast of Japan,* Yoshiko Yamamoto provided a
description of the masked visitors (see Figure 43), the behavior of
the Namahage, and the functions they provide for the cohesive-
ness of the village, including shaping the behavior of the children.[32] Her thoughts closely parallel Frank Cushing's description
of the Zuni monster kachinas, Atoshle (see Figure 44) and his wife
Suyuki (see Figure 45), here paraphrased by Barton Wright in
Kachinas of the Zuni:

> *In January when Atoshle and his wife visit the children, he
> carries a large blood-stained knife, which he uses to sweep the
> hair back from his bulging eyes, leaving his hair smeared with
> blood. His wife carries a basket on her back and a long crook
> for catching children. The Koyemshi usually accompany them.
> As they draw near a house, Atoshle rushes toward it and then
> withdraws and rushes again, striking the door with his knife*

Figure 43. *Japanese Namahage mask, Oga Peninsula*

Figure 44. *Zuni kachina: Atoshle*

Figure 45. *Zuni kachina: Suyuki*

on the fourth approach. The inhabitants may beat drums or clang tin pans together in a futile effort to frighten him away. Once inside, he berates the children in a chilling falsetto voice that can be heard throughout the village and often makes them perform the duties they have been avoiding. The threat of being carried off in a basket to be eaten later is used with great effect, and, occasionally, Atoshle will add to this horror by pretending to bite one of the adults present. The monsters are eventually bought out with meat from the household and are forced out, where they make their way to the next place as every youngster they meet rushes to hide.[33]

In both Japan and Zuni, the masked monsters traditionally appear at the same time of year, in mid-January, after the New Year's ceremony. Their arrival is preceded and announced by a bonfire on a hill the night before. Both are associated with purification, and with protecting fruit trees, especially peach trees.[34] Both sets of monsters are considered visitors from the land of the dead; both carry knives and other weapons and make unusual, threatening vocal sounds. The masks of both have horns, exaggerated bulging eyes, and horse hair falling down around a bearded face. Both have assistants to help frighten the children, and to collect the goods given by parents to appease the monsters who threaten to eat children—the bad children who do not behave. The masks and the ceremonies are associated with men's secret societies.

Are the masked monsters of the Namahage ceremonies in Japan related to the masked monsters of the Uwanaga (ground-cleansing) ceremonies in Zuni?[35] The sequence and timing of their activities, their appearance, functions, and effectiveness as a means of social control seem exceptionally parallel. One more piece of the puzzle.

In Japan the traditional Namahage masks and ritual are now much diminished; few communities keep up the tradition, although some have made the Namahage ceremony into a tourist event including masks in museums (see Figure 46). In Zuni, the kachina masks, dances, and ceremonies are increasingly elaborate, and private, though it is said the Atoshle and Suyuki monsters rarely come anymore.[36]

However, the knowledge and the fear are clearly perpetuated in a picture by the late Phil Hughte, a Zuni artist, entitled *"Here comes Atoshle!"* (see Figure 47). It portrays four Koyemshi (Mudheads, or clowns) and Atoshle and his wife Suyuki in a modern setting, masks, bloody knives, and all.

All human societies devise ways to shape their children into behaving respectfully, but how many terrify them with masked monsters with bulging eyes who carry bloody weapons, shrieking as they approach? And how often are the monsters paid off by parents in mid-January after a ceremonial fire on a hillside with a ritual protecting peach trees? And how many are performed by men in a secret society?

Finally, what about the peach trees? Both the Namahage and the Uwanaga ceremonies include protection of the peach orchards by the monsters en route down the mountain after the bonfire the night before. Peach pits have been found in excavations in the Southwest, and peach orchards were noted by early Spanish explorers of the American Southwest. Where did the peaches come

Figure 46. *Namahage mask*

Figure 47. *Here comes Atoshle!*

from? Peach trees are not easily established; indeed, a complex cluster of knowledge is required for their cultivation and maintenance.

Although the Spanish are credited with introducing peach
trees to the Southwest,[37] the Spanish words *melacotone* and *du-
razno* do not sound like the Zuni word *mo:chiqa* at all. And no specific reference in Spanish to a time and place for the actual
introduction by the Spanish has been found. Peaches are assumed
to be European, but in fact they were first domesticated in China
by 3000 B.C. Might peaches have been introduced from the west
before the Spanish arrived? From China via Japan rather than
from China via Spain?

Elsie Parsons reported that two Hopi men were spared by the
Spanish in a 1700 massacre because they knew about growing
peaches.[38] She also noted the Hopi made clay images of peaches,
and prayer sticks for their protection.

Of further interest is the description of the Zuni peach orchards provided by Matilda Stevenson. During her time in Zuni in
the late nineteenth century, peaches were raised in the foothills
where there was more moisture. The trees were, she reported,
small, many of them "not over three feet in height, some even
less." Harvesting the peaches was a delightful family event in
those days, and large quantities were dried for the winter (see
Figure 48).[39]

The most comprehensive reference to Zuni peach orchards is
by T. J. Ferguson in *Historic Zuni Architecture and Society*.[40] In the
1880s there were many orchards among the cliffs and terraces
near Zuni, and it has been proposed that the great kivas were built
in the peach orchard villages to escape from Spanish authorities.
At least two peach orchard villages have been located along the
bases and sides of mesas in defensive positions in the Zuni River
valley. These villages may have been refuge sites for ceremonial
practices, built hidden away so the Zuni could practice their religion. During the eighteenth century, they were the largest of the
seasonally occupied settlements.

However, the peach orchard villages cease to be occupied now.
Ferguson reported that only a few stumps from peach trees remain, and noted, "The best archaeological evidence that there
were once peaches at the settlement comes from the peach stones
that are in the middens."[41]

Figure 48. *View in Zuni circa 1885, with drying fruit in foreground*

At Zuni, near the base of Dowa Yalanne (Corn Mountain), is evidence of an ancient peach orchard. The Japanese word for peach is *momo;* the Zuni root word for spherical object is *mo* and the Zuni word for peach is *mo:chiqa* (*mo,* "round object," *chiqa,* "sweet") sweet round object. Is it not possible that Zuni peach trees and the ceremony associated with protecting them are of Japanese origin? Of course, DNA testing and dating of pollen and pits could resolve the question of the source of the very early peach orchards in the American Southwest.

The four clusters of cultural data presented in this chapter bring together a combination of features that paint a larger picture and tease the mind with the possibility that additional evidence may be embedded in the well-documented Zuni culture and the even more-documented medieval Japanese culture.

The Zuni merger of Japanese cultural concepts does not stop with kinship terms, clans, genderlects, and monsters. Complex Asian religious concepts were also incorporated by the Zuni Pueblo peoples of the Southwest.

CHAPTER NINE

COSMOLOGY
AND RELIGION:
KOKKO AND
KAMI

C lan names, kin terms, and ceremonies move with people in discrete, complex clusters of information; they do not wander about aimlessly in isolated fragments. Certain Zuni religious concepts and terms suggest that the western contingent of the search for Itiwanna included Japanese pilgrims whose religious views and practices merged with those held by the population already in the Southwest when they arrived.

Study of Japanese religions reveals a remarkable history of creatively reworking old concepts with new ones, framing a strong philosophical foundation for the next source of ideas. Religions, like waves and currents, words and genes, came to the Japanese islands from the north, the south, and the west, bringing concepts of shamanism, Taoism, Confucianism, and Buddhism to complement Shinto, which is considered the traditional religion. The term *amalgamation* of numerous traditions is appropriate when studying the history of Japanese religion[1] and amalgamation also applies to the Pueblo region of the American Southwest. The late Pueblo Indian anthropologist Alfonso Ortiz refers to the "unique cultural syntheses from elements of diverse provenance."[2] The religious complexities of the area's twenty Pueblo tribes continue to challenge scholars.

The Zuni religion is known for its intricacy, well documented in the late nineteenth and early twentieth centuries. Anyone who has experienced a religious event in Zuni—whether a public ceremonial dance, a private prayer, or a gift of food offered to the ancestors—knows that something powerful is embedded in the spirituality of this middle place of the world.

If contemporary Zuni kinship, language, and biology are the result of mergers in the recent past, then elements of Shinto, Taoism, and Buddhism might be identifiable in the cosmology and ceremonies of these Pueblo peoples.

And they are.

No one can reconstruct the sequence of events in Japan and in Zuni that led to the cluster of shared concepts and words, but religions do have histories, just as genes and languages do; colorful threads of ideas are woven into conceptual tapestries of theological systems. The Zuni religion reveals a merging of many ideas from a myriad of sources.

COMMON DISTANT ROOTS

Native American Indian religions evolved long before the thirteenth-century Asian contact I propose. Some basic elements, like shamanism, were probably brought by Native Americans from their places of origin, including Northeast Asia; other ideas were elaborated as various populations arrived and settled throughout the New World. Spiritual creativity is part of the great human phenomenon of an intelligent species on the move.

Japan may have received some basic and early ideas, like shamanism, from the same sources in Asia as did Native Americans. For one example of a shared word, in Japan a Buddhist priest is called *shamon*, a linguistic adaptation of a North Asian word, *shaman*, itself derived from the Sanskrit word now widely applied to Native American traditional practitioners called medicine men and women. Shamanism includes themes of magical acts, powers received through visions and trances, and curing skills performed by part-time specialists. Zuni religion includes some shaman-like practices of magic and witchcraft that are probably quite ancient in origin and predate more recent Asian sources, influences, and words that seem woven into their intricate religious system.

SHINTO KAMI AND ZUNI KOKKO

Shinto and Zuni religion are based on animism and ancestor worship; both include a spiritual world richly populated by hundreds of named deities, called *kami* in Japanese and *kokko* in Zunian. Both envisage a three-dimensional universe divided into high, middle, and low.[3] Both are characterized by polytheism, daily offerings to the ancestors, regular ceremonies for fertility and harvest, ritual washing, reverence for hundreds of shrines, annual pilgrimages to sacred sites, and prayers to the sun.[4] Shinto and Zuni also share exceptionally elaborate New Year ceremonies (see Figure 49).[5] Although renewal rites and New Year celebrations are common among world cultures, some celebrate with more flair than others. Japan and Zuni may be near the upper end of the scale for their annual focus on New Year events.[6]

Figure 49. *Painting of four Shalako*

SHARED RELIGIOUS TERMS

One Japanese word for ancestors is *kojin*. The Zuni employ both the Hopi word *kachina*[7] and their own word, *kokko*, which means god, deity, and ancestor.[8] *Kokkokwe* means "god clan" in Zuni: *kokko* meaning "god" and *kwe*, "clan" or "society."[9] In Japanese, *kogoshi* refers to "god-like"; a recently deceased emperor, considered a god, is referred to as *Kōkō*.

The highly ranked Zuni clown (Galaxy) fraternity is called *Ne'wekwe*. The Zuni word for "clown" is *newe* (also called *Koyemshi*, or Mudhead). The Japanese word for "clown" is *niwaka*.

Zuni and Shinto religions share a concern over the navel. This center point of the body is referred to as "the source of life" in Zuni.[10] *Zu* is "stomach" or "navel" in Zuni; *zo* is the Japanese word for "viscera," and *eso* is the word for "navel." In Kyoto, Japan (see Map 17), a shrine and a six-sided rock called Eso Ishi (navel stone) marked the exact center of the city in A.D. 793 on the eve of the Heian period when Kyoto became the capital (see Figures 50 and 51). The Zuni also have a sacred stone, located under a kiva in the old village, that marks what they believe to be the exact center of the world. The stone is so sacred neither picture nor written description is available.

A common reference in Zuni religion is to the "sun crossing over the sky." The verb "to cross over" is *yato;* in Japanese it is *yoko*.[11]

A Zuni priest is called *shiwani;* a Shinto priest is *shanin, shinkwan,* or in rural areas, *shawani,* a word derived from Sanskrit.

Shinto priests, *shawani,* and Zuni priests, *shiwani,* call on deities and ancestors to bring rain. The Japanese word for rain is *ame*. The Zuni word for rain is *ami;* Zuni rain-making priests are *uwanami*.[12]

YIN-YANG

When I prepared a table entitled "Zuni Directional Relationships" for Robert Redfield's course on social anthropology at the University of Chicago in 1957, I had not heard of yin-yang or Taoism. My chart (see Table 5) was based exclusively on reading

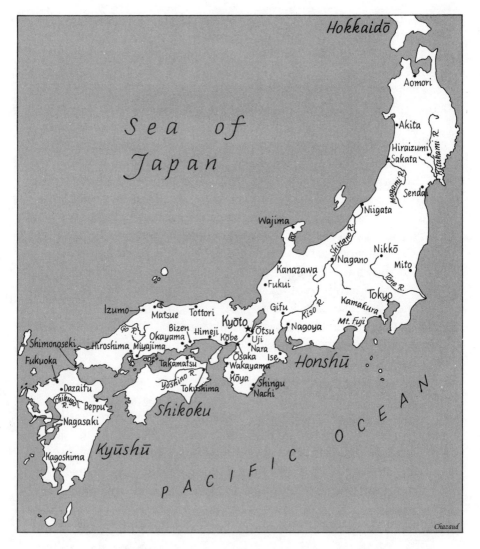

Map 17. *Japan: Modern cities on three major islands.*

Figure 50. *Rokkaku-dō. Sacred Temple for Pilgrims, Kyoto*

Figure 51. *Eso Ishi. Navel stone. Kyoto*

TABLE 5
ZUNI DIRECTIONAL RELATIONSHIPS

DIRECTION	CLANS	ELEMENTS	SEASON	COLOR
NORTH	Grouse Crane Evergreen-oak Yellowwood	Wind	Winter	Yellow
WEST	Bear Coyote Springherb Red-top plant	Water	Spring	Blue
SOUTH	Tobacco Maize plant Badger	Fire	Summer	Red
EAST	Deer Antelope Turkey	Earth	Autumn	White
ZENITH UPPER	Sun Sky Eagle			Many-colored
NADIR LOWER	Frog Water Rattlesnake			Black
MIDDLE	Parrot-Macaw			Many-colored

NAME	BEAST GOD	CHARACTER-ISTICS	PRIEST-HOODS	OTHER RELATIONS
Elder brother	Mountain lion, Cougar	Masterfulness and destructiveness; War and destruction	Shiwanni of the North—highest priesthood	Chief priest
Younger brother of the North	Bear	War cure; Hunting	Priesthood of the Bow and of the Hunt	Idols for Bow priests to be carved by Bear clan
Younger brother of the West	Badger	Husbandry and medicine	Shiwanni of the South	Assistant to priest must be a Badger
Younger brother of the South	Wolf	Magic and religion	Shiwanni of the East	Chief from Antelope clan; direction of Katchina—Deer clan
Younger brother of the East	Eagle	Life preservers	Shiwanni of the Zenith	Sun priest—most revered man; keeper of calendar
Younger brother to all	Mole, Gopher	Life makers	Shiwanni of the Nadir	
Brother to all		Mythic dance, drama—Kaka		

Compiled by Nancy Yaw, 1957. Sources included, primarily, Cushing 1882, 1896, and 1920 and Stevenson 1904 major Zuni ethnographies and it diagrammed the associations of directions with clans, elements, seasons, colors, beast gods, characteristics, priesthoods, and other relations.[13]

I learned later that the Zuni and the Japanese religions share a concern about totality, harmony, integration, and cohesion.[14] Specifically, both the Asian yin-yang and the Zuni religion emphasize avoiding calamities and keeping the right relations with the major elements.[15] In both systems, the arrangements of houses and things within the house *(feng-shui)* are influenced by directional orientation.[16] Both yin-yang and the Zuni religion provide a dual organization of the universe. In China and Japan,[17] the yin represents the *kwei,* the female or material substantial soul of the earth. The yang is the *shen,* the male or immaterial soul of heaven, the sky. Yin is dark and of the earth; yang is light and of heaven.[18] Accounts of Zuni cosmology reveal a similar duality between sky and earth, male and female, light and dark.[19] Frequent references are made to Earth Mother and Sky Father.

Although simple systems of direction-color correspondence exist among other North American Indians[20] including the Navaho, Hopi, Cherokee, and Aztec (see Table 6), the idea seems particularly pervasive and elaborate among the Zuni. Eggan stated, "It is evident that the Zuni have tended to organize much of the world on a basis of six directions; not only were the clans so organized in Zuni thinking but also kivas, societies, corn, prey animals, seasons, and colors."[21]

Frank Cushing reported that the six Zuni towns before consolidation at Itiwanna were organized in relation to direction and

TABLE 6
DIRECTIONS AND COLORS: ASIAN AND AMERICAN

	YIN-YANG	ZUNI	AZTEC	HOPI	NAVAJO	JAVA	TIBET
NORTH	Black	Yellow	Black	White	Black	Black	Green
EAST	Blue	White	Red	Yellow	White	White	Blue
SOUTH	Red	Red	Blue	Red	Blue	Red	Yellow
WEST	White	Blue	White	Blue	Yellow	Yellow	Red

were ruled from a central tribe and town through priest-chiefs.[22] One of the Zuni town names was Matsaki, a common place name in Japan referring to pine trees. Pine trees are present in the Zuni area; in fact they play a role in religious ceremonies, as they do in Japan.

Through their all-inclusive directional orientation, the A:shiwi (Zuni) relate themselves to the rest of the world, or, the rest of the world to themselves—one great interrelated life, oriented to the middle.[23] Powerful and complex concepts fasten the system together.

Until recently, the Japanese had a similar, intricate system of directional relationships called *onmyō-dō*, based on yin-yang concepts that originally came from China. By the first century A.D., the Chinese system involved not only directions and colors, but also the elements and constellations, passions and virtues, viscera, apertures, and other parts of the body. The system spread throughout the Far East.[24] In Japan, a government department of yin-yang was established in A.D. 675, and by the eighth century, yin-yang concepts were distributed among the general populace.[25]

Although the practice of this cosmology generally has been discontinued in Japan, some remnants of the color-direction themes may still be displayed at special times such as the celebration of Prince Shōtoku's birth. Shōtoku (574–621) was a statesman and religious leader instrumental in shaping early Japanese Buddhism, including advocacy of a strong lay leadership and a social consciousness that included all classes. In March 1998, I observed banners of five colors hung along the front of the Hōryū-ji Temple (see Figure 52) near Nara, the first capital of Japan, and also at the Rokkaku-dō, a six-sided temple in Kyoto that was supposedly established by Shōtoku Taishi.[26] The color sequence is the same as that on Tibetan prayer flags: green, purple, white, red, and yellow.

What is the probability that any two groups living in a four-seasoned, temperate environment would orient their lives in the same manner? Some scholars attribute the basic directional system in the Americas to an introduction by the original migrants from Asia many thousands of years ago. That might explain the wide distribution of the simple direction-color relationship, but why the unusual detail, pervasiveness, and complexity at Zuni? Further, why is the Zuni system so much more complete than those of other Native American groups? Is it because the original

Figure 52. *Hōryū-ji temple with banners*

details were lost by other tribes? Or because only fragmented pieces of the complex system moved outward from a Zuni center?

Table 6 reveals variations within North America between cardinal points and associated colors. Note that variations also occur in the Far East, where the origin of the system is *known* to be Chinese.[27] In short, although the elementary idea of a direction-color association is widespread in North America and in East Asia, the specific correspondences appear highly variable within both areas.

The links between the Zuni system and the formerly complex Japanese system provide additional interest because of their pervasiveness in everyday life in both cultures, and because numerous words associated with yin-yang in Zuni appear to be cognate with Japanese *onmyō-dō*, demonstrating that the ideas and the words came to North America already associated and inherently linked with the system (see Table 7). A few examples follow.

In the nineteenth century, two sets of Zuni words were used for directions, one ritualistically and the other familiarly. The religious word for "West," *k'ya-lishiinkwin,* referred to "direction of

TABLE 7
ZUNI AND ASIAN YIN-YANG

	DIRECTION	SEASON	COLOR	ELEMENT	CHARACTERISTIC
ZUNI	South	Summer	Red	Fire	Husbandry and medicine
JAPANESE	South	Summer	Red	Fire	Creativeness
ZUNI	East	Autumn	White	Earth	Magic and Religion
JAPANESE	West	Autumn	White	Metal	Care
ZUNI	West	Spring	Blue	Water	Hunting and War Cure
JAPANESE	East	Spring	Blue	Wood	Anger
ZUNI	North	Winter	Yellow	Wind	War and Destruction
JAPANESE	North	Winter	Black	Water	Fear

the home, or source of mists and waters, or the sea"[28] and also to "blue like the great world of waters."[29] The everyday word for "West" in Zuni is *kalishi*. The Japanese word for "West" is *nishi* (the Chinese word is *shi*).

The phonemic correspondence of /l/ and /n/ (kalishi to nishi) is also noted in a word for "South": in Zuni, *alaho*, and, in Old Japanese, *uma-no-ho* (alaho and uma-*no*-ho). The Zuni word for "East" is *temakoha;* the *koha* ending is derived from *kohakwa*, meaning "white," the color that is also associated with East in the Zuni system (East-white; *temakoha*).[30] *Tema* by itself denotes "East," as does *atuma* in Old Japanese.[31]

The concept of creativeness is associated in both systems (Zuni cosmology and yin-yang) with summer, South, and red. In Zuni, badger, *tonushi,* is also linked to South and fire *(akli).* In Japan, badger is *tanuki,* and fire, *hi.* One important Zuni deity, K'yaklu, is referred to as "Keeper of the rituals of creation."[32] One Japanese word for creation, the beginning of the world, is *kaibyaku,* a word borrowed from Chinese.

THE MIDDLE

The concept of "middle," the center of the world, is a major focus for the Zuni, as well documented in their migration story and their continuing commitment to Itiwanna, their exact center point of the universe. In the religious language of Zuni, "middle" is *wanakwin;* in Japanese, *mannaka.* This /w/ and /m/ correspondence also exists in the names of important gods concerned with the middle of the world. The Shinto "Deity Master of the August Center of Heaven" is Ame-no-*mi*-naka-nushi-no-kami.[33] The Zuni "Maker and Container of all, the All-father Father" and the great "he-she imitator of life, pervading all space" is Awo-na-*wi*-lo-na.[34] (Note two more /m/ to /w/ shifts.)

The Japanese language incorporated a large contingent of new words (about 55% of the modern vocabulary) and also writing from China during the Nara period, the eighth century. The borrowing included the word *naka,* and the symbol for "middle" is 中. The Japanese word *mannaka* includes the Chinese word *naka* and an Austronesian prefix /ma-/, which is retained in modern Japanese to enhance and emphasize root words. (Another example is *makkuro,* "very black"; *ma-* means "very" and *kuro,* "black.")

This symbol for "middle" appears at El Morro (see Figure 53), along with other petroglyphs and some writings by early Spanish explorers and members of American expeditions.[35] El Morro, located east of Zuni, was the location of a village, Atsinna, until the thirteenth century, when it was abandoned, and the people presumably moved to one of the Zuni villages.

China, from its standpoint, is the Middle Kingdom, and the first symbol in the compound word for "China," 中, means "middle." Although China perceived itself so, other countries did not view it in that light. India, for example, and Buddhism in particular, did not allocate "Middle Kingdom" to any one area of the world. The idea of the "Middle Path," the "Middle way," however, is a basic tenet in Buddhism.[36] The Zuni sought the middle road all the way to Itiwanna, the exact center *(wannaka)* of the universe.

Additional concepts and words related to the religious systems further support the Japanese-Zuni link. The center, the middle,

Figure 53. *Atsinna village ruins at El Morro, New Mexico*

TABLE 8
ZUNI MATRILINEAL CLAN NAMES

		ZUNI (CLAN)		JAPANESE
CRANE	North	Kalakta	(kwe)	karancho
CROW	North	Kwalasi	(kwe)	karasu
BADGER	South	Tonashi	(kwe)	tanuki
DEER	East	Shohita	(kwe)	shika

and earth in the Japanese yin-yang system are associated with the "spleen," *hi no zō*. *Zō* refers to the viscera. In Zunian, "stomach" is *zu*.

Zuni matrilineal clans related to three directions are represented by four species whose Zuni names appear cognate with Old Japanese (see Table 8).[37]

The Breath and the Deer

In addition to the basic Taoist concepts of yin-yang, an especially unique feature of this ancient Chinese cosmology was introduced to Japan and may also have reached Zuni: the special qualities of breath, called *qi* in Chinese,[38] *ki* in Japanese, and *pinna* in Zuni.

The *qi* or breath concept may be seen on animal and human figures embossed on certain Japanese bronze bells called Dōtaku (see Figure 54), produced in the Yayoi period, 300 B.C.–A.D. 300. Of the 430 bronze bells found so far, 53 have distinct pictorial representations; the deer is the most common motif. A series of four bells with a total of thirty-four scenes are of special interest because in addition to deer, they depict mantis, frogs, spiders, dragonflies, turtles, heron, and people, many with a line from the mouth to the midbody.[39] (The Kagawa bell best illustrates this possible "breath" or "heartline.")

Garrick Mallery noted the similarities between the figures on a Dōtaku bell he saw in Takoka, Japan, in 1891 and certain figures in North America pictographs, especially in the American Southwest, reported in his volume called *Picture-Writing of the American Indians* (see Figure 55). Could it be that the heartlines featured so prominently on Zuni pottery and fetishes are associated with the concept of the breath, *pinna?*[40]

Figure 54. *Dōtaku (bell-shaped bronze), Japan*

Here are some examples of *pinna:* Zuni men exchange a breath greeting upon meeting; gifts are received through a breath thanks, and animals, especially deer, are illustrated with the distinctive Zuni "heartline," the breath connection from the mouth to the center of the body (see Figure 56). Matilda Stevenson reported that every Zuni is taught that in "inhaling the sacred breath from his fetishes or in breathing upon the plumes he offers to the gods he is receiving from A'wonawil'ona the breath of life or is wafting his own breath prayers to his gods. . . ."[41]

Parsons provided references to breath, detailing the times the blessing is breathed *in,* and the times the blessing is breathed *out.* Especially interesting is the breath blessing from deer bones during the ceremony for snow and the initiation by the Wood Society.[42]

The deer with the heartline is a special characteristic, recognizable always as Zuni. Cushing referred to the line as the en-

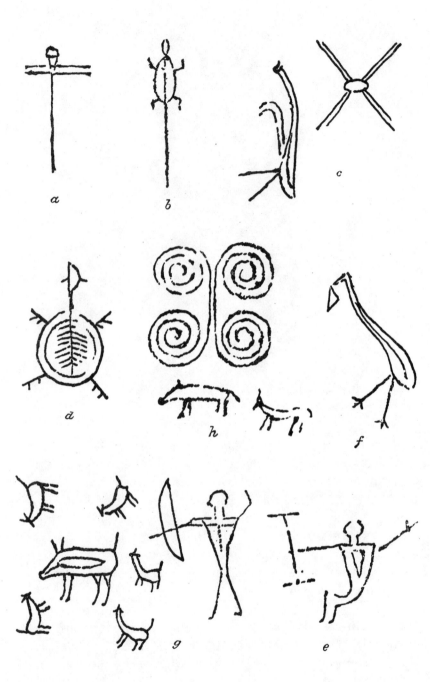

Figure 55. *Pictures on Dōtaku bronze bell, Japan*

Figure 56. *Deer with heartline on Zuni ceramic drum*

Figure 57. *Sacred deer joining a picnic, Nara Park, Japan*

trance trail of the deer's source of life. Sometimes it is called a "heartline" and other times a "breathline" or "lifeline."

Clearly the deer is sacred both in Zuni and in Japan. In Zuni this status is reflected in ritual surrounding the hunt and in other ceremonies, such as Shalako. Likewise, the deer continues a sacred position in Japan, especially at Nara where hundreds wander the park, protected and respected, as messengers of the God of Kasuga (see Figure 57).[43] Perhaps the words for deer (*showita* in Zunian and *shika* in Japanese) and their associated concepts are related as well.

BUDDHISM

The name of the leader of the highest-ranked Zuni religious society, the Galaxy (Ne'wekwe) fraternity, is Bitsitsi. One Japanese word for Buddha is Butsu.[44]

Matilda Coxe Stevenson observed that in Zuni, Bitsitsi is "held in high regard by the people"[45]; his regal appearance creates an aura of reverence and silence. He speaks "with the heart," not with the lips. Bitsitsi sometimes is referred to sitting or standing with his arms folded[46] (see Figure 58). Further suggestion of the Asian origin of this deity is provided by a topknot of hair tied with corn husks on his forehead,[47] a practice continued today.[48]

One version of the great migration narrative reports that soon after Bitsitsi's creation, the A:shiwi began their ascent to the outer world."[49] Another variation credits Bitsitsi with providing leadership in the search for the center. Indeed, Bitsitsi is still known and highly respected by the Zuni because he saved them from famine.[50] Perhaps his arrival coincided with the end of a twenty-five-year drought, well documented by dendrochronology as occurring between A.D. 1276 and 1302. This exceptionally dry period was followed by a forty-year rainy interval and by the suddenly increased organizational complexities reported for Pueblo IV: new irrigation system, flurry of new construction, consolidation of people, new social institutions, and the introduction of a new religious system.[51]

If Bitsitsi is a Native American Butsu, a reincarnated Buddha,

Figure 58. *Bitsitsi, director of Newekwe (Galaxy) Fraternity*

this would explain his authority, his leadership in the migration, and his continued recognition and respect in the modern day. If the new religion was perceived to have brought rain (*ami* in Zunian, *ame* in Japanese), then other aspects might have been more easily incorporated. The arrival of new people with new ideas may explain why the Zuni area increased in population whereas other Anasazi-related settlements declined and were abandoned.

However, Bitsitsi is not the central figure among the many deities that populate the Zuni religious world. He is sometimes called by another name, Payatuma. He appears only once a year, five days after Shalako, part of the big winter solstice religious ceremony. The rain priests *(uwanami)* and other Shinto features appear stronger in Zuni, at least as reported in the major early ethnographies of the Pueblo. This apparent subordination suggests that Buddhism may have been added relatively late in the series of events that shaped the Zuni religion.

THE CHACO CONNECTION

One of the last of many stopping places of the Zuni on their long search for the very center of the universe was Chaco Canyon north of Zuni, a place they called Kiwihtsi Bitsulliya.[52] *Kiwihtsi* is one of three Zunian words that means "Ceremonial Center"; also, *kiwitsine* connotes "secret chamber," a place for secret ceremonies. The word *kimitsu* in Japanese means "secrecy." (*Kibi* is a Japanese word for secrets.) The shift of /m/ in Japanese to /w/ in Zuni appears in other religious words, a fact that strengthens the probability that *kiwihtsi* and *kimitsu* are cognates (see Table 9). As noted earlier, Bitsu is close to Butsu (Buddha); *lliya* means "dwelling place" in Zunian. These correlations suggest that Kiwihtsi Bitsulliya, Chaco Canyon, was a ceremonial secret dwelling place of Buddha. Bitsitsi may have been one of the deities the Zuni brought with them from the Chaco Canyon area following the demise of the Anasazi culture (see Figure 59).

A second word that contemporary Zuni use for ceremonial center is *kiva,* which is a Hopi term, recently adopted by Zuni and other Pueblo peoples. Somehow *kiva* has superseded other Pueblo terms, perhaps only since 1891 when Powell, director of

TABLE 9
COMPARISON OF RELIGIOUS WORDS

ENGLISH	ZUNI	JAPANESE
Middle	wanaka	mannaka
West	kalishi	nishi
East	tema	atuma
South	alaho	umanoho
Zuni god	Awo-na-wi-lona	
Shinto god		Ame-no-mi-naka-nushi-no-kami
Keeper of the Creation Rituals	K'yaklu	
Creation		kaibyaku
stomach	zu	zō
great god	kokkothlana	
godlike		kogoshi
God	kokko	
The Late Emperor		Kōkō
meeting, clan	kwe	
society		kwai
clan, guild		be
clown	newe	niwa
rain	ami	ame
rain priest	shiwani	
Shinto priest		shinkwan, shawani
cross over	yato	yoko
diety	Bitsitsi	
Buddha		Butsu
secret chambers	kiwitse	
secrecy		kimitsu
ceremonial center	upa (stupa)	sotoba

Figure 59. *Pueblo Bonito. Chaco Canyon, New Mexico*

the Bureau of Ethnology, wrote to Victor Mindeleff, who was doing architectural studies of the Pueblos, and directed him to cease using the word *estufa* when referring to Pueblo ceremonial centers, because *estufa* means "stove" in Spanish, clearly an inappropriate word for a sacred and secret center. *Kiva* has become the "official" term used by anthropologists and most Pueblo Indians since then.[53]

A third word for "religious place" in Zunian is *upa*, which may be a derivative of *stupa*, a Sanskrit word associated with Buddhist temples. Since Zunian does not have the consonant cluster /st/, to drop the foreign sound /st/ would be easier than trying to say it, leaving *upa* as the reference to a sacred place. The Japanese language made a different adaptation to the same Sanskrit word by inserting a vowel, consistent with the CV pattern, and changing the /p/ to the more common sound /b/: The Japanese word for stupa is *sotoba*, or *toba*, a term now associated more with Buddhist grave markers than with Buddhist temples.

Here is a speculative thought: Are the "estufas" of Chaco Canyon, those many circular stone structures first recorded in detail by Simpson in 1849, possibly *stupas?* Was the Anasazi remarkable architectural and engineering accomplishment possibly a series of Buddhist monasteries? The Zuni word for Matilda Stevenson's friend, We'hwa, the accomplished priest who was male but dressed in women's clothing, was *llamana.* Was he a modern *lama,* a celibate monk?

Recall from the first chapter, the passage recorded in the first written record in Japan, *Kojiki,* A.D. 712. The theme of expansion of power appeared as a motif of civilizing people to the east who needed it (from an emperor's standpoint), bringing them law and justice. The idea of a "center," six directions, and eight cords suggested Chinese influence, including concepts of yin-yang. The passage seemed to anticipate a missionary zeal characteristic of some later sects of Buddhism.

Like a tsunami of ideas, a sequence of ideologies from the great traditions—Taoism, Confucianism, and Buddhism–reached Japan with a series of impacts. New ideas were creatively modified and incorporated, adding to, but not eliminating, the personal shrines and numerous *kami* of Shinto.

I am convinced similar processes occurred in North America where new ideas continued to arrive by sea and by land over the millennia and during recent centuries. Native Americans, like other peoples of the world, assessed, modified, and adapted some of what came their way. They did not live in a vacuum of isolation from each other or from the Old World.

The correspondences introduced here suggest that the Zuni religious system is unusually complex today because it shares a link with Shinto and includes elements from Taoism and Buddhism. Native American gods and rituals were incorporated as the pilgrims moved eastward from the west coast, integrating with other tribal groups searching for the middle, Itiwanna, the exact center of the universe. "Our gods are more powerful than your gods," the war gods and priests declared, as they continued east, looking for a stable, earthquake-free place to settle.

CHAPTER TEN

THE CHRYSANTHEMUM AND THE SWORD REVISITED

"They are our enemies," said a Zuni leader as he contemplated the implications of my findings shortly after my second presentation to the Zuni Council in 1988. He had been a prisoner of the Japanese during World War II.

"Not in the thirteenth century," I commented, quietly.

And not now.

More than fifty years since the end of World War II, we pause to assess the impact of half a century of recovery and changing human and economic relationships. Think about the Zuni-Japanese connection in the late thirteenth century, in the early 1940s, and now.

WORLD WAR II

Between February 1941 and March 1946, 213 Zuni men, almost 10% of the 1941 village population of 2,205, left their safe and conservative pueblo for war service. More would have been drafted, but the governor of the pueblo, the secular council, and the council of high priests formally requested, and won, deferment for men who held certain important religious offices.[1]

In 1947–48, two anthropologists, John Adair and Evon Vogt, interviewed thirteen Navaho veterans, six Zuni veterans, and others for a comparative study of different responses to the draft, the war, and the return of veterans.[2] The Navaho and the Zuni differed sharply in how the draftees were prepared to depart for the war, in religious behavior while gone, and in methods for managing the reentry home. They varied in ways clearly shaped by their different cultural patterns.

Before leaving their pueblo, the Zuni draftees received a brief blessing ceremony with prayers to protect them, performed by a bow priest, the traditional war leader. Many carried sacred prayer meal with them, and said prayers in the Zuni language during combat. Back in the pueblo, priests prayed for the protection of the men, and as one reported, "That is why so few of the Zuni men were killed."[3] Four members of the 1988 council were veterans of World War II. Two were prisoners of the Japanese, and one, Virgil Wyaco, served in the European arena and included a chapter about his survival in *A Zuni Life. A Pueblo Indian in Two Worlds*[4] (see Figure 60).

When the veterans returned, they were met outside the village and a cleansing rite, *hanasema isuwaha* (translated as "bad luck get rid of it"[5]) was performed. The reentry ceremonies were secret, and the returnees at first were treated with suspicion, sometimes ridicule, as social pressures shaped their reorientation into pueblo life.

The postwar period was not easy for these Zuni veterans. They had to recover from many traumas: the original separation from the pueblo; the times of combat and injury; the death of friends and family[6]; and the severe social constraints placed on them by this very conservative pueblo when they returned.[7] These Zuni veter-

Figure 60. *Photo of Zuni veteran Virgil Wyaco*

Figure 61. *Memorial Day Parade, Zuni, 1991*

ans and their families have a World War II link with Japan in addition to the thirteenth-century one. They, and veterans from later wars, gather annually for a Memorial Day Parade (see Figure 61).

Los Alamos, one of the four research centers of the Manhattan Project that developed the atomic bombs, is located in the state of New Mexico. This presents yet another connection with Japan.

"They are our enemies," Japanese can also say about Americans.

But not in the thirteenth century.

And not now.

PATTERNS OF CULTURE

In 1934 Ruth Benedict wrote *Patterns of Culture* about the peaceful Zuni of New Mexico, the unpleasant Dobu of New Guinea, and the fierce Kwakiutl of the northwest coast of North America. She drew on other scholarly work on Dobu and Kwakiutl,[8] but Benedict had personal experience in Zuni. For several summers in the 1920s she lived with her friend, Ruth Bunzel, while both did original research in the pueblo.[9] Benedict's comparison of these three cultures—the Zuni, Dobu, and Kwakiutl—in a highly readable publication provided the general public with a factual basis for a heightened awareness of marked cultural diversity among human groups; it remains a landmark of creative thinking in social sciences.

Twenty years after her Zuni field experience, Benedict worked during World War II with a team of social scientists at the Office of War Information and the Office of Strategic Studies in Washington, D.C. She and others had the challenge of trying to understand Japan's national character—at a distance. Fieldwork in Japan was impossible at the time, but she interviewed many Japanese Americans and read extensively about Japan. Americans were puzzled by the paradoxes that seemed endemic to Japanese culture and personality, and Benedict sharpened the understanding by analyzing the apparent dual characteristics within Japanese culture, symbolically represented by a willingness to die by the sword, yet also a keen interest in the beauty of the chrysanthemum. Like *Patterns of Culture*, Benedict's 1946 publication *Chrysanthemum and the Sword: Patterns of Japanese Culture* became a classic.

Fifty years later at the 1996 annual meeting of the American Anthropological Association, a session entitled "The Chrysanthemum and the Sword at 50: A Critical Retrospective on Anthropological Theory, Area Studies, and Public Policy" provided an assessment of the continuing, and somewhat puzzling, influence of the book. Even today Japanese find it a fascinating commentary on what Americans thought about the Japanese in the late 1940s; many believe those ideas persist today. Benedict's book is still popular in Japan, and often recommended reading for Americans interested in Japan.

Although Benedict studied both cultures, the Zuni and the Japanese, apparently she did not compare them. Cultural differences, not similarities, and certainly not similarities between small tribes and large nations separated by oceans, shaped the research focus of her day.[10]

Anthropologists have done a good job documenting human variations—linguistic, cultural, and biological—throughout the twentieth century; a detailed record about hundreds of distinct populations is an intellectual heritage to be celebrated. Now, I propose we complement that effort, indeed utilize it, by considering human similarities and developing paradigms for understanding commonalities between cultures. Are some human similarities between disparate groups the result of a shared psychic unity of the species? Do some observed commonalities stem from genetically programmed species-specific phenomena? Are they accidents? Innovations? Or the results of selected diffusion of ideas and traits across the earth? How are surprising correlations to be proved or rejected? How are striking resemblances to be discussed?

Here is a test.

THE CHRYSANTHEMUM, THE ROSETTE, AND THE GLAZE

The Chrysanthemum

I believe the symbol of the chrysanthemum appears in both Zuni and Japan as part of a cluster of cultural *patterns,* to use Ruth Benedict's concept. I am convinced the Zuni "sacred rosette" noted on pottery and Shalako robes was derived from the Japanese mon (crest) for the chrysanthemum, which was imported from China. At Nara, Japan, the sixteen-petal emblem is associated with Prince Shōtoku and continues to be affiliated with the Buddhist temple complex he established there. When the capital was moved to Kyoto at the beginning of the Heian period, the chrysanthemum design continued as a motif, as noted in the reconstruction of the Nijo Castle (see Figure 62).

The chrysanthemum is not indigenous to Zuni, but neither was it indigenous to Japan. Rather, it was introduced from China or Korea during the first centuries A.D.; by the Kamakura period, A.D. 1185–1333, it appeared as a motif on many forms of decoration.[11] This distinctive Japanese crest is sometimes found on porcelain, as the chrysanthemum floating in a stream, conveying a wish that hunger and thirst will not be a part of one's life. One Japanese version of "the chrysanthemum boy," Sennin Kikugido, includes a theme of error, banishment, a profusion of chrysanthemums, and leaves in the stream, which conveyed power and allayed hunger and thirst. Water used to wash off writing on the leaves became an "elixir of everlasting youth."[12]

Figure 62A. *Ninomaru Palace, Nijo Castle, Kyoto, Japan*

Figures 62B and 62C. *Detail of entrance, Nijo Castle*

This raises the possibility that the chrysanthemum design, the Zuni rosette, was part of the sequence in the story about how Bitsitsi "saved the people from famine by finding and returning the Corn Maidens." Could it not be that the chrysanthemum motif was introduced in Zuni as one in a cluster of cultural traits associated with a Japanese form of Buddhism, similar to the way the same motif was introduced to Japan from China?

The Japanese imperial crest of modern times is the chrysanthemum consisting of sixteen petals round a central calyx and the tips of sixteen others behind them, in a circle *(kikumon)* (see Figure 63). Variations appear in different contexts, over a long time period. For example, the imperial design is found on an elegant reliquary from the Kamakura period, 1185–1333, a cast bronze vessel with the chrysanthemum in the center of the lid (see Figure 64).

One of the variations of the *kiku* crest found on Japanese porcelain is the twelve-petal flower with a circle around it, but the more traditional imperial crest has sixteen petals.[13] The chrysanthemum design figures on the curtains of a painting of the Battle of Minatogawa in 1333.[14] Japanese art features the crest in many settings: ceramics, paintings, banners, temple tiles, embroidery, weaving, and silver. Many variations (see Figure 65) exist today.

By the eleventh century A.D., the high-ranking courtier developed family crests for the formal costume worn at the imperial court. These family crests came to be used for formal occasions, with one crest in the center of the back, one on the back of each sleeve, and one each on the left and right front.

When the warrior class took over the government at the end of the twelfth century, samurai used their emblems as identification on banners, flags, weapons, and hanging screens. It was not until the Meiji period (1868–1912) that the crest representing any form of the chrysanthemum became the exclusive symbol of the imperial family.[15]

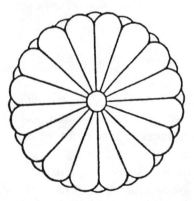

Figure 63. *The Japanese imperial emblem*

Figure 64. *Top of imperial reliquary, Kamakura period*

Figure 65. *Sample of variations of Japanese* kikumon *(chrysanthemum crest)*

The Zuni Sacred Rosette

Zuni pottery is rich in diversity of form and design. The time depth and continuity of local ceramic techniques are great, and Zuni potters tend to be conservative with tradition.

A book entitled *Gifts of Mother Earth: Ceramics in the Zuni Tradition* by Margaret Hardin provides eight examples of the sacred rosette on pottery, including a drawing of the Zuni "medallion" with sixteen petals and an elaborate border.[16] Variations of the motif (see Figure 66) are found on many fine olla (water jars) (see Figure 67).

James Stevenson referred to the design as a sacred rosette or "hepak'inne."[17] Ruth Bunzel, who also studied Zuni pottery, referred to it as a "sacred rosette" and as a figure that also appears in other contexts.

Two fine collections of Zuni pottery, one at the School of American Research and the other at the Laboratory at the New Mexico Museum in Santa Fe, provide documentation for many medallions with the small center, bounded by scallops and circles; no other pueblo tribe uses this motif.[18]

The rosette occurs in other contexts sacred to the Zuni. It appears on the robes of the Shalako (see Figure 68): clear, distinct, many petals.

Might the rosette be borrowed from the Catholic Church? The Catholic presence in the American Southwest dates to 1540, so there has been ample time for selected designs to be adopted.

Figure 66. *The Zuni sacred rosette*

Figure 67. *Zuni water jar with sixteen petals, circa 1850*

Figure 68. *Zuni rosette on the border of Shalako robe*

The extent to which the Zuni separate their religious ceremonies and symbols from anything Catholic was best described by
Cushing in the late nineteenth century. He informed us that the
Zuni remove all traces of Catholicism, speak no Spanish near the
sacred *kokko,* and politely but firmly usher out any one showing
up at the Pueblo during their religious ceremonies.[19]

I conclude that the Zuni rosettes on Shalako robes are not European in origin. Nor is the medallion on olla jars of Catholic vintage. No Zuni would stitch a Catholic symbol on sacred regalia, nor
paint a Catholic symbol on a olla water jar. But does it mean, by
default, that the design is Japanese in origin?

Another question must be asked: When did the sacred rosette
first appear in the Southwest? If the Zuni medallion is *not* Catholic,
and *not* European in origin, when and where is the earliest evidence of its appearance?

Susan Kenegy addressed the question of the Zuni deer and
medallion-style pottery designs in an article published in the *New
Mexico Studies in the Fine Arts.*[20] She reported that the deer with the
heartline, *binnanne,* seems to be ascribed to local native sources,
but the origin of the medallion, the *hepak'inne,* is not so clearly
identified (see Figure 69). James Stevenson thought the rosette
might have been introduced by Europeans, or derived from the
sunflower in nature.[21] Alfred Kroeber thought both designs were
from European contact, but reported the Zuni believed they were
native.[22] Clara Tanner noted that the rosette or medallion motif is
"quite different from native pueblo design and may well be a
Spanish-influenced theme" and suggested it may have been inspired by embroidered altar cloths.[23] Kenegy agreed that external
sources *may* explain the prevalence of the rosette in Zuni, but
puzzles about a pictograph drawn in the Rito de los Frijoles area,
located less than two hundred miles from Zuni, which shows a
multilobed circular flower within a larger scalloped frame.[24]

Other examples Kenegy found are dated to the Pueblo IV period, A.D. 1300–1600, for example, at the Pottery Mound site in
Rio Puerco Valley where a series of medallions are painted on
kiva walls.[25]

R. L. Carlson reported that the medallions can be traced back
to St. Johns polychrome of the upper Little Colorado during the
twelfth century. This reference and site are significant for the

Japanese-Zuni hypothesis because this is also where the earliest glaze appears.[26]

Further, Kenegy suggested the medallion may be related to the Zuni creation myth, the ordering of the universe, and their detailed stories about the search for the middle place. After listing the ways the Zuni divide their world into two opposing spheres, she stated that the medallion reflects the way the universe was seen: "as being structured in a circular manner, radiating to the above, the north, northwest, west, southwest, south, below, and so forth, with Zuni as the central place or center of the circle." An interview Kenegy had with a Zuni person in March 1978, led to this statement: The medallion is a " 'flower design designating the creation point or the center of the universe.' "[27]

This may explain why the circular rosette motif is exclusive to contemporary Zuni art; at Zuni the theme of centrality and the integration of parts with the middle are most elaborately developed. Perhaps other Pueblo groups had the rosette motif at an earlier time, and modified or lost it. Or perhaps it has been the intellec-

Figure 69. *Zuni olla with rosette and deer breathline*

tual property of Zuni thinking for the last seven centuries, introduced by the pilgrims from the Pacific. As Frank and Harlow noted, the large rosette is "a uniquely Zuni adaptation of the motif."[28] It stands out as a distinct feature of Zuni pottery.

The paintings by Duane Dishta in the book *Kachinas of the Zuni* by Barton Wright illustrate at least thirteen examples of the sacred rosette (see Figure 70). They appear on the White Kachina, Shi-tsukia; the cloak of the Shalako, the Courier of the Gods; Kiaklo; the Red Warrior of the South; the White Warrior of the East; the White Kianakwe of the East; the Mountain Sheep Kachina; the Big-Horned Kachina; the Double-faced Kachina; the Corn Dance Drummer mask; the Ne'wekwe Kokothlanna (the Big Kachina of the Galaxy Society); the Big Kachina of the Fire Society; and Shumaikoli, the Blind God.[29]

Finally, one example of the Zuni medallion on a breast-shaped water canteen was analyzed by Cushing in 1886. He reported the name for the ceramic canteen was me'hetonne, and suggested the word was related to breast, *mewe,* and associated with water, the adult "milk" (see Figure 71).[30] The Japanese word for breast is *mune.* (Recall the frequent shift of Japanese /n/ to Zuni /w/ noted earlier.)

Figure 70. *Zuni dragonfly and medallion on warrior robes*

Figure 71. *Zuni rosette on water canteen*

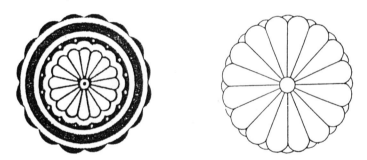

Figure 72. *Zuni sacred rosette and Japanese* kikumon

In both cultures, the many petalled medalion appears associated with center, longevity, and water—yet another topic to further research.

Might the ancestors of the Zuni include ancestors of the Japanese imperial family? Is this an example of a cluster of ideas associated with Buddhism and royalty shared on both sides of the Pacific? Is this a case of the completely independent innovation of similar concepts and design motifs? I know of only two cultures that make a sacred symbol out of a many-petalled flower rosette: the Japanese and the Zuni (see Figure 72).

Other topics with potential for comparative research include textiles, crests, Kabuki costumes, and Noh masks with Pueblo forms and designs, such as the dragonfly and crane.[31]

Glaze Paint on Pots

Generations of scholars have provided detailed ceramic analysis in both the American Southwest and Japan. Were some of the remarkable pottery traditions in the Zuni area creative responses to new ideas introduced from Japan?

The Japanese have the earliest pottery tradition in the world, beginning about 10,500 B.C. Much later, new ceramic methods from China and Korea were added to an already rich repertoire. For example, the three-glaze polychrome of the Tang period in China was introduced to Japan by the eighth century A.D.

Two kinds of glazes suddenly appeared in the Zuni area for a short time: The first, glaze on red (A.D. 1300–25), was followed by what is called Pinnawa glaze on white (A.D. 1325–50.)[32] Both these glazes continued until about 1400, and then they disappeared until about 1630 when glaze on red reappeared at the major Zuni settlement of Hawikuh.[33]

Several facts are important. Glaze does not appear earlier anywhere in North America, and it does not last long after its sudden introduction just west of the Zuni area in the late thirteenth century.[34] In addition, the paint and glaze techniques on the early wares were highly refined; they were rapidly distributed east to the Rio Grande pueblos, then deteriorated, and were completely abandoned at Zuni. The knowledge of how to apply glaze paint after the first firing appears to have been introduced in the late thirteenth century; local creative adaptations were made, and then skill and knowledge declined and disappeared.

The earliest comprehensive study of glazed pottery in the American Southwest was reported in 1917 by Leslie Spier of Columbia University; he used pottery classifications to a create a chronology of Zuni ruins.[35] He found two-color paint and three-color paint followed by a rather sudden appearance of two- and three-color glazed ware,[36] and he concluded that the glaze decoration was a borrowed trait, from somewhere.[37] Spier also noted that black glaze sometimes appears as vivid green.[38] He was the first to use pottery sequences as stratigraphic tools of chronology and the first to report that the glazes appear simultaneously with the pueblo type of settlement.

Professor Emil Haury of the University of Arizona studied lead-glaze pottery techniques and also reported that they occurred first in the Zuni area, but he thought they were indigenous.[39]

Erik K. Reed's review of pottery sequences confirmed a transition at the end of the thirteenth century from St. Johns polychrome to Zuni glazes; the technique lasted about 150 years.[40] The timing and uniqueness of the glaze are distinct enough to be used as an indicator of both time and contact between areas in the Southwest.

A well-known ceramic specialist, Anna O. Shepard, proposed two origins for American Indian glazes: the Pueblo area and Mesoamerica. The two techniques are sufficiently different that the discovery, she presumed, must have been independent in each area. She also pointed out how difficult a glaze is to acquire.[41] Glaze is a glass that is exceptionally unpredictable and hard to control. Temperature and mixture proportions, for example, are critical to the outcome. She admitted that it is "surprising" to find a lead-glaze paint in the Pueblo region, but she believed it was an accidental discovery.[42]

J. J. Brody, professor of art at the University of New Mexico, noted the change in pottery beginning in the 1200s in the Mogollon area of east-central Arizona and west-central New Mexico. He referred to "a variety of alien traditions" that were creatively and almost simultaneously modified and transformed by the Mogollon. Among the new traditions were glaze paints.[43]

Thus far, one scholar (Spier) believed glaze was introduced as a borrowed trait, from somewhere undetermined, and two scholars (Haury and Shepard) claimed it was an unusual, but indigenous development. Brody allowed that it may have been introduced.

Glazed pottery is most unusual in North America. Walter Hough, in a 1928 article on the lead-glaze–decorated pottery of the Pueblo area, questioned whether it was an indigenous art[44]; he also noted a religious preference for green glaze. Although there was an apparent great demand for green as a decorative element in Pueblo ceramics, attaining the color was difficult. The glazes were hard to obtain and the firing demanded such high technical skill (similar to smelting metal) that Hough concluded that the process was not an indigenous art. He wondered whether the glaze could have had a European origin, but found that the lead glaze predated Spanish arrival. It appears too early to be explained by Spanish influence.

Was the lead glaze in the Zuni area an accidental occurrence? Or part of a cluster of techniques that came into the area in the late thirteenth century? The earlier examples were more finely executed than the later ones, suggesting loss of technical skill over time. The glaze suddenly appeared; the quality of glaze deteriorated; the glaze went away. These are characteristics of introduced technology: sudden, with no precedent; loss of quality; and disappearance.

The lead glazes of Zuni may be an example of an extremely rare independent innovation, or, alternatively, a cluster of pottery techniques that reached Zuni during the late thirteenth century, along with the new irrigation methods, changed settlement patterns, kachina cults, and modified physical characteristics. At least one thing is clear: Glaze was an anomaly, and it still is.

Japan also had a lead-glaze tradition. Originally from China, lead glaze was introduced to Japan by Korean or Chinese pottery experts near the present-day city of Nara. From there the technology spread to other areas including southern Kyushu, where green glaze was the preferred color until the end of the twelfth century.

The early glazes of the Nara period (A.D. 710–793) included three-color wares, usually green, white, and yellowish brown (similar to the Chinese Tang polychromes), but green-glazed ceramics became more favored during the Heian period, A.D. 794–1184. These glazes were painted on after the pots had been fired once; the second firing was at a relatively low temperature of about 750 to 800 degrees centigrade. There appears to be some association of green glaze with religious ceremonial use.

According to a specialist in Japanese ash and lead-glazed ceramics, Richard Mellott of the Asian Museum in San Francisco, the green-glazed wares continued to be preferred throughout the Heian period. The composition of the colored glaze was 30% to 45% silica and 50% to 60% lead flux, with the addition of small amounts of copper oxide for green or iron oxide for the yellowish brown.[45]

Finally, did new pottery techniques introduced to the American Southwest in the late thirteenth century also introduce the word *sale* to go with them? *Sale* in Zuni and *sara* in Japanese refer to a special category of open dish.[46]

A PRISM FOR PERSPECTIVE

The implications of these puzzles from the past, the Zuni enigma, are large. How we respond to new ideas like this one is more important than what happened in the past, whether in the thirteenth century or in World War II.

In the future, genetic studies may reveal biological links to widely separated populations. A tiny fluke of a genetic contribution from an unknown distant ancestor may be the source of success for our descendants, if, for example, a slight selective advantage of that tiny fluke is played out following some future epidemic or cosmic disaster. And that genetic material may come from a population on another continent.

Each of us harbors at least one mutation, a little mistake in the ordering of the proteins that make up the DNA that gives messages to the genes. That small error probably is not significant (most mutations are not) but even a slight rearrangement of a single protein at a critical genetic juncture can set off a vulnerability to a particular disease. What if that disease and associated gene fragment currently are being studied in connection with a different population in another country?

Here is an example. In Chapter 6 on the biological evidence for a Japanese-Zuni connection, the "Zuni disease," a serious kidney disease called mesangiopathic glomerulonephritis, was discussed. If a breakthrough in the cause and treatment of the disease is found in Japan, and the Zuni are proved to be related to the Japanese, and that biological link includes the same genetic vulnerability in both populations, it clearly behooves the Zuni to know about any new treatment, diagnosis, and knowledge developed about the disease in Japan. Knowledge of links in the past may assist survival in the future.

Now is a good time to reconsider and appreciate our shared heritages. Maintaining human heterogeneity may provide some important selective advantages; continuing mixing of populations may be a sound idea if we want to enhance the survival of our children.

When our shared and varied genetic makeups become better understood, the knowledge will help map the details of prehistoric movements. Linguistic analysis may reassociate disparate languages and reconstruct the approximate timing of the introduction of new items and new customs, as reflected in the lexicon. Clusters of cultural complexes identified in archeological sites may emerge with new and surprising messages about specific origins.

If the thesis presented here is correct, what consequences follow?

If you are one of 8,800 Zuni tribal members, you suddenly have a lot of distant relatives. Not just in Japan where 140 million Japanese live, but all over the world where Japanese nationals have migrated. I anticipate some Zuni and other Pueblo Indians will welcome an opportunity to meet and visit, to talk and compare notes on Shinto, Buddhism, ancestors, architecture, lexicon, and biology. Native American scholars with Japanese scholars. Zuni *shiwani* with Japanese *shawani.*

If you are Japanese, you find unexpected links across the Pacific, over the desert, and into the mountains of the North American continent. Quite a pilgrimage your ancestors took, many years ago.

If you are a descendant from other Native American tribes, you may want to consider the possibility that some of your ancestors came by boat across the ocean and along the coasts, too— not only across the Pacific, but also across the Atlantic.

Perhaps those Africa vegetables so important now in South America did not float all by themselves across the Atlantic. Africans may have lived along the African coasts longer than human beings have lived anywhere else in the world, and they may have arrived to the New World long before slave trade began. Might those be African features that we see on the famous Olmec figures in Mexico? Or might they be Chinese? Southeast Asian?

The larger message suggested by the Zuni enigma and my proposed theory of Japanese pilgrims traveling across the Pacific is one of a creative mixture of genes, language, and culture through adaptive processes by an intelligent species moving across a shared planet. Contemporary concepts of ethnicity and political boundaries are but temporary states masking the universal human links among us all.

AFTERWORD

ITIWANNA:
THE CENTER OF
THE UNIVERSE

The name Itiwanna is what the Native American residents at Zuni call their place; the word refers to the exact center of the universe. Itiwanna may be derived from a composite of Chinese and Japanese words: *ittei/mannaka* or *itten/mannaka.* The root *ittei* in Japanese means "fixed, definite, certain." It usually is used with the postposition particle *no,* which makes it an adjective. Another word, *itten,* refers to a point, a spot. Another meaning of *itten* in Japanese is "the whole sky, the heavens, the firmament."

Recall that in Japanese, *ma-* is a prefix that provides enhancement to the root word *naka,* a term derived from Chinese. *Mannaka* is the Japanese word for "middle." Is it not conceivable that a combined and compressed form of *ittei (n)mannaka* (the very exact center point of the whole sky, heavens, and firmament) could be Itiwanna, the place the pilgrims from the Pacific sought and found, the center of the world?

The people of Itiwanna call themselves A:shiwi. The more

common label, Zuni, is the term originally given to them by near-by Pueblo people who speak a completely different language, Keresan. *Pueblo* is a Spanish word for the numerous compact, permanent settlements the Spaniards found in the Southwest during their sixteenth-century explorations. In stating that this book has been about the *A:shiwi* who live at *Itiwanna,* the *Pueblo* of *Zuni,* six different languages are used: English, Zunian, Chinese, Japanese, Spanish, and Keresan. Thus, an international theme is symbolically reflected in one word: Itiwanna.

In raising questions about human mobility across lands and seas and about the creative mix of cultures that resulted, this book has considered Zuni as one surprising example.

The findings presented here do not in any way undermine the intelligence of Native Americans, nor question the unique characteristics of each tribe. The people indigenous to the Americas, like all peoples across the world, responded creatively yet selectively to new ideas from many sources. Increasing evidence indicates that Native Americans also made contributions abroad during prehistoric times: Crops such as the sweet potato, corn, coca, and tobacco appear in the Old World in surprising contexts.

Nor does this theory assume exceptional Japanese arrived in North America. They may have been ordinary fishermen, or perhaps mavericks who were run out of the country. The religious and political developments at the end of the Heian period (twelfth century) provide a likely time for a purposeful departure. The pilgrims from Japan who landed on North America's west coast may have come for the same reasons the pilgrims from Europe arrived on the east coast a few centuries later: to escape religious persecution while seeking freedom in a new land.

Some readers will find this theory with a thousand themes wild speculation, especially if it touches lightly on a topic of their personal expertise. After all, I have not even begun to fully address all the ins and outs of genetics, linguistics, archeology, religious beliefs, and all the related topics. Other readers may find no adequate discussion of alternative explanations; I am counting on the skeptics to provide those in glorious detail. Still other readers may wonder why, with all the different kinds of evidence marshalled here, the Japanese-Zuni connection was not discovered, reported, and confirmed long ago.

Clearly some areas are more speculative than others, and surely future investigations will prove parts of the proposition wrong. I followed an initial hunch in many directions; it was an intriguing safari of ideas, but the result is a broad-brushed sketch demanding further investigation. The data are presented with a strong conviction, knowing that each part can be challenged. But I believe this one small, multifaceted puzzle, the Zuni enigma, can lead to larger understandings among us all.

This book is about a pilgrimage that ended up at Zuni in the late thirteenth century, the beginning of the period called Pueblo IV. Suppose there was more than one pilgrimage, and the one that ended at Zuni was one of the last? If it was not the only prehistoric migration that brought new arrivals to the area, where might we look for evidence of others?

These findings may not be conclusive, but together they are suggestive; clearly, further research on dozens of topics in many academic disciplines is necessary. Especially important in future research and discussion will be participation by Native Americans from many tribes with Asians from many countries. Surely now it is time to address the probability of multiple arrivals to the Americas over the centuries.

ENDNOTES

INTRODUCTION

1. Davis, Nancy Yaw. 1992. The Zuni Enigma. New England Antiquities Research Association. *NEARA Journal* 27(1–2):39–55. Later reprinted in *Across before Columbus? Evidence for Transoceanic Contact with the Americas prior to 1492.* Donald Y. Gilmore and Linda S. McElroy, eds. New England Antiquities Research Association, Edgecomb, Me.: NEARA Publications, 1998. Pp. 125–140.
2. Abegg, Lily. 1952. *The Mind of East Asia.* London: Thames and Hudson.

CHAPTER 1

1. The similarities of the Zuni system with yin-yang of Taoism and *onmyō-dō* of Japan are discussed in Chapter 9.

    See Tsunoda, Ryusaku, William Theodore de Bary, and Donald Keene, comp. 1958. *Sources of the Japanese Tradition.* New York: Columbia University Press. Pp. 59–60.
2. *The Shiwi Messenger* was established in 1995.
3. This 45-bed hospital, completed in 1976, is overseen by the Zuni-Ramah Health Board, and contracts for services with the Public Health Service office located in Albuquerque.
4. Established in 1979 by Donald Eriacho, who later became governor of the pueblo from 1994 through 1998.
5. An example of the control the Zuni have over their lands, history, religion, and resources is reflected in the Zuni Archeology Program, initiated in 1976. Zuni live on one of the most-documented reservation lands in North America.
6. Eggan, Fred. 1979. Pueblos: Introduction. Pp. 224–235 in *Handbook of North American Indians.* Vol. 9, *Southwest.* A. Ortiz, vol. ed. W. C. Sturtevant, general ed. Washington, D.C.: Smithsonian Institution. P. 230.
7. In the spring of 1995, the Zuni Tribal Office Directory listed 150 telephone numbers for specific functions. Over 300 Zuni were employed by the tribe; non-Zuni residents with special expertise are hired as consultants for specific jobs.

    An unpublished 1995 report by Jim Ostler, then manager of the

Pueblo of Zuni Arts and Crafts Cooperative, is indicative of the economic success of this enterprise. The wholesale market reached from Tokyo to Paris, and 3 retail stores were maintained: in Zuni and in San Francisco and Venice, California. The high quality of authentic Zuni arts generates significant income for the commumity. The cooperative was begun in 1984, and by 1994, and business assets had grown to over $1,000,000 and sales had grown to $1,600,000.

8. For a general overview about the tribe, see Spencer, Robert F., Jesse D. Jennings, et al. 1965. *The Native Americans*. New York: Harper & Row, Pp. 303–318.

9. The Zuni anthropologist Edmund Ladd (1979a) explained the complex interconnections of the Zuni social, religious, and political systems and how they are linked to the ceremonial and religious cycles and to the kin and clan system in Zuni Social and Political Organization. Pp. 482–491 in *Handbook of North American Indians*. Vol. 9, *Southwest*.

10. Modern foods are available in the local stores and in major shopping centers in nearby Gallup, but certain foods such as corn, bread, and mutton continue to be prepared, distributed, and consumed in traditional ways, eaten at ceremonial times.

11. The Zuni Public School District was created in 1980 by the New Mexico State Board of Education at the request of the Zuni Tribe. In 1995, over 2,000 students attended 9 different schools, including 2 church-related programs. West, James B. February 1995. Letter to applicants. Zuni Public School District.

12. Complete site records, artifact catalogs, historical photos, and many unpublished documents are held in the library, which includes over 1,500 entries.

    The A:shiwi A:wan Museum and Heritage Center is an ecomuseum established in 1990, operated by an independent board.

    In addition to preparing traveling exhibits, the Pueblo of Zuni Arts and Crafts Cooperative and the museum have produced museum catalogs and several books on Zuni pottery, fetishes, and jewelry. Hughte, Phil. 1994. *A Zuni Artist Looks at Frank Hamilton Cushing*. Zuni, N.M.: Pueblo of Zuni Arts and Crafts and the A:shiwi A:wan Museum and Heritage Center. Nahohai, Milford and Elisa Phelps. 1995. *Dialogues with Zuni Potters*. Photography by Dale W. Anderson. Zuni, N.M.: Zuni A:Shiwi Publishing. Ostler, James, Marian Rodee, and Milford Nahohai. 1996. *Zuni. A Village of Silversmiths*. Zuni, N.M.: Zuni A:Shiwi Publishing and the University of New Mexico. Rodee, Marian and James Ostler. 1990. *The Fetish Carvers of Zuni*. Maxwell Museum of Anthropology and Pueblo of Zuni Arts and

Crafts. Albuquerque: Maxwell Museum of Anthropology, University of New Mexico.

13. In the late 1990s, the Zuni Council was considering how much to link their lives with the larger world, and how much to focus on maintaining their isolation, their religion, and their independence as a sovereign Indian nation.

　　The balance between openness and exclusiveness must be managed carefully. Elegant, high-quality jewelry, fetish carvings, pottery, and paintings provide income for many families, so public relations are important. Each council manages the inherent tensions differently.

14. Murdock, George P. 1953. *Ethnographic Bibliography of North America.* 2nd ed. New Haven: Human Relations Area Files. Pp. 158–160, 322.

15. Ladd 1979a. P. 482.

16. Ortiz, Alfonso. 1979. Introduction. Pp. 1–4 in *Handbook of North American Indians.* Vol. 9, *Southwest.* P. 1.

17. There is a peculiar leap of logic in association with the pithouses-to-pueblo transition, called PPT. But it is one established theme in Southwest archeology. See Gumerman, George J., ed. 1994. *Themes in Southwest Prehistory.* Santa Fe: School of American Research Press. *Kiva* is a Hopi word, now applied to all Pueblo ceremonial centers. An alternative (and earlier) term, *estufa,* ("stove" in Spanish) is discussed in Chapter 9, and an alternative source of the word is proposed. Ceremonial centers called *estufas* may be *stupas,* religious structures associated with Buddhism.

18. Frazier, Kendrick. 1986. *People of Chaco. A Canyon and Its Culture.* New York: W. W. Norton.

19. Ferguson, T. J. and E. Richard Hart. 1985. *A Zuni Atlas.* Norman: University of Oklahoma Press. P. 26; Kintigh, Keith W. 1985. *Settlement, Subsistence, and Society in Late Zuni Prehistory.* Anthropological Papers of the University of Arizona. No. 44. Tucson: University of Arizona Press.

20. Ferguson and Hart 1985:26.

21. For a history of Pueblo-Spanish relations to 1821, see Simmons, Marc. 1979. History of Pueblo-Spanish Relations to 1821. Pp. 178–193 in *Handbook of North American Indians.* Vol. 9, *Southwest.* For an account of the Pueblo Revolt, consult Sando, Joe S. 1979. The Pueblo Revolt. Pp. 194–197 in *Handbook of North American Indians.* Vol. 9, *Southwest.* For a summary and references to Zuni prehistory and history to 1850, see Woodbury, Richard B. 1979. Zuni Prehistory and History to 1850. Pp. 467–473 in *Handbook of North American Indians.* Vol. 9, *Southwest.*

22. The Friars were again expelled from the village in 1846, and the church building was abandoned until 1967 when the National Park Service assisted with the restoration. The interior is well known for the remarkable paintings of Zuni masked gods, *kachinas*, by Alex Seowtewa.

23. For a detailed list of incidents of violence in the Zuni area from 1539 to 1889, consult Ferguson and Hart 1985:59–61.

24. For general references to Japanese history, consult Imamura, Keiji. 1996. *Prehistoric Japan. New Perspectives on Insular East Asia.* Honolulu: University of Hawai'i Press; Hall, John Whitney. 1968 [1991]. *Japan from Prehistory to Modern Times.* Center for Japanese Studies. Ann Arbor: University of Michigan; Collcutt, Martin, Marius Jansen, and Isao Kumakura. 1988. *Cultural Atlas of Japan.* New York: Facts on File.

CHAPTER 2

1. Ferguson, T. J. and E. Richard Hart. 1985. *A Zuni Atlas.* Norman: University of Oklahoma Press. P. 26

2. Cushing, Frank H. 1920. *Zuni Breadstuff.* Indian Notes and Monographs 8. New York: P. 216.

3. Quam, Alvina, transl. 1972. *The Zunis: Self-portrayals by the Zuni People.* Albuquerque: University of New Mexico Press. P. 112; Tedlock, Dennis, transl. 1972. *Finding the Center: Narrative Poetry of the Zuni Indians, from Performances in Zuni, by Andrew Peynetsa and Walter Sanchez.* Lincoln: University of Nebraska Press. Pp. 288, 291, 292.

4. The migration story is such a pervasive theme in Zuni literature, it seems ethnologists almost competed to find informants to document it. First there was Frank Cushing who lived in the pueblo from 1879 to 1884, and published a long narrative of migration (40 pages) in 1896. About the same vintage, but based on data from different informants, Matilda (Tillie) Stevenson published another version in 1904, followed by the next generation—Ruth Bunzel in 1932 and Elsie Parsons in 1939. A third generation of scholarship emerged in 1972 with Dennis Tedlock's translated narrative poetry of the Zuni, called *Finding the Center.* That same year Alvina Quam included a translation of the search in the book *The Zunis: Self-portrayals by the Zuni People.* Finally, Barton Wright's 1988 edited and illustrated book called *The Mythic World of the Zuni,* derived from the original 19-century account by Cushing, begins a second century of printed variations of the Zuni migration story. Stevenson, Matilda (Coxe). 1904. The Zuni Indians: Their Mythology, Esoteric Fraternities, and Cere-

monies. Pp. 3–634 in *23rd Annual Report of the Bureau of American Ethnology for the Years 1901–1902*. Washington, D.C.: U.S. Government Printing Office; Parsons, Elsie (Clewes). 1939. *Pueblo Indian Religion*. 2 vols. Chicago: University of Chicago Press; Bunzel, Ruth L. 1932b (1984). Zuni Origin Myths. Pp. 545–609 in *47th Annual Report of the Bureau of American Ethnology for the Years 1929–1930;* Wright, Barton, ed. 1988. *The Mythic World of the Zuni. Written by Frank Hamilton Cushing.* Albuquerque: University of New Mexico Press.

5. Quam 1972:149.
6. Ferguson and Hart 1985. See Appendices 1 and 2.
7. Ferguson and Hart 1985:21.

   This research was presented to the U.S. Court of Claims in support of a lawsuit that sought payment for lands taken from the tribe without compensation. A settlement was made in 1990 for $25 million.

8. Bunzel noted, "The Zunis are as much preoccupied with the origins and early history of their people as were, for instance, the ancient Hebrews. . . ." Bunzel 1932b:547.

   Others have compared the narrative to the epics of Homer. Ferguson and Hart 1985:xi.

9. For references to induction into the Bow Society, see Green, Jesse, ed. 1990. *Cushing at Zuni. The Correspondence and Journals of Frank Hamilton Cushing. 1879–1884.* Albuquerque: University of New Mexico Press. Pp. 392, note 39; 178–182. This membership allowed Cushing to hear and record the prayers and songs in a secret religious language, which he reported as ancient and obsolete. As discussed in Chapter 9, the religious language includes many Japanese words.

10. For a compilation of his writings, and overview of his life, consult Green 1990.

    For a contemporary Zuni perspective, good humor, and commentary on Cushing, see Hughte, Phil. 1994. *A Zuni Artist Looks at Frank Hamilton Cushing.* Zuni, N.M.: Pueblo of Zuni Arts and Crafts and the A:shiwi A:wan Museum and Heritage Center.

11. Cushing, Frank. 1896. Outlines of Zuni Creation Myths. Pp. 321–447 in *13th Annual Report of the Bureau of American Ethnology for the Years 1891–1892.* Washington, D.C.: U.S. Government Printing Office. This summary is drawn specifically from pp. 379–430.

12. The same relationship was noted in the Zuni council chambers. On either side of the governor are the two next-ranking members of the council: the younger leader, the head councilman, to his right, and an older gentleman, the lieutenant governor, on his left. The governor is called "father."

13. Cushing's narrative, in classic late-nineteenth-century prose, describes the terror created: "The heights staggered and the mountains reeled, the plains boomed and crackled under the floods and fires, and the high hollow-places, hugged of men and the creatures, were black and awful, so that these grew crazed with panic and strove alike to escape or to hide more deeply." Cushing 1896:389.

14. How many places just inland from the coast of California would this describe? Note the similarity of the words for mountain: *yala* in Zuni and *yama* in Japanese. Cushing 1896:390.

15. This may describe Mono Lake in eastern California. Cushing 1896:390.

16. *Shipololo* means "to be foggy" in Zuni. Cushing 1896:390.

17. One Zuni word for corn is *towa*. In Japanese, it is *tomorokoshi*. The phonemic shift from /w/ to /m/ is common. See Chapter 7. Corn is assumed to be a recent introduction to Japan, but since growing evidence indicates corn reached India by the 13th century, or before, the possibility of this American vegetable reaching Japan needs also to be considered. (See Johannessen, Carl L. 1998. Maize Diffused to India before Columbus Came to America. Pp. 111–125 in *Across before Columbus? Evidence for Transoceanic Contact with the Americas prior to 1492.* Donald Y. Gilmore and Linda S. McElroy, eds. New England Antiquities Research Association. Edgecomb, Me.: NEARA Publications.

18. Cushing 1896:398.

19. The conch shells, common in the Pacific, have been found in archeological sites in the Southwest, dating back to A.D. 900, and they are still used in Zuni rituals. Conch shells are also used in Buddhist rituals and by the *yamabushi,* the mountain priests near Kyoto, Japan.

20. Suggested etymology: *kami* means "deity," or a "deified hero" in Japanese; *mosa* has the meaning of "a stalwart, a man of valour (courage)." *Kawimosa* perhaps connotes "courageous hero" in Zuni. Note yet another shift of /m/ to /w/.

21. Here is an example of the suffix *-atchi,* which means "more than one" in Japanese. It means "two" in Zunian.

22. Brother-sister marriage, a widespread story theme, also appears in the Japanese version of creation. Aston, W. G., transl. 1972. *Nihongi. Chronicles of Japan from the Earliest Times to A.D. 697.* Tokyo, Japan: Charles E. Tuttle. Pp. 6–34; Chamberlain, Basil Hall, transl. 1981. *The Kojiki. Records of Ancient Matters.* Rutland, Vt.: Charles E. Tuttle. P. li.

23. Cushing 1896:404. In this passage, note the reference to the mountains, a recurring theme during the search. Mountains play an im-

portant religious role in Shinto and in Japanese Buddhism, especially in association with pilgrimages.

24. For another version of the story, see Wright 1988:58.

25. Cushing 1896:405. These southern relatives of the Zuni may be a large group in northern Mexico, whose language is also an isolate.

26. Note reference here to the special qualities of the blind: "Though thou be blind, yet thou hearest all." Cushing 1986:407. Susan Matisoff (1978), professor of Japanese at Stanford, refers to the the Buddhist tradition of recognition of the special characteristics of the blind in *The Legend of the Semimaru. Blind Musician of Japan.* New York: Columbia University Press.

27. This may be an example of a Native American story that has been incorporated into this story of the pilgrims' search for the middle of the world, or it may be adopted from the Japanese Buddhist tradition of the supernatural characteristics of the blind.

    Also motifs of part of this story are similar to the well-known myth in North America about the blind man who is rescued by the loon and led back to his people.

28. The marked differences recognized in Japan for the elder and younger brothers are also found in Zuni kinship terms. See Chapter 8.

29. Cushing 1896:415. Here note the Zuni root *hanhli* and Japanese *hani*. The exact meaning of *Hán'hlipink'ya* has not been analyzed, but Cushing indicated the word means "Place of Sacred Stealing." One of the meanings of Japanese *hani* is "a criminal intent." Many of the names of stopping places along this journey from the west to east may be composed of 12th-century Japanese place names—yet another topic for the specialists.

30. The Priesthood of the Bow is the one that initiated Cushing, the major source for this narrative. This priesthood is associated with the west, and I suspect a cluster of words, designs, and symbols link this priesthood more closely to 12th-century Japan than may be the case with other priesthoods. The Priests of the Bow were guardians of the Zuni migration, the warriors who cleared the way for the eastward-moving migration. Were they the A:shiwi equivalent to samurai?

31. Colton, Harold S. 1932. Sunset Crater: The Effect of a Volcanic Eruption on an Ancient Pueblo People. Reprinted in R. I. Ford, ed. 1987. *The Prehistoric American Southwest. A Source Book. History, Chronology, Ecology and Technology.* New York: Garland Publishing.

32. Cushing 1896:424. With only this much of a description, the exact location cannot be identified. However, the spectacular Mesa Verde

ruins are north of the present-day Zuni in southern Colorado. If those ruins were abandoned about the time the Zuni were gathering their forces together for the final move to the middle place, we can at least speculate that the survivors included people from the Anasazi region. The name *heshotayalawa* means "dwellings in the mountains" in Zunian.

33. Cushing 1896:424–425.

34. "Their kin-names on the rocks thereabout." One of the pictographs painted in red high on the cliff to the left of the White House in Canyon de Chelly is a clear symbol for the sun—in Japanese kanji: 日.

    The Japanese kanji for rice field, 田, is also found in petroglyphs. Other examples of writing appear in Owens Valley, California, where complex symbols such as *Ni o*, referring to two Buddhist kings who guard the temple, appear. To my knowledge no one has yet studied petroglyphs and pictographs with early Asian writing systems in mind.

35. Stevenson, Matilda. 1904. The Zuni Indians: Their Mythology, Esoteric Fraternities, and Ceremonies. Pp. 3–634 in *23rd Annual Report of the Bureau of American Ethnology for the Years 1901–1902*. Washington, D.C.: U.S. Government Printing Office. Pp. 407–408.

36. Cushing 1896:426–427. *Shohko* is the Zuni word for "flute"; *shakuhachi* is the Japanese word for "bamboo flute."

37. See Map 8 and Appendix 1 in Ferguson and Hart (1985) for contemporary names for these stops.

38. *Matsaki* is a common Japanese place name, referring to "pine trees," *matsu*. Pine trees are significant in Chinese and Japanese Buddhism. No etymology for the Zuni place name Matsaki is available, but pine trees grow in the vicinity.

39. Another narrative, found in Matilda Stevenson's 1904 work, "The Zuni Indians," provides additional details of places passed, based on different informants, but highlighting similar detail and descriptive character of the migration story:

    After emerging from the fourth world place (Place of Origination, or Beginning: Chimik'yana'kya dey'a), the People who became the Zuni walked to the following places: gaming-stick spring, gaming-ring spring, Ne'wekwe baton spring, spring with prayer plume standing, cat-tail place, moss spring, muddy spring, sun-ray spring, spring by many aspens, shell place, dragon-fly place, flower place, place of trees with drooping limbs, fish spring, young-squash spring, and listening spring.

Here a segment of the Stevenson version of the Zuni narrative provides a sense of the continuing detail of the story:

Narrator: "They passed between the mountains. It is far to the middle of the world.

. . . Kiäklo (Kyaklu) now recounts the travels of the ancients to the Middle of the world."

Kiäklo: "We come this way. We come to a large lake; here we get up and move on. We come to a valley with watercress in the middle; here we get up and move on.

We come to the stealing place; here we get up and move on.

We come to the houses built in mesa walls; here we get up and move on.

We come to the last of a row of springs; here we get up and move on.

We come to the middle of a row of springs; here we get up and move on."

The story continues on and on, identifying more places where they stopped: after the middle of a row of springs, the house of Kolowisi, watercress place, a small spring, a spring in a hollow place in a mound, hidden by tall bending grasses, ashes spring, high-grass spring, rainbow spring, place of the Shalako, place with many springs, moss place, stone-lodged-in-a-cleft place, stone-picture place, poison-oak place, spring in a mesa wall, rush place, place of bad-smelling water, sack of meal hanging place, blue-jay spring, Corn Mountain, spring at the base of the mesa, ant-entering place, vulva spring, spring high in the mountain, Apache spring, coyote spring, salt place, place with fumes like burning sulphur, ant place. And then:

"We come to the Middle place." (Ítiwanna kwi)

In all, thirty-six locations are named in this account. Stevenson 1904:78–88.

40. Cushing 1896:428–430.
41. Cushing 1920:218.
42. One brief version of the finding of the middle place is stated in a book by the Zuni people, *The Zuni Self-portrayals*:

> *They (the priests) called upon the water spider to find the middle place. The water spider came from the north and it stretched its legs until its body lay upon the center. Then upon that exact spot the village was built. Under the houses*

where the priests now spend their fasting days, there lies the
heart of the earth, the middle place. Quam 1972:113.

43. Ferguson and Hart 1985:126.

44. Ferguson and Hart 1985:126.

45. Possible prehistoric explorations to North America by Chinese have been the source of speculation in the past. References include Mertz, Henriette. 1953. *Pale Ink. Two Ancient Records of Chinese Exploration in America.* Chicago: Ralph Fletcher Seymour; Thompson, Gunnar. 1989. *Nu Sun. Asian-American Voyages 500 B.D.* Fresno, Cal.: Pioneer Publishing; and Thompson, Gunner. 1994. *America Discovery. Our Multicultural Heritage.* Seattle, Wash.: Argonauts Misty Isles Press.

46. Tsunoda, Ryusaku, William Theodore de Bary, and Donald Keene, Comp. 1958. *Sources of the Japanese Tradition.* New York: Columbia University Press. Pp. 66–68. See original translation by Aston W. G. 1972. *Nihongi. Chronicles of Japan from the Earliest Times to* A.D. *697.* Tokyo, Japan: Charles E. Tuttle. Pp. 110–132.

47. See Tsunoda et al. 1958:67.

48. Some leaders included Kūya (903–72), Genshin (942–1017), and later, Hōnen (1133–1212), Nichiren (1222–82), Ippen (1239–89). Hori, Kyotsu. 1967. The Mongol Invasions and the Kamakura Bakufu. Ph.D. dissertation in political science. Columbia University. P. 73; Kitagawa, Joseph M. 1966. *Religion in Japanese History.* New York: Columbia University Press. P. 76.

49. Anesaki, Masaharu. 1930. *History of Japanese Religion.* London: Kegan Paul, Trench, Trubner. P. 202.

50. Kitagawa 1966:71–77; Dobbins 1989:424–29; Sansom 1958:224–28.

51. The major earthquakes in California and in Japan in 1994 and 1995 highlight the vulnerability of these areas to the periodic disruption of the earth's crust and the extensive ramifications on humans that earthquakes can have. Both areas on either side of the Pacific are located on the "Rim of Fire." Both have had many earthquakes in the past and will continue to share the risk of many more in the future.

52. Sansom, George. 1958. *A History of Japan to 1334.* Stanford: Stanford University Press. P. 75.

53. Hazard, Benjamin Harrison, Jr. 1967. Japanese Marauding in Medieval Korea: The *Wakō* Impact on Late Koryo. Ph.D. dissertation in history. University of California, Berkeley. P. 90.

54. Hazard 1967:329–330.

55. Sansom 1958:393.

56. Sansom 1958:417.

CHAPTER 3

1. Frazier, Kendrik. 1986. *People of Chaco. A Canyon and Its Culture.* New York: W. W. Norton. See especially pp. 210–212.
2. This is one of many puzzling aspects of the earlier Southwest cultures. Of the 20 fish taxa identified on Mimbres pottery, 18 are of marine origin. Jett and Moyle suggested that Mimbres traders traveled 1,500 kilometers from the New Mexico Mimbres Valley to the Gulf of California and back. Twelve of 14 shell species found in Mimbres sites are from the Panamic Province (including the Gulf of California) and 1 species is from the Pacific coast.

   The fish motifs are quite realistic and make up about 11 % of the animals on the pottery. The fish motif also seems to be associated with mortuary bowls.

   The Mimbres culture apparently was linked with the Anasazi at Chaco, as was its demise.

   See Jett, Stephen C. and Peter B. Moyle. 1986. The Exotic Origins of Fishes Depicted on Prehistoric Mimbres Pottery from New Mexico. *American Antiquity* 51:688–720.

   (The Zuni do not, traditionally, eat fish, a fact that may be related to the story about the children lost in the river; the children became water animals. Also the link to the Lake of the Dead, where all Zuni go at the time of death, again perhaps explains the disdain for eating marine products. Cremation and putting the ashes in pots or in the river was also a custom in the past.)

   For other references on Mimbres, see Fewkes, Jesse Walter. 1990b (1914–1924). *The Mimbres Art and Archaeology.* With an introduction by J. J. Brody. A reprint of 3 essays, published by the Smithsonian Institution between 1914 and 1924. Albuquerque: Avanyu Publishing; LeBlanc, Steven A. 1983. *The Mimbres People. Ancient Pueblo Painters of the American Southwest.* London: Thames and Hudson; and Brody, J. J. 1977. *Mimbres Painted Pottery.* Santa Fe: School of American Research. Albuquerque: University of New Mexico Press.
3. Jett, Stephen C. 1964. Pueblo Indian Migration: An Evaluation of the Possible Physical and Cultural Determinants. *American Antiquity* 29:281–300; Eggan, Fred. 1950. *Social Organization of the Western Pueblos.* Chicago: University of Chicago Press; Woodbury, Richard B. 1956. The Antecedents of Zuni Culture. *Transactions of the New York Academy of Sciences.* Second series. 18(6):557–563.

   Marie Wormington stated that the Village of the Great Kivas, 16 miles from Zuni, was begun in the 11th century and "after a time, due

to the arrival of new people, the community increased in size."
Wormington, H. Marie. 1959. *Prehistoric Indians of the Southwest.* (4th
printing.) Denver: Denver Museum of Natural History. P. 101.

4. Adler, Michael A., ed. 1996. *The Prehistoric Pueblo World,* A.D.
1150–1350. Tucson: University of Arizona Press.

5. Kintigh, Keith. 1985. *Settlement, Subsistence, and Society in Late Zuni
Prehistory.* Anthropological Papers of The University of Arizona. No.
44. Tucson: University of Arizona Press. P. 113.

6. Kintigh, Keith. 1996. The Cibola Region in the Post-Chacoan Era. Pp.
131–144 in *The Prehistoric Pueblo World A.D. 1150–1350.* P. 136.

7. Adams, E. Charles. 1991. *The Origin and Development of the Pueblo
Katsina Cult.* Tucson: University of Arizona Press.

8. An intriguing controversy has been generated by Christy and
Jacqueline Turner's book *Man Corn. Cannibalism and Violence in the
Prehistoric American Southwest* (1999). Extensive analysis of skeletal
collections from 76 sites, many associated with the Anasazi, especially in the sphere of Chaco, led the authors to propose a Mesoamerican connection for over three centuries (900–1200) of violence,
human sacrifice, and cannabalism in the Southwest. I suggest an alternative explanation for the butchered bones: the possibility of Buddhist sky burial, a ritualized manner of disposing of bodies after
death. See Jack Weatherford *Savages and Civilization. Who Will Survive?* (1994) for a description of the Tibetan sky burial custom of cutting up the body on a rock platform above the villages and feeding
the parts to the vultures. Do the remaining bones have similar marks
to the ones the Turners (and others) have studied? Or does sky burial butchering leave a different kind of signature? (Not many bones
have been found in association with Chaco. Perhaps the vultures did
a very good job.)

9. The link between the Mogollon and the Zuni has long been recognized by others (Ferguson, T. J. and E. Richard Hart. 1985. *A Zuni
Atlas.* Norman: University of Oklahoma Press. P. 27.) Here I simply
add the Japanese component. Perhaps the Arizona area should also
be searched for evidence of this late migration. Do the Hopi, Pima,
Papago, and Havuspai, for example, also have traditions of migration
and coming from the ocean to the west?

10. At the nearby Acoma-Laguna area to the east of Zuni, the appearance
of glaze also marks the beginning of Pueblo IV. In Pueblo III it was
absent; in Pueblo IV it is there. Roney, John R. 1996. Eastern San
Juan Basin, Acoma-Laguna Area. Pp. 145–169 in *The Prehistoric
Pueblo World A.D. 1150–1350.* Pp. 145, 163.

11. Bandelier, Adolph F. A. 1892. An Outline of the Documentary History

of the Zuni Tribe. *Journal of American Ethnology and Archaeology* 3(1):1–115.

12. In 1972 Fred Eggan, an eminent scholar of the region, late professor of anthropology at the University of Chicago, raised the question with others, "Where and when did the Pueblo people originate?" He concluded there was little agreement but "the twelfth and thirteenth centuries are the critical periods" especially in the Rio Grande area. Indeed his assessment led him to state, "Today the evidence for diversity of origin for the prehistoric Pueblo cultures seems greater than ever." Eggan, Fred. 1972. Summary. Pp. 287–305 in *New Perspectives on the Pueblos.* A. Ortiz, ed. A School of American Research Book. Albuquerque: University of New Mexico Press. P. 305.

Subsequent research has further confirmed Eggan's observations. Now consideration must be given to the proposal that the diversity of origins included Japanese pilgrims and their entourage arriving by the late 13th century.

Other descendants of the Anasazi probably include all the Pueblo groups in New Mexico and the Hopi in Arizona, but this is beyond the scope of my theory at this time. I suggest here that the Western Pueblos (both Hopi and Zuni) share sharp distinctions from the Eastern Pueblos partly because they incorporated the newcomers after the collapse of Anasazi.

13. Colton, Harold S. 1941. Prehistoric Trade in the Southwest. *Scientific Monthly* 52(April):308–319.

14. Vargas, Victoria D. 1995. *Copper Bell Trade Patterns in the Prehispanic U.S. Southwest and Northwest Mexico.* Arizona State Museum Archeological Series 187. Tucson: University of Arizona.

Dorothy Hosler's work on New World metallurgy assumes independent development, initially begun in South America and then traded northward to West Mexico. To my knowledge, no one has yet analyzed and compared the content, shapes, and quality of bronze and copper bells found in the Americas with those found in Southeast Asia, Japan, or China, where bells were first innovated by the Shang Dynasty. Celia Heil, however, has begun insightful observation of the role of metal items especially in connection with Purhepecha religion in Michoacan, Mexico, and raises significant questions about possible Asian connections. Bells appeared in Michoacan in the 10th century, along with many other metal items such as rings, tweezers, and axes. See Heil, Celia. 1998. The Significance of Metallurgy in the Purhépecha Religion. Pp. 43–51 in *Across before Columbus? Evidence for Transoceanic Contact with the Americas prior to 1492.* Donald Y. Gilmore and Linda S. McElroy, eds. New England Antiquities Research Association. Edgecomb, Me.: NEARA Publications; Hosler, Dorothy. 1988. Ancient West Mexican Metallurgy: South and Central American Origins and West Mexican Transformations. *American Anthropologist* 90:832–855. Palmer, J. W., M. G. Hollander, P. S. Z. Rogers, T. M. Benjamin, C. J. Duffy, J. B. Lambert, and J. A. Brown. 1998. Pre-Columbian Metallurgy: Technology, Manufacture, and Microprobe Analysis of Copper Bells from the Greater Southwest. *Archaeometry* 40(2):361–382.

15. Heizer, Robert F. 1978b. Trade and Trails. Pp. 690–693 in *Handbook of North American Indians.* Vol. 8, *California.* R. F. Heizer, vol. ed. W. C. Sturtevant, general ed. Washington, D.C.: Smithsonian Institution.

16. Colton 1941:318.

17. Ferguson and Hart 1985:53.

18. Cushing, Frank H. 1920. *Zuni Breadstuff.* Indian Notes and Monographs 8. Museum of the American Indian, Heye Foundation. New York: Pp. 216–217.

19. For detail of these visits see Green, Jesse, ed. 1979. *Zuni. Selected Writings of Frank Hamilton Cushing.* Foreword by Fred Eggan. Lincoln: University of Nebraska Press. Pp. 408–425; Green, Jesse, ed. 1990. *Cushing at Zuni. The Correspondence and Journals of Frank Hamilton Cushing. 1879–1884.* Albuquerque: University of New Mexico Press. Pp. 16–17, 218–222.

20. Roscoe, Will. 1991. *The Zuni Man-Woman.* Albuquerque: University of New Mexico Press.

21. This was one of Puccini's less successful operas and the only one with an American theme. Near the beginning of Act 1, Jake Wallace, the roving minstrel, sings "Old Dog Tray." The song was apparently a modified rendition derived from "The Festive Sundance," sung by Cushing in 1898. Cushing's version was recorded by Carlos Troyer and published by Arthur George Farwell in 1904. In response to Puccini's request for Indian songs, Sybil Seligman sent him the Troyer version in 1907 in time to be incorporated for the opera's first performance at the New York's Metropolitan Opera on December 10, 1910. For an analysis of the song and its original source see Atlas, Allan W. 1991. Belasco and Puccini: "Old Dog Tray" and the Zuni Indians. *Musical Quarterly* 75(3):362–398.

22. Woodward, Arthur. 1932. A Modern Zuni Pilgrimage. *The Masterkey* 6:44–51.

23. Heizer, Robert Fleming 1978a. Introduction. Pp. 1–5 in *Handbook of North American Indians.* Vol. 8, *California.* P. 3.

24. Luomala, Katherine. 1978. Tipai-Ipai. Pp. 592–609 in *Handbook of North American Indians.* Vol. 8, *California.* Pp. 601, 604.

25. For an example of the sophistication of modern scientific analysis of ceramics in the Southwest (including for example, petrography, x-ray fluorescence), consult Mills, Barbara J. and Patricia L. Crown, eds. 1995. *Ceramic Production in the American Southwest.* Tucson: University of Arizona Press.

26. The California archeologists attend the meetings of the Society of California Archeology; archeologists from Texas, Arizona, and New Mexico attend the meetings of the Southwest Archeologists; and archeologists from these respective regions organize regional meetings at the national meetings of the Society for American Archeology.

27. Ruby, Jay W. 1970. Culture Contact between Aboriginal Southern California and the Southwest. Unpublished Ph.D. dissertation in anthropology. University of California, Los Angeles.

28. Ruby 1970:xiv.

29. Ruby's own interest began when he found Southwest ceramic sherds in the Big Tujunga site in Los Angeles County. Ruby, Jay. 1964. Occurrence of Southwestern Pottery in Los Angeles County, California. *American Antiquity* 30:209–210.

    In all, 56 locations in southern California contained ceramics from the Southwest, an average of 1.9 pottery types for each site, and Pacific coast species of shells appear in the Southwest in great numbers. (For example, in 1896 J. Walter Fewkes published an article "Pacific Coast Shells from Tusayan Pueblos" in *American Anthropologist* 9:359–367.) (*Tusayan* was the 19th-century term for one Hopi group in Arizona.) Ruby also identified 50 southwestern sites with shells found in them (Ruby 1970:377–378) and noted "the number of shells in most Anasazi sites exceed by tenfold the number found in most Puebloid sites" (Ruby 1970:49).

    In Hohokam locations, 13 different species of southern California shells were excavated. Once the shells arrived in the Southwest, they were probably redistributed within the region.

30. Kroeber, A. L. 1925. *Handbook of the Indians of California.* Bureau of American Ethnology Bulletin 78. Washington, D.C.: U.S. Government Printing Office. Kroeber, A. L. 1928. Native Culture in the Southwest. University of California Publications in American Archaeology and Ethnology Vol. 23, No. 9. Pp. 375–398. Berkeley: University of California; Strong, William D. 1927. An Analysis of Southwestern Society. *American Anthropologist* 29:1–61 (see especially pp. 52–56).

31. The Navaho are better known for their sand paintings than are other Southwest, or California, groups. Peter Gold brings our attention to significant similarities between Navaho and Tibetan mandalas and

sand paintings. See Gold, Peter. 1994. *Navajo and Tibetan Sacred Wisdom. The Circle of the Spirit*. Rochester, Vt.: Inner Traditions.

32. Steward, Julian H. 1953. Evolution and Process. Pp. 313–326 in *Anthropology Today*. A. L. Kroeber, ed. Chicago: University of Chicago Press.

33. Hawley, Florence M. 1937. Pueblo Social Organization as a Lead to Pueblo History. *American Anthropologist* 39:506, 520; Parsons, Elsie (Clews). 1939. *Pueblo Indian Religion*. Vol. II. Chicago: University of Chicago Press. P. 989.

34. Jeancon, J. A. 1923. *Excavations in the Chama Valley, New Mexico*. Bureau of American Ethnology Bulletin 81. Washington, D.C.: U.S. Government Printing Office. Pp. 33–34. Bourke, John G. 1884. *The Snake-dance of the Moquis of Arizona*. New York: Charles Scribner's Sons. P. 242.

    Captain John G. Bourke, who was in the Southwest in 1880s, reported that the abalone shells found at Hopi in the 1880s were obtained from the seashore, at least until "recently." He also noted the Hopi were making pilgrimages every 4 or 5 years, although he was skeptical until he met an Indian from the Pueblo of Jemez who said he had worked for 2 years in the "little town of Santa Barbara."

35. Bandelier was sent to the Southwest in 1880 by the Archaeological Institute of America to gather information and to investigate ruins. His novel *The Delight Makers* was published in 1890.

36. Ruby 1970. On Ruby's Map V, one trail passing from the Southwest to southern California crosses near Needles, California, and another much farther south, east of San Diego.

CHAPTER 4

1. Cushing, in his discussion about 2 or more groups of peoples merging, noted the dominant role of the Zuni who came from the west:

    The intrusive or western branch is, strange to say, although least numerous, the one most told of in the myths, the one which speaks throughout them in the first person; that is, which claims to be the original Shiwi or Zuñi. Of this branch it is unnecessary to say much more here than the myths themselves declare, save to add that it was, if not the conquering, at least for a long time the dominant one.

    Cushing, Frank H. 1896. Outlines of Zuni Creation Myths. Pp. 321–447 in *13th Annual Report of the Bureau of American Ethnology for the Years 1891–1892*. Washington, D.C.: Pp. 343.

2. Arnold, Jeanne E. 1995. Transportation Innovation and Social Complexity among Maritime Hunter-Gatherer Societies. *American Anthropologist* 97:733–747. Arnold argued convincingly that water transportation by large canoes supported the development of trade and political, economic, and social complexity among the Chumash of the Channel Islands and the Nootka of coastal Canada. The production and distribution of coastal shells represented one theme of success and power, especially among the Chumash.

3. Winchester, Simon. 1991. *Pacific Rising. The Emergence of a New World Culture.* Prentice-Hall. Pp. 40–41.

4. Ramage, Colin S. 1994. El Niño. Pp. 78–85 in *The Enigma of Weather.* A Collection of Works Exploring the Dynamics of Meteorological Phenomena. New York: Scientific American.

5. Epstein, Paul R., ed. 1999. *Extreme Weather Events: The Health and Economic Consequences of the 1997/98 El Niño and La Niña.* The Center for Health and the Global Environment. Boston, Mass.: Harvard Medical School.

6. Finney, Ben. 1985. Anomalous Westerlies, El Niño, and the Colonization of Polynesia. *American Anthropologist* 87:9–26. P. 23.

7. Betty J. Meggers (1976) of the Smithsonian Institution noted the tradition of American archeologists of accepting diffusion by land, but not sea travel, in Yes If by Land, No If by Sea: The Double Standard in Interpreting Cultural Similarities. *American Anthropologist* 78:637–639.

8. This occurred in the vicinity of 44–42 degrees North, 178–06 degrees East. For details and maps consult Ebbesmeyer, Curtis C. and W. James Ingraham, Jr. 1994b. *Drifting Objects. Atlas of Pilot Charts. North Pacific Ocean.* 3rd ed. Washington, D.C.: Defense Mapping Agency, U.S. Department of Defense. NV Publication 108.

9. Harrell, Debera C. 1994. "Toys Drift into Ice." Seattle Post-Intelligencer in *Anchorage Daily News,* November 28, pp. B1, B2; Ebbesmeyer, Curtis C. and W. James Ingraham, Jr. 1994a. Pacific Toy Spill Fuels Ocean Current Pathways Research. *EOS, Transactions, American Geophysical Union* 75(37):425–427.

10. Location: 48–00 degrees North, 161–00 degrees West.

11. Ebbesmeyer, Curtis C. and W. James Ingraham, Jr. 1992. Shoe Spill in the North Pacific. *EOS, Transactions, American Geophysical Union* 73(34):361–365; Ebbesmeyer and Ingraham 1994a; Sullivan, Walter. 1992. "If the Shoe Floats, Follow It." Science Times. *New York Times,* September 22, p. B5.

12. Bowen, B. W., F. A. Abreau-Grobois, G. H. Balazs, N. Kamezaki, C. J. Limpus, and R. J. Ferl. 1995. Trans-Pacific Migrations of the Logger-

head Turtle *(Caretta caretta)* Demonstrated with Mitochrondrial DNA Markers. *Proceedings of the National Academy of Sciences, USA* 92:3731–3734.

13. Arnold 1995; Quimby, George I. 1985. Japanese Wrecks, Iron Tools, and Prehistoric Indians of the Northwest Coast. *Arctic Anthropology* 22(2):7–15; Also see Thompson, J. Eric S. 1951. Canoes and Navigation of the Maya and Their Neighbors. *Journal of the Royal Anthropological Institute* 79:69–78; Epstein, Jeremiah F. 1990. Sails in Aboriginal Mesoamerica: Reevaluating Thompson's Argument. *American Anthropologist* 92:187–192. Finney, Ben. 1976. *Pacific Navigation and Voyaging.* Polynesian Society Memoir No. 39. Wellington, New Zealand: Polynesian Society; Finney, Ben. 1994. *Voyage of Rediscovery. A Cultural Odyssey through Polynesia.* Berkeley: University of California Press.

14. Brady, William. 1995. Personal communication; Kitka, Herman. 1997. Speech at the opening of the Sitka Tribe's Community Center, May 23.

15. Collcutt, Martin, Marius Jansen, and Isao Kamukura. 1988. *Cultural Atlas of Japan.* New York: Facts on File. P. 16.

16. Arnold 1995.

17. Evidence of agriculture among some northwest coast tribes was discussed at the American Association for the Advancement of Science meeting in Seattle, 1997. Could it have been brought by someone from Asia?

18. McCartney, Allen P., Hiroaki Okada, Atsuko Okada, and William B. Workman. 1998. Introduction. North Pacific and Bering Sea Maritime Societies. The Archaeology of Prehistoric and Early Historic Coastal Peoples. *Arctic Anthropology* 35(1):1–5; Workman, William B. and Allen P. McCartney. 1998. Coast to Coast: Prehistoric Maritime Cultures in the North Pacific. *Arctic Anthropology* 35(1):361–370.

19. Riley, Carroll L., J. Charles Kelley, Campbell W. Pennington, and Robert L. Rands. 1971. *Man across the Sea. Problems of Pre-Columbian Contacts.* Austin: University of Texas Press.

20. One of the most impressive and well-researched topics was the worldwide distribution of the chicken: George F. Carter. 1971. Pre-Columbian Chickens in America. Pp. 178–218 in *Man across the Sea.*

   When I prepared a proposal for a session entitled "Pre-Columbian Asian Influences and Creative Native American Responses" for the 1992 American Anthropological Association's annual meeting held in San Francisco, it was turned down. The only comment I could elicit from the Program Chair was she had been informed "pre-Columbian issues had been discussed before and dismissed for lack of evidence, so why bring it up again."

21. Schwerin, Karl H. 1970b. *Winds across the Atlantic. Mesoamerican Studies.* No. 6. University Museum. Carbondale, Ill.: Southern Illinois University; Whitaker, Thomas W. 1970. Endemism and Pre-Columbian Migration of the Bottle Gourd, *Lagenaria siceraria* (Mol.) Standl. Pp. 320–327 in *Man Across the Sea.*

22. Johannessen, Carl L. 1998. Maize Diffused to India before Columbus Came to America. Pp. 111–125 in *Across before Columbus? Evidence for Transoceanic Contact with the Americas prior to 1492.* Donald Y. Gilmore and Linda S. McElroy, eds. New England Antiquities Research Association. Edgecomb, Me.: NEARA Publications.

23. Baker, Herbert G. 1971 Commentary: Section III. Pp. 428–444 in *Man Across the Sea.*

   The themes of the conference include inadequate evidence, counterevidence, and the problems of overenthusiastic amateurs messing things up. Linguistics was recognized as possibly having some place in the future, but physical anthropological evidence was not possible to consider because any data on modern populations after "four centuries of massive contact can hardly produce anything but suspect data." Riley et al. 1971:452. The editors concluded that "there is no hard and fast evidence for any pre-Columbian human introduction of any single plant or animal across the ocean from the Old World to the New World, or vice-versa." Riley et al. 1971:452–453.

24. Heizer, Robert Fleming. 1941. Archeological Evidence of Sebastian Rodriguez Cermeño's California Visit in 1595. *California Historical Society Quarterly* 20:315–328; Hanna, Warren L. 1979. *Lost Harbor. The Controversy over Drake's California Anchorage.* Berkeley: University of California Press.

25. Keddie, Grant R. 1990. *The Question of Asiatic Objects on the North Pacific Coast of America: Historic or Prehistoric?* Contributions to Human History, No. 3. Pp. 1–26. Victoria, British Columbia: Royal British Columbia Museum.

26. Akin, Marjorie Kleiger. n.d. The Noncurrency Functions of Chinese *Wen* in America. P. 21.

27. No. 78559. ACC 730, collected by Emmons on April 5, 1902, acquired from the Taku tribe located near Juneau, Alaska.

28. Akin, Marjorie Helen Kleiger. 1992. Asian Coins in the North American West: A Behavioral System Approach to Numismatic Analysis. Unpublished Ph.D. thesis. University of California, Riverside. Appendix D, Pp. 331–336. For another example of Chinese coins on

Tlingit armor, see the leather tunic from Hoonah, Alaska in Fitzhugh, William W. 1988. Comparative Art of the North Pacific Rim. Pp. 294–312 in *Crossroads of Continents. Cultures of Siberia and Alaska.* William Fitzhugh and Aron Crowell, eds. Washington, D.C.: Smithsonian Institution Press. P. 231.

29. Sansom, George. 1958. *A History of Japan to 1334.* Stanford: Stanford University Press. P. 423–24.

30. Benjamin Harrison Hazard, Jr. (1967) wrote an unusual dissertation at the University of California, Berkeley, on Japanese pirates, entitled "Japanese Marauding in Medieval Korea: The *Wakō* Impact on Late Koryo." His discussion about currency includes this: The demand for coins in Japan increased and Sung coins were imported, despite specific prohibition in Japan against the use of Chinese coins in 1194; also the Sung Chinese had an earlier edict in 1142 against the export of Chinese coins. Indeed the Sung in 1219 commanded that coins not be used in foreign trade at all, but that silk, brocade, porcelain, and lacquerware be the media of exchange. However, despite these efforts in both China and Japan to limit coin currency, Japan experienced an increasing shift from barter to a money economy during the late Heian and early Kamakura period. Hazard 1967:24–25.

31. For a history of coinage, see Grierson, Philip. 1975. *Numismatics.* New York: Oxford University Press. Pp. 55–71 for Chinese coins and pp. 65–70 for Japanese coins.

32. Fitzhugh, William W. 1988. Comparative Art of the North Pacific Rim. Pp. 294–312 in *Crossroads of Continents.* P. 307.

33. Fitzhugh 1988:312.

34. Although there has been little serious academic discussion yet, over 5,100 citations on questions and studies on transpacific topics appear in Sorenson, John L. and Martin H. Raish. 1996. *Pre-Columbian Contact with the Americas across the Oceans. An Annotated Bibliography.* 2nd ed, revised. 2 vol. Provo, Utah: Research Press.

35. Kirk and Daugherty stated:

   Tools from the Ozette houses included chisels with blades of beaver teeth, and of steel. Presumably, the metal came across the Pacific Ocean from Japan on shipwrecked junks. A piece of bamboo about a foot long and four inches in diameter suggests trans-Pacific drift.

   Kirk, Ruth with Richard D. Daugherty. 1978. *Exploring Washington Archaeology.* Seattle: University of Washington Press. P. 100.

36. Stenger, Alison T. 1991. Japanese-Influenced Ceramics in Precontact Washington State: A View of the Wares and Their Possible Origin. Pp.

111–122 in *The New World Figurine Project*. Vol. 1. T. Stocker, ed. Provo, Utah: Research Press.

37. For an excellent summary of the presence of iron along the northwest coast as reported by the first explorers, consult Emmons, George Thornton. 1991. *The Tlingit Indians*. Seattle: University of Washington Press and American Museum of Natural History. Pp. 183–189.

   Any major museum exhibit with ethnographic materials from the northwest coast cultural area reveals many pieces of iron, on the tips of spears, hooks, and sometimes whole blades. Are they possibly from prehistoric sources? Are they Japanese iron and steel? Or Chinese? See exhibits at the American Museum of Natural History and Chicago's Field Museum for a few examples.

38. Beardsley, Richard K. 1954. *Temporal and Areal Relationships in Central California Archaeology*. University of California Archaeological Survey Reports 24, 25. Berkeley: University of California.

39. Fink, Colin G. 1941. Division of Electrochemistry, Department of Chemical Engineering, Columbia University. Personal correspondence to Allen L. Chickering of Chickering and Gregory in San Francisco July 3, 1941.

   The detailed report and analysis from the chemist could not be located at the museum, so we are left wondering what may have happened to it. We have only letters indicating it had been submitted, and the spikes returned.

   The same summer the spikes were found (1941), a hoax was played by a student, possibly Alan Treganza, on a fellow graduate student, Richard Beardsley. Treganza, who was working with Gifford at the museum that summer, may have planted an Asian decorated piece of fine shell under a skull in a site Beardsley was excavating, causing quite a flurry of excitement. (The item was traced to a 1941 acquisition at the Museum, later a part of an exhibit on hoaxes prepared by Frank Norick.)

   Because the anthropology department at the University of California, Berkeley has had a significant role in the development of anthropology over the years, including dismissing interest in Asian influence in North America, I am left wondering if the source of that position, and the emotional basis for it, stemmed partly from the events of early summer in 1941, and World War II in the Pacific, which began in December 1941.

40. Olson, Ronald L. 1930. *Chumash Prehistory*. University of California Publications in American Archaeology and Ethnology. Vol. 28, No. 1. Berkeley: University of California Press.

41. Olson 1930:21.
42. Pierson, Larry J. 1979. New Evidence of Asiatic Shipwrecks off the California Coast. Unpublished manuscript. University of San Diego; Pierson, Larry J. and James R. Moriarty. 1980. Stone Anchors: Asiatic Shipwrecks off the California Coast. *Anthropological Journal of Canada* 18:17–23.
43. The numbers of the metal items in the museum collection include a bronze statuette (1-37056), a sword (255378), and the spear head (1-225214).
44. Chartkoff, Joseph L. and Kerry Kona Chartkoff. 1984. *The Archaeology of California*. Stanford: Stanford University Press. P. 255. These authors mention that the Spanish were apparently the first non-Indians to arrive in California, but qualify this statement by allowing the possibility that "Asians may have sailed across the Pacific and accidentally or deliberately reached the coast of California earlier. The evidence for this is ambiguous at best, and if any such visits took place they made no impact on native cultures." Chartkoff and Chartkoff 1984:251–252.

CHAPTER 5

1. Wood, Jim. 1980. Early Asians May Have Sailed to West. *San Francisco Sunday Examiner & Chronicle,* July 13, 1980, Section A, p. 8.
2. For a discussion of the feasibility of such voyages in ancient times, see Meggers, Betty J. 1998. Jomon-Valdivia Similarities: Convergence or Contact? Pp. 11–22 in *Across before Columbus? Evidence for Transoceanic Contact with the Americas prior to 1492.* Donald Y. Gilmore and Linda S. McElroy, eds. New England Antiquities Research Association. Edgecomb, Me.: NEARA Publications. Pp. 16–17.
3. Associated Press. 1995. "Ocean Crossing." *Anchorage Daily News,* September 26. P. 2.
4. Goodenough, Ward H. 1953. *Native Astronomy in the Central Carolines.* Philadelphia: University Museum, University of Pennsylvania; Finney, Ben. 1994. *Voyage of Rediscovery. A Cultural Odyssey through Polynesia.* Berkeley: University of California Press.
5. The Aleuts, for example, have the expression "when the tide goes out, the table is set." Anyone able to move, old and young, can harvest a tidal crop of edibles. See also Dixon, E. James. 1993. *Quest for the Origins of the First Americans.* Albuquerque: University of New Mexico Press. P. 123.
6. Laughlin, William S. 1980. *Aleuts: Survivors of the Bering Land Bridge.*

Case Studies in Cultural Anthropology. New York: Holt, Rinehart and Winston. Pp. 21, 69. Mann, Daniel H., Aron L. Crowell, Thomas D. Hamilton, and Bruce P. Finney. 1998. Holocene Geologic and Climatic History around the Gulf of Alaska. *Arctic Anthropology* 35(1):112–131. Crowell, Aron L. and Daniel H. Mann. 1996. Sea Level Dynamics, Glaciers, and Archaeology along the Central Gulf of Alaska Coast. *Arctic Anthropology* 33(2):16–37. Josenhans, Heiner, Daryl Fedje, Reinhard Pientiz, and John Southon. 1997. Early Humans and Rapidly Changing Holocene Sea Levels in the Queen Charlotte Islands-Hecate Strait, British Columbia, Canada. *Science* 277:71–74.

7. Levy, Matthys and Mario Salvadori. 1995. *Why the Earth Quakes. The Story of Earthquakes and Volcanoes.* New York: W. W. Norton. Pp. 24, 37.

8. Bodies of water are supportive of rich renewable resources, and are conducive to mobility of all sorts of other things, including tsunami, plants, animals, people, and diseases such cholera, which as recently as 1991 spread up the west coast of South America, across the Isthmus of Panama, and down the east coast of South America. Colwell, Rita. 1996. "Global Climate: Emerging Diseases and New Epidemics." American Association for the Advancement of Science Presidential Address. Baltimore, Md. February 10.

9. Jett, Stephen. 1971. Diffusion versus Independent Development. Pp. 5–53 in *Man across the Sea. Problems of Pre-Columbian Contacts.* Carroll Riley et al., eds. Austin: University of Texas Press.

10. Doran, Edwin, Jr. 1971. The Sailing Raft as a Great Tradition. Pp. 115–138 in *Man across the Sea.* This chapter brings together descriptions, sketches, and maps illustrating the distribution of sailing crafts worldwide.

11. For an annotated listing of Heyerdahl's prolific publications (49), consult Sorenson, John L. and Martin H. Raish. 1996. *Pre-Columbian Contact with the Americas across the Oceans. An Annotated Bibliography.* 2nd ed., revised. Provo, Utah: Research Press. Pp. 444–454.

In 1999 another expedition on a balsa wood raft was attempting the Pacific crossing. A 4-man American-led crew on the *La Manten,* a 60-foot raft, left Ecuador for Mexico, anticipating leaving Mexico and crossing the Pacific to Hawaii. Kotler, Jared. 1999. "Oceangoing Raft Crew Seeks to Prove Points." Associated Press. *Anchorage Daily News,* January 6, p. A6.

12. Heizer, Robert F. and William C. Massey. 1953. Aboriginal Navigation off the Coasts of Upper and Baja California. Pp. 289–311 in Anthropological Papers, No. 39. Bureau of American Ethnology. Bulletin

151. Washington, D.C.: Smithsonian Institution; Arnold, Jeanne E. 1995. Transportation Innovation and Social Complexity among Maritime Hunter-Gatherer Societies. *American Anthropologist* 97:733–747.

13. Dixon 1993.

14. Fladmark, K. R. 1979. Routes: Alternative Migration Corridors for Early Man in North America. *American Antiquity* 44:55–69; Fladmark, K. R. 1983. Times and Places: Environmental Correlates of Mid-to-Late Wisconsin Human Population Expansion in North America. Pp. 13–42 in *Early Man in the New World.* Richard Shutler, ed. Beverly Hills: Sage Publications.

15. Dillehay, Tom. 1997. *Monte Verde: A Late Pleistocene Settlement in Chile.* Washington, D.C.: Smithsonian Institution Press.

16. Meltzer, David J. 1997. Monte Verde and the Pleistocene People of the Americas. *Science* 276:754–755.

17. Dixon proposed that humans may not have just stayed put, sitting on their ocean-going skills for another 30,000 years after getting to Austronesia and before another eastward voyage. Rather, perhaps many events that occurred over that 30,000-year period led to periodic successful trips to South America, and northward. Dixon 1993:129.

18. Dixon further stated, "Advances will also require courage on the part of researchers who discover information that does not fit accepted scientific paradigms. These researchers must risk criticism and rejection from other scientists as they challenge accepted models and present alternative interpretations." Dixon 1993:132.

19. Collcutt, Martin, Marius Jansen, and Isao Kumakura. 1988. *Cultural Atlas of Japan.* New York: Facts on File. P. 16.

20. Imamura, Keiji. 1996. *Prehistoric Japan. New Perspectives on Insular East Asia.* Honolulu: University of Hawai'i Press.

21. Meggers, Betty J., Clifford Evans, and Emilio Estrada. 1965. *Early Formative Period of Coastal Ecuador; The Valdivia and Machalilla Phases. Smithsonian Contributions to Anthropology.* Vol. 1. Washington, D.C.: Smithsonian Institution; Estrada, Emilio and Betty J. Meggers. 1961. A Complex of Traits of Probable Transpacific Origin on the Coast of Ecuador. *American Anthropologist* 63:913–939; Meggers 1998.

22. J. Edward Kidder (1959), an archeologist and art historian, in *Japan before Buddhism.* New York: Frederick A. Praeger. P. 165.

23. Furuta, Ryoichi and Yoshikazu Hirai. 1967. *A Short History of Japanese Merchant Shipping.* Duncan Macfarlane, transl. and annot. Tokyo: Tokyo News Service. See also Collcutt et al. 1988:15–16.

24. Sansom, George. 1958. *A History of Japan to 1334.* Stanford: Stanford University Press. Pp. 137–138. Much more is known about Chinese junks, voyages, and ships than is available in translation on Japan-

ese ships. See Steiner, Stan. 1977. China's Ancient Mariners. *Natural History* 86(10):48–63; also, Chinese Academy of Sciences. 1983. *Ancient China's Technology and Science.* Institute of the History of Natural Sciences. China Knowledge Series. Beijing, China: Foreign Languages Press. In the chapter on shipbuilding (pp. 479–503), we learn that 200 to 300 types of Chinese wooden junks have been described in historical records. The best-known sea-going vessels in ancient China (dating first to the Warring States Period 475–221 B.C.) were the "sand ship," "bird ship," Fujian ship, and Guangdong ship.

Early in the 15th century, Zheng He made 7 voyages to the South Seas in 20 years, stopping at ports in more than 30 countries. On each voyage he took a fleet of 100 to 200 ships, of which from 40 to 60 were called "treasure ships." (The fleet carried over 17,000 men.) These ships were about 150 meters long from stem to stern, their rudder posts 11.07 meters long, each carrying 12 sails, the largest of the sand ships. Institute of the History of Natural Sciences 1983:486.

25. Sansom 1958:442–450. Estimates include 100,000 people and 3,500 boats on the second attack. Sansom 1958:450.

26. Hall, John Whitney. 1968 [1991]. *Japan from Prehistory to Modern Times.* Center for Japanese Studies. Ann Arbor: University of Michigan. The first invasion may have included 30,000 Mongols and Koreans; the second, reported 140,000 men. Hall 1968 [1991]:92–94.

27. When shipping on the Inland Sea was thriving in the 8th century, commerce was "afflicted by piracy." At the end of the Heian period, a Japanese named Tadamori made his name by "the suppression of the pirates and it was regarded as a great achievement." Furuta and Hirai 1967:17.

28. Hazard, Benjamin Harrison, Jr. 1967. Japanese Marauding in Medieval Korea: The *Wakō* Impact on Late Koryo. Ph.D. dissertation in history. University of California, Berkeley. P. 322.

29. Sansom 1958:168.

30. Hori, Kyotsu. 1967. The Mongol Invasions and the Kamakura Bakufu. Ph.D. dissertation in political science. Columbia University. P. 65.

31. Murray, Dian H. 1987. *Pirates of the South China Coast 1790–1810.* Stanford: Stanford University Press. Also, the skills of fishermen-turned-pirates for part of the year may have been modeled after the pirates of the South China seas who received support from an elite population on shore, cultivated political allies, and developed forms of patronage as a strategy for fishermen to make ends meet during lean months of the year.

32. Furuta and Hirai 1967:31.

33. Tsunoda, Ryusaku and L. Carrington Goodrich. 1951. *Japan in Chinese Dynastic Histories.* Perkins Asiatic Monograph No. 2. South Pasadena, Cal.: P.D. and Ione Perkins. Pp. 60–61.

34. Kakubayashi, Fumio. 1981 Japanese Drift Records and the Sharp Hypothesis. *Journal of Polynesian Society* 90:515–524. Further, in the 13th century, Korean sources report that a Japanese monk accompanied by a large party on a pilgrimage to China was blown off course and returned to Japan in 1263. Also in 1263, a Japanese merchant ship was wrecked off the Korean coast and the crew were assisted in their return to Japan. Hazard 1967.

35. Hazard 1967:61. Although no detailed description of the plank boats of Japan was found, a comparative analysis between the Chumash plank boats may reveal independent development of similar construction, or perhaps, an adaptation by the Chumash of boat making without iron brackets. The California coast plank boats were sewn together with deer sinew or milkweed fibers and caulked with a tar-pitch mixture. See Arnold 1995:737; Heizer and Massey 1953:300–303.

36. Nuttall, Zelia. 1906. *The Earliest Historical Relations between Mexico and Japan (from Original Documents Preserved in Spain and Japan).* University of California Publications in American Archaeology and Ethnology. Vol. 4, No. 1. Berkeley: University of California Press. Pp. 1–45. Although this reference is old, it is full of refreshing detail of a period little known in America, and as such remains a rare document in English. What happened to the baptized Japanese on the 1613 embassy to Mexico?

37. Culin, Stewart. 1920. Japanese Discovery of Alaska, "Kwankai-ibun", the Wonderful News of Circumnavigation. *Asia Monthly* 20:365–372, 436.

38. Brooks, Charles Wolcott. 1964. *Japanese Wrecks Stranded and Picked up Adrift in the North Pacific Ocean.* Fairfield, Wash.: Ye Galleon Press. (Originally printed in 1876 in *Proceedings of the California Academy of Sciences,* No. 6.)

39. A little figuring gives us the following numbers: 22,670 ships with an average of 10 on board equals perhaps a total of 226,700 Japanese involved in shipping in 1874, about 1 in 1,500 residents, not counting those on small fishing boats. Although this is just an estimate, it is indicative of an island nation with knowledge and investments involving the seas and trade.

40. Brooks 1964:8.

41. One unusual exception is reported in a 1991 book by Katherine Plummer, *A Japanese Glimpse at the Outside World 1839–1843. The Travels*

of Jirokichi in Hawaii, Siberia and Alaska. Adapted from a translation
of *Bandan.* Richard A. Pierce, ed. Alaska History No. 36. Fairbanks,
Alaska: Limestone Press. Jirokichi was one of 4 survivors of the *Cho-jamaru* found drifting off California in 1839. His story was told to
Koga Kinichiro in *Bandan* (Stories of Barbaric Places), which is, ac-cording to Plummer, the most valuable narrative among the Japan-ese "stories of sea-drifting" called *hyoryu monogatari.*

42. Quimby, George I. 1985. Japanese Wrecks, Iron Tools, and Prehis-toric Indians of the Northwest Coast. *Arctic Anthropology* 22(2):7–15.
P. 13. (One wonders if some of those iron blades ended up on Santa
Rosa Island found much later by R. Olson.)

43. Kakubayashi 1981.

44. The earliest books in Japanese refer to people who also arrived in
Japan from the south. For example in *Nihonshoki* (A.D. 720), 2 men
and 2 women arrived in 654; and in 657, 2 men and 4 women drifted
to Japan from a location south, perhaps Thailand.

45. Kakubayashi 1981:520.

46. Ekholm, G. F. 1953. A Possible Focus of Asiatic Influence in the Late
Classic Cultures of Mesoamerica. Memoirs of the Society for Amer-ican Archaeology, No. 9. 18:72–97. P. 88.

47. Hori 1967: 81–83.

CHAPTER 6

1. The goal of the Human Genome Project is to complete the mapping
by 2005. By 1997 about half of 70,000 to 100,000 genes had been
mapped, and about 2% of human genetic material had been se-quenced. Of 3 billion base pairs, only 60 million have been analyzed.
See especially, Rowen, Lee, Gregory Mahairas, and Leroy Hood. Se-quencing the Human Genome. *Science* 278:605–607 and the rest of
this *Science* issue on the human genome.

2. Tsuji, Tadashi. 1958. Incidence and Inheritance of the Carabelli's
Cusp in a Japanese Population. *Japanese Journal of Human Genetics*
3:21–31. P. 24.

3. Turner, Christy G., II. 1987. Late Pleistocene and Holocene Popula-tion History of East Asia Based on Dental Variation. *American Jour-nal of Physical Anthropology* 73:305–321. P. 313.

4. Sofaer, J. A., J. D. Niswander, C. J. MacLean, and P. L. Workman.
1972. Population Studies on Southwestern Indian Tribes. V. Tooth
Morphology as an Indicator of Biological Distance. *American Journal
of Physical Anthropology* 37:357–366.

5. Pinto-Cisternas, Juan and Hernan Figueroa. 1968. Genetic Structure of a Population of Valparaiso. II. Distribution of Two Dental Traits with Anthropological Importance. *American Journal of Physical Anthropology* 29:339–348.

6. Suzuki, Makoto and Takuro Sakai. 1964. Shovel-shaped Incisors among the Living Polynesians. *American Journal of Physical Anthropology* 22:65–72. P. 67.

7. Sofaer et al. 1972:363.

8. Sofaer et al. 1972:360.

9. Scott, G. Richard, Rosario H. Yap Potter, John F. Noss, Albert A. Dahlberg, and Thelma Dahlberg. 1983. The Dental Morphology of Pima Indians. *American Journal of Physical Anthropology* 61:13–31; Scott, G. R., S. Street, and A. A. Dahlberg. 1986. The Dental Variation of Yuman Speaking Groups in an American Southwest Context. Pp. 305–319 in *Teeth Revisited: Proceedings of the VIIth International Symposium on Dental Morphology*. Paris, 1986. D. E. Russell, J. Santoro, P. Sigogneau, and D. Russell eds. *Mémoires du Muséum National d'Histoire Naturelle, Paris* (série C)53:305–319.

10. Spuhler, James N. 1979. Genetic Distances, Trees, and Maps of North American Indians. Pp. 135–183 in *The First Americans: Origins, Affinities, and Adaptations*. W. S. Laughlin and A. B. Harper, eds. New York: Gustav Fischer.

11. Here is an example of one of Turner's basic assumptions: "Recall that all native Americans have to be descended from the limited number of North China hunting bands that drifted into severely restrictive late Pleistocene northeast Siberia." Turner 1987:311.

    He assumed, wrongly I believe, that all of the American Indians came across the Bering Strait. See Greenberg, Joseph H., Christy G. Turner, II, and Stephen L. Zegura. 1986. The Settlement of the Americas: A Comparison of the Linguistic, Dental, and Genetic Evidence. *Current Anthropology* 27:477–497. Also note the apparent reservations about dental analysis now held by Cavalli-Sforza, L. Luca, Paolo Menozzi, and Alberto Piazza. 1994. *The History and Geography of Human Genes*. Princeton, N.J.: Princeton University Press.

12. Turner 1987.

13. This trend appears to be part of an evolutionary response to domestication of our species. Heavy bones, thick crania, and large teeth have become less necessary since the agricultural revolution.

14. Turner, Christy G., II. 1985. Expression Count: A Method for Calculating Morphological Dental Trait Frequencies by Using Adjustable Weighting Coefficients with Standard Ranked Scales. *American Journal of Physical Anthropology* 68:263–267.

15. Roberts, Frank H. H., Jr. 1932. *The Village of the Great Kivas on the*

Zuni Reservation, New Mexico. Bureau of American Ethnology Bulletin 111. Washington, D.C.: U.S. Government Printing Office; Seltzer, Carl. 1944. *Racial Prehistory in the Southwest and the Hawikuh Zunis.* Papers of the Peabody Museum of American Archaeology and Ethnology, Harvard University. 23(1). Cambridge, Mass.

16. In comparing pit-dwelling people with the later pueblo remains, Roberts reported, "The skeletal remains show striking contrasts. . . . The long heads represent Basket Maker survivals, the broad heads Pueblo infiltration." Roberts, Frank H. H., Jr. 1931. *The Ruins at Kiatuthlanna Eastern Arizona.* Smithsonian Institution. Bureau of American Ethnology Bulletin 100. Washington, D.C.: U.S. Government Printing Office. P. 174.

17. Seltzer 1944:9, 32–33. Seltzer further compared the Old Zuni Hawikuh measurements on 17 features and 8 indices with those reported on 174 Pecos crania, and also with other populations in the Southwest. Most surprising was his finding that the 11 crania of the Bonito-Chaco Canyon group showed "virtual identity with the Old Zuni in ten out of twelve measurements and four out of six indices," which he found indicative of a fundamental physical relationship between them. Seltzer 1944:17.

18. Imamura, Keiji. 1996. *Prehistoric Japan. New Perspectives on Insular East Asia.* Honolulu: University of Hawai'i Press. Seltzer 1944:25, 33.

19. Szathmary, Emoke J. E. 1993. Genetics of Aboriginal North Americans. *Evolutionary Anthropology* 1:202–220. This article makes a strong case for considering many different kinds of biological data.

20. Of course, dead ends in our hominid past happened too, and some isolated populations became extinct. For example, modern humans probably do not manifest many full-blown Neanderthal genes. Earlier pockets of that branch of hominids merged or were displaced by Cro-Magnon, a wholly modern species, by 50,000 years ago, leaving the more remote and specialized classic Neanderthals to meander about in ultimate sexual isolation and demise. Or, so goes one side of the continuing debate of the fate of Neanderthal.

   Some populations that arrived to North America may have met a similar fate.

21. Newman, Marshall T. 1962. Evolutionary Changes in Body Size and Head Form in American Indians. *American Anthropologist* 64:237–257. P. 253.

22. Spuhler 1979.

23. Ushijima, Yoichi. 1954. The Human Skeletal Remains from the Mitsu Site, Saga Prefecture, a Site Associated with the 'Yayoishiki' Period of Prehistoric Japan. *Quarterly Journal of Anthropology* 1(3-4):273–303.

24. Rogers, Spencer L. 1963. *The Physical Characteristics of the Aboriginal*

La Jollan Population of Southern California. San Diego Museum Papers. No. 4. San Diego: Museum of Man.

25. Perhaps there were many occasions for Japanese, Polynesian, Chinese, and Korean admixture with North American Indians over the long prehistory of North America. Surely the example of admixture I am proposing between Japanese and a population that became the Zuni is not the only occasion of biological merger of different populations. If there was Japanese admixture at Hawikuh relatively late in North American prehistory, then perhaps there was earlier, perhaps much earlier, mixture along the Pacific coast. Perhaps the skeletons recovered from the Anasazi sites also should be reconsidered and compared with Japanese, Chinese, and Tibetan skeletal remains, and contemporary physical characteristics.

26. Relatively little information is available about the physical anthropology of any prehistoric people in southern California.

27. Garn, Stanley M. 1961 (1969 ed.). *Human Races.* Springfield, Ill.: Charles C. Thomas. P. 40.

28. Watanabe, S., S. Kondo, and E. Matsunagi, eds. 1975. *Anthropological and Genetic Studies on the Japanese. Human Adaptability.* Vol. 2. Japanese Committee for the International Biological Program. Tokyo: University of Tokyo Press. Pp. 77–85.

29. Brown, K. S., B. L. Hanna, A. A. Dahlberg, and H. H. Strandskov. 1958. The Distribution of Blood Group Alleles among Indians of Southwest North America. *American Journal of Human Genetics* 10:175–195. P. 177.

30. Workman, P. L., J. D. Niswander, K. S. Brown, and W. C. Leyshon. 1974. Population Studies on Southwestern Indian Tribes. IV. The Zuni. *American Journal of Physical Anthropology* 41:119–132.

31. Workman et al. 1974:126.

32. *The most striking observation . . . is the high frequency of type B in the ABO system. . . . In order to test for stratification with respect to the B gene the frequencies of genes at other loci were determined for individuals with type O and type B. The more recent the intermixture, the more likely type B individuals would have gene frequencies closer to Caucasian values, assuming B to be derived from Caucasian gene flow. No differences were found among B and O individuals and we must conclude that if B came in by gene flow, it is of quite distant origin. Workman et al. 1974:126.*

33. Also, the incidence of the red cell acid phosphatase allele (pA and pB) is nearly identical. The gene frequency of pA is 0.199 in one

Japanese study and 0.208 in Zuni. The numbers and percentages are as follows:

		n = 612*				n = 660	
Japan	A	26	4.2%	Zuni	A	32	4.8%
	BA	192	31.4%		BA	210	31.8%
	B	394	64.4%		B	418	63.3%

*The Japanese sample is one of 26 studies on Japanese populations listed on Table 3.1-1 entitled "Red cell acid phosphatase types in Japan." Watanabe, Kondo, and Matsunagi 1975:110–111. This study was based on a Tokyo sample similar in size to the Zuni sample. Neither population has the phenotype involving C. The Zuni data are from Workman et al. 1974:124.

34. Hoy, Wendy E., Donald M. Megill, and Michael D. Hughson. 1987. Epidemic Renal Diseases of Unknown Etiology in the Zuni Indians. *American Journal of Kidney Diseases* 9:485–496; Hughson, Michael D., Don M. Megill, Suzanne M. Smith, Kenneth S. K. Tung, Gerald Miller, and Wendy E. Hoy. 1989. Mesangiopathic Glomerulonephritis in Zuni (New Mexico) Indians. *Archives Pathological Laboratory Medicine* 113:148–157.

35. Hoy et al. 1987:494.

36. Troup, G. M., R. L. Harvey, R. L. Walford, G. S. Smith, and P. Sturgeon. 1973. Analysis of the HL-A, Erythrocyte and Gamma Globulin Antigen Systems in the Zuni Indians of New Mexico. Pp. 339–344 in *Histocompatibility Testing 1972.* J. Dausset and J. Colombani, eds.

37. Watkins, David I., Stephen N. McAdam, Xiaomin Liu, Clarice R. Strang, Edgar L. Milford, Cindy G. Levine, Theodore L. Garber, Alex L. Dogon, Carol I. Lord, Steven H. Ghim, Gary M. Troup, Austin L. Hughes, and Norman L. Letvin. 1992. New Recombinant HLA-B Alleles in a Tribe of South American Amerindians Indicate Rapid Evolution of MHC Class I Loci. *Nature* 357:329–333.

38. Belich, Mônica P., J. Alejandro Madrigal, William H. Hildebrand, Jacqueline Zemmour, Robert C. Williams, Roberto Luz, Maria Luiza Petzl-Erler, and Peter Parham. 1992. Unusual HLA-B Alleles in Two Tribes of Brazilian Indians. *Nature* 357:326–329.

CHAPTER 7

1. For a sense of the debate and the controversy, see Ross, Philip E. 1991. Trends in Linguistics. Hard Words. *Scientific American.*

264(4):138–147; Greenberg, Joseph H. 1990. The American Indian Language Controversy. *Review of Archaeology* 11(2):5–14; Goddard, Ives. 1987. Comments on book review of *Language in the Americas.* *Current Anthropology* 28:656–657.

2. Zunian uses more prefixes than does modern Japanese, which has lost most of its former prefix morphemes, originally derived from an early foundation in the large language family called Austronesian.

3. Swadesh, Morris. 1952b. Lexico-statistic Dating of Prehistoric Ethnic Contacts; With Special Reference to North American Indians and Eskimos. *Proceedings of the American Philosophical Society* 96:452–463.

4. For a critique of the lexicostatic method, see Hymes, Dell H. 1960. Lexicostatistics So Far. *Current Anthropology* 1(1):3–34, 41–44.

5. Swadesh, Morris. 1966. Personal communication. February 20.

   In a second letter, dated March 18, 1966, Swadesh invited me to study with him at Edmonton that summer. However, I was by then married, had one child, and was active in my university teaching career in Anchorage.

6. Nichols, Johanna. 1992. *Linguistic Diversity in Space and Time.* Chicago: University of Chicago Press; Nichols, Johanna. 1994. Language at 40,000 BC. Paper presented at the American Association for the Advancement of Science annual meeting, San Francisco, February 21.

7. Jacobsen, William H., Jr. 1989. The Pacific Orientation of Western North American Languages. Paper presented at the Circum-Pacific Prehistory Conference, Seattle, Washington.

8. Powell, John Wesley. 1891. Indian Linguistic Families of America North of Mexico. Pp. 1–142 in *7th Annual Report of the Bureau of American Ethnology for the Years 1885–1886.* Washington, D.C.: U.S. Government Printing Office; Sapir, Edward. 1929. Central and North American Indian Languages. Pp. 138–141 in *Encyclopedia Britannica.* Vol. 5. 14th ed. New York: Encyclopedia Britannica Company. (Reprinted in 1949 in pp. 169–178 in *Selected Writings of Edward Sapir in Language, Culture, and Personality.* David G. Mandelbaum, ed. Berkeley: University of California Press.)

9. Newman, Stanley S. 1964. Comparison of Zuni and California Penutian. *International Journal of American Linguistics* 30:1–13; Hale, Kenneth and David Harris. 1979. Historical Linguistics and Archeology. Pp. 170–177 in *Handbook of North American Indians.* Vol. 9, *Southwest.* A. Ortiz, vol. ed. W. C. Sturtevant, general ed. Washington, D.C.: Smithsonian Institution. P. 173.

10. Like Fladmark (1979, 1983), who addressed the archeological evidence of possible north-to-south migrations, neither Nichols nor Jacobsen considered south-to-north possibilities, nor was the whole

issue of ocean navigation discussed. Somehow island hopping across the central North Pacific seems to be more palatable to both linguists and archeologists who share a growing and recent interest in coastal mobility of prehistoric peoples in North America. These advocates of "multiple coastal colonization" noted the clustering of languages, and specific language features linking the Pacific Rim area. Fladmark, K. R. 1979. Routes: Alternative Migration Corridors for Early Man in North America. *American Antiquity* 44:55–69; Fladmark, K. R. 1983. Times and Places: Environmental Correlates of Mid-to-Late Wisconsin Human Population Expansion in North America. Pp. 13–42 in *Early Man in the New World*. Richard Shutler, ed. Beverly Hills: Sage Publications.

Nichols, like James Dixon, envisioned the possibility of a population in the Americas by 35,000 years ago, or earlier. Dixon, E. James. 1993. *Quest for the Origins of the First Americans*. Albuquerque: University of New Mexico Press.

11. Renfrew encouraged a new synthesis of modern linguistics and archeology that share an emphasis on scientific procedures. Of course he was addressing Indo-European languages and archeology, which are better known and documented than what is available in North America. But still, he provided inspiration and a model for what might also be applied to the Pacific Rim. Renfrew, Colin. 1987. *Archaeology and Language. The Puzzle of Indo-European Origins*. London: Jonathan Cape.

12. Torroni, Antonio, Theodore G. Schurr, Margaret F. Cabell, Michael D. Brown, James V. Neel, Merethe Larsen, David G. Smith, Carlos M. Vullo, and Douglas C. Wallace. 1993. Asian Affinities and Continental Radiation of the Four Founding Native American mtDNAs. *American Journal of Human Genetics* 53:563–590.

13. A *cognate* is a word that is genetically related to another in a shared protolanguage. In this study it is not always clear what words may be cognate and what words may be loan words, borrowed after the initial separation. This technicality I cannot resolve. Perhaps others can.

14. Ringe, Donald A., Jr. 1992. On Calculating the Factor of Chance in Language Comparison. *Transactions of the American Philosophical Society* 82:1–110.

15. This was a problem I had with Greenberg's and Newman's work with Penutian. In my Zunian-Japanese analysis, I deal only with words with exact meanings, not approximate ones. Yet some linguists seem to give themselves considerable liberty to fish around for similar categories of words. Greenberg, Joseph H. 1971. Unpublished note-

books. Vol. 8. Penutian. Stanford University Library; Greenberg 1990; Newman 1964:1–13.

16. Specific references on the status of Zunian include Sapir 1929: 171; Greenberg, Joseph H. 1953. Historical Linguistics and Unwritten Languages. Pp. 265–286 in *Anthropology Today. An Encyclopedic Inventory.* A. L. Kroeber, chair. Chicago: University of Chicago Press. P. 282; Ramer, Alexis Manaster. 1996. Tonkawa and Zuni: Two Test Cases for the Greenberg Classification. *International Journal of American Linguistics* 62:264–288; Newman, Stanley. 1954b. American Indian Linguistics in the Southwest. *American Anthropologist* 56:626–634. P. 630; Newman 1964; Hale and Harris 1979: 173; Woodbury, Richard B. 1979. Zuni Prehistory and History to 1850. Pp. 467–473 in *Handbook of North American Indians.* Vol. 9, *Southwest.* P. 468; Greenberg, Joseph H. 1987. *Language in the Americas.* Stanford: Stanford University Press. Pp. 144, 380; and Ruhlen, Merritt. 1987. *A Guide to the World's Languages.* Vol. 1, *Classification.* Stanford: Stanford University Press.

17. Sapir 1929: 171.

18. Whorf, Benjamin and George L. Trager. 1937. The Relationship of Uto-Aztecan and Tanoan. *American Anthropologist* 39:609–624. P. 609.

19. Greenberg 1953: 283.

20. Trager, George L. and Felicia E. Harben. 1958. North American Indian Languages. Classification and Maps. Studies in Linguistics, Occasional Papers 5. Buffalo, N.Y.

21. Newman 1964.

22. Greenberg 1987:144, 380.

23. Woodbury 1979:468.

24. Charles F. Hockett, Professor Emeritus of Cornell University, an established scholar of human languages, advised me to drop attempts to find genetic relationships and focus instead on the possibility of loan words. Personal communication. June 17, 1987.

25. Hattori, Shiro. 1948. The Relationship of Japanese to Ryukyu, Korean, and Altaic Languages. *Transactions of the Asiatic Society.* Third Series. 1:101–133; Shibatani, Masayoshi. 1990. *The Languages of Japan.* (Cambridge Language Surveys.) Cambridge: Cambridge University Press. Pp. 94–118.

26. Shibatani 1990:94.

27. Matisoff, James A. 1990. Discussion Note. On megalocomparison. *Language* 66:106–120. Pp. 114–115.

28. Shibatani's chapter on dialects, 1990:185–214.

29. Johanna Nichols noted this as a general characteristic of the Pacific Rim. Nichols 1992.

30. Miller, Roy Andrew. 1967. *The Japanese Language.* Chicago: University of Chicago Press; Miller, Roy Andrew. 1971. *Japanese and the Other Altaic Languages.* Chicago: University of Chicago Press; Miller, Roy Andrew. 1980. *Origins of the Japanese Language. Lectures in Japan during the Academic Year 1977–78.* Seattle: University of Washington Press.

31. One of the Austronesian prefixes that continues to be expressed in modern Japanese is /ma-/ which means "very" or "really," a morpheme providing emphasis.

32. Shibatani 1990:117.

33. Unlike biochemical research, which is thriving in the 1990s, comparative linguistics appears in need of new energy devoted to something other than the "bickering" noted by Shibatani 1990:118; Matisoff 1990; and Cavalli-Sforza, L. Luca, Paolo Menozzi, and Alberto Piazza. 1994. *The History and Geography of Human Genes.* Princeton, N.J.: Princeton University Press.

34. Newman, Stanley. 1958. Zuni Dictionary. *International Journal of American Linguistics* 24(1): Part II.

35. Bunzel, R. L. 1935. Zuni. Pp. 385–515 in *Handbook of American Indian Languages,* Part 4. New York: J. J. Austin.

36. Bunzel, R. L. 1933. *Zuni Texts.* American Ethnological Society Publication 15:1–285.

37. Stevenson, Matilda (Coxe). 1904. The Zuni Indians: Their Mythology, Esoteric Fraternities, and Ceremonies. Pp. 3–634 in *23rd Annual Report of the Bureau of American Ethnology for the Years 1901–1902.* Washington, D.C.: U.S. Government Printing Office.

38. Cushing, Frank H. 1882. Zuni Social, Mythic and Religious Systems. *Popular Science Monthly* 21 (June): 186–192; Cushing, Frank H. 1896. Outlines of Zuni Creation Myths. Pp. 321–447 in *13th Annual Report of the Bureau of American Ethnology for the Years 1891–1892.* Washington, D.C.: U.S. Government Printing Office; Cushing, Frank H. 1920. *Zuni Breadstuff.* Indian Notes and Monographs 8. New York: *Museum of the American Indian, Heye Foundation.*

39. Hepburn, James Curtis. 1903. *A Japanese-English, English-Japanese Dictionary,* abridged. 2nd ed. Tokyo: Z.P. Maruya. London: Truber.

40. For example, less than 20 years after Ruth Bunzel's work, Stanley Newman stated that her phonemic analysis does not "differ radically" from his but he added, "I must admit that I have found Bunzel's transcribed material highly unreliable." Newman 1954:63.

41. Later, Newman wrote an article on the religious and slang usages, introduced later in Chapters 8 and 9. Newman, Stanley. 1955. Vocabulary Levels: Zuni Sacred and Slang Usage. *Southwestern Journal of Anthropology* 11:345–354.

42. Of about 209 Native languages spoken in North America in 1995, only 46 were spoken by a significant number of children. One of them was Zuni. See "Table 2. Status of the Native Languages of North America in 1995" in Goddard, Ives. Introduction. 1996a. Pp. 1–16 in *Handbook of North American Indians.* Vol. 17, *Languages.* I. Goddard, vol. ed. W. C. Sturtevant, general ed. Washington, D.C.: Smithsonian Institution. P. 3.

43. Zengel, Majorie Smith. 1962. Literacy as a Factor in Language Change. *American Anthropologist* 64:132–139.

44. According to Newman (1958:1), each of these vowels in Zunian has an equivalent long sound. According to Bunzel (1935:436), the duration of a vowel is determined by syllabic stress; that is, there are 2 kinds of syllables, strong and weak, and the weak syllables end in short vowels.

45. One Japanese dictionary lists 2 dipthongs, /ai/ and /au/. Bunzel (1935:357) includes the same 2, but Newman does not list either. Newman, Stanley. 1965. *Zuni Grammar.* University of New Mexico Publications in Anthropology. No. 14. Albuquerque: University of New Mexico Press. P. 13; Newman 1958:1.

    For a detailed discussion of Japanese phonetics, consult Shibatani 1990:158–184. There are many dialect differences within the language.

46. Bunzel 1935:432. As further demonstration of the difficulties of different orthographies at various times, one Japanese dictionary (Hepburn 1903) lists /ng/ as a separate sound. Newman did not include /ng/, but Bunzel (1935:433) noted that /n/ sometimes becomes /ng/ before k. Newman, Stanley. 1996. Sketch of the Zuni Language. Pp. 483–506 in *Handbook of North American Indians.* Vol. 17, *Languages.* P. 485; Newman 1958:1.

47. Sansom, George. 1928. *An Historical Grammar of Japanese.* Oxford: Clarendon Press. P. 500; Shibatani 1990:167.

48. Shibatani 1990:161–162; Newman 1958: 1; 1996:485.

    Certain phonemes occur in some positions, and not in others. For example, the sound /p/ and the sound /r/ rarely occur in the initial position, that is, at the beginning of a word. Overall the /p/ is rarely used, and a documented shift of the sound first to /h/, then to /w/ is reported (Shibatani 1990:167). This may have also occurred in Zunian.

49. For a discussion of the lack of attention given to the study of loan words in Native American languages, consult Callaghan, Catherine A. and Geoffrey Gamble. 1996. Borrowing. Pp. 111–116 in *Handbook of North American Indians.* Vol. 17, *Languages.*

50. Sansom 1928:315; Bunzel 1935:439.
51. Bunzel 1935:440.
52. These words are especially relevant to the migration story.
53. Adjective: cold
54. Sansom 1928:86.
55. Bunzel 1935:455.
56. Sansom 1928:191.
57. Bunzel 1935:513.
58. Bloomfield, Leonard. 1933. *Language.* New York: Holt, Rinehart and Winston. P. 116; Hattori 1948:120; Bunzel 1935:438; Newman 1958:1.

    The languages sound alike even to a novice. Several Public Health Service personnel who had lived in Japan commented to me that they were startled when they first arrived in Zuni. The language "sounds" like Japanese to them.
59. Bunzel 1935:430; Miller, Laura. 1989. The Japanese Language and Honorific Speech: Is There a Nihongo without Keigo? *Penn Linguistics Review* 13:38–46; Miller, Laura. 1994. The Discourse of Japanese Workers and Folklinguistic Theories of Honorifics. Presented at a meeting of the American Anthropological Association. Shibatani 1990:371–380.

CHAPTER 8

1. A rare and insightful discussion of social merger is found in Owen, Roger C. 1965. The Patrilocal Band: A Linguistically and Culturally Hybrid Social Unit. *American Anthropologist* 67:675–791.
2. This subfield was developed by some key British anthropologists who were especially influential at the University of Chicago: for example, R. H. Radcliffe-Brown, Raymond Firth, Bronislaw Malinowski; the next generation, Fred Eggan; and the next, David Schneider.
3. The complexities of kinship terminology in many small-scale societies include crafted reciprocity mechanisms that often are associated with each category of kin.
4. This term refers to the social requirement to marry outside one's own clan.
5. Ladd, Edmund. 1979a. Zuni Social and Political Organization. Pp. 482–491 in *Handbook of North American Indians.* Vol. 9, *Southwest.* A. Ortiz, vol. ed. W. C. Sturtevant, general ed. Washington, D.C.: Smithsonian Institution.
6. Ladd 1979:483.
7. Schneider, David M. and John M. Roberts. 1956. *Zuni Kin Terms.* Uni-

versity of Nebraska, Laboratory of Anthropology Notebook 3. Lincoln: University of Nebraska. (Reprinted by Human Relations Area Files Press, New Haven, Conn.)

8. Lowie, Robert H. 1935. *The Crow Indians.* New York: Rinehart.

9. Schneider and Roberts 1956:15.

10. Zunie, Willard. 1999. Personal communication, May 5.

11. This word has changed recently to mean more "old hag" or "my old lady," and is good for a chuckle. Stanley Newman referred to the word *okacciki* meaning "the old lady, the old woman" in his discussion of slang words. Newman, Stanley. 1955. Vocabulary Levels: Zuni Sacred and Slang Usage. *Southwestern Journal of Anthropology* 11:345–354. P. 352.

12. Sansom, George. 1928. *An Historical Grammar of Japanese.* Oxford: Clarendon Press.

13. Eggan, Fred. 1950. *Social Organization of the Western Pueblos.* Chicago: University of Chicago Press. P. 187.

14. Ladd 1979:485.

15. Bennett, John W., Herbert Passin, and Robert K. McKnight. 1958. *In Search of Identity. The Japanese Overseas Scholar in America and Japan.* Minneapolis: University of Minnesota Press. P. 229.

16. Watts also reported the conservative nature of the kinship groups, noting great continuity of clans and names over time. For example, of 16 clans identified by Cushing over a hundred years ago, she found 14 still exist. Of the 22 kinship terms reported by Kroeber in 1916, 16 continue in active use. Watts, Linda K. 1988. Relational Terminology and Household-Group Role Structure at Zuni. Paper read at the 87th annual meeting of the American Anthropological Association, November 19; Kroeber, Alfred L. 1916b. The Speech of a Zuni Child. *American Anthropologist* 18:529–534.

17. Anthropologist Alfred Kroeber visited the Pueblo of Zuni in 1916 and wrote an article based on his observations of the speech of a Zuni child, Robert Lewis, who later became the governor of the pueblo for 4 terms. By the age of 2, young Robert recognized the significance of certain age categories, and used them appropriately. Kroeber 1916:531.

18. Ladd 1979a:484.

19. Laura Miller wrote an insightful article about *keigo,* a system in Japanese honorific speech patterns so highly valued that many books are written to help persons learn the appropriate words for special situations. This elite aspect of the language is not learned by all Japanese, but mastery of its subtleties is deemed necessary for success. Miller, Laura. 1989. The Japanese Language and Honorific

Speech: Is There a Nihongo without Keigo? *Penn Linguistics Review* 13:38–46.

20. Bunzel 1935:438; Newman 1955:346; Kroskrity, Paul V. 1983. On Male and Female Speech in the Pueblo Southwest. *International Journal of American Linguistics* 49:88–91.

21. Shibatani, in a section on separate men's and women's speech, discussed how that separation is especially marked in first person pronominal forms. Politeness in women's speech includes honorifics, speech levels, and different verbal endings. A system of polite forms is learned after childhood, and has to be taught. Shibatani. 1990:371–374; 379–380. In Japanese there is a well-known avoidance of direct confrontation, which is part of the social politeness. This leads to ambiguous expressions.

22. Tannen, Deborah. 1990. *You Just Don't Understand: Women and Men in Conversation.* New York: Morrow.

23. If the Japanese-speaking pilgrims on their way to the middle place encountered and adopted Penutian-speaking California people, primarily women, and if the Penutian language was linked to Japanese in the ancient past, perhaps this explains why the Zuni language has not been identified as related to any other Native American language. The other Penutian-related languages continued to change away from the protolanguage, but Japanese and Zuni were relinked, and perhaps recharged with similarities through an intensive first-hand contact in the 13th century.

24. Tsunoda, Ryusaku, William Theodore de Bary, and Donald Keene, comp. 1958. *Sources of the Japanese Tradition.* New York: Columbia University Press. Pp. 20–22. For other versions, see Ohnuki-Tierney, Emiko. 1993. *Rice as Self. Japanese Identities through Time.* Princeton, N.J.: Princeton University Press. P. 52.

   Another example of Japanese twins refers to Izanagi and Izanami, paired male and female deities, who figure importantly in the creation stories. A comparative analysis of twins in myth remains for others to explore; the dichotomy of the mountain and sea, and the theme of the elder and the younger brother also need analysis.

25. Kitigawa, Joseph M. 1987. *On Understanding Japanese Religion.* Princeton, N.J.: Princeton University Press. Pp. 20, 37, 71, 101.

26. Hurst, G. Cameron, III. 1988 (1974). The Structure of the Heian Court: Some Thoughts on the Nature of "Familial Authority" in Heian Japan. Pp. 39–59 in *Medieval Japan. Essays in Institutional History.* John W. Hall and Jeffrey P. Mass, eds. Stanford: Stanford University Press.

27. Hurst 1988 (1974):43–45.

    In the early Nara period (710–793), the Fujiwara clan split into four lineages: northern, southern, ceremonial, and capital branches. After the Nara period, only the northern branch continued to be important politically. In fact, that northern branch came to dominate all other kinship groups in Heian political society, through maternal connection. The efforts to make Japan more like China simply did not work, partly because the *uji*—the "clans"—provided Japan with a special local sieve that allowed a distinctive Japanese character to persist even with things introduced from China.

    In a footnote, Hurst lists the *uji* that maintained a measure of clan unity during the Nara and Heian periods: O, Minamoto, Fujiwara, Tomo, Takashina, Tachibana, Nakatomi, Imibe, Urabe, Koshiji, Sugawara, and Wake (note the CV patterns here). Although the *uji* continued during the Heian period, the main functional unit during that time was the household, and some were powerful.

28. See Chapter 7 for the Chinese origin of /kwe/, meaning "society."

29. De Visser, M. W. 1908. The Fox and Badger in Japanese Folklore. *Transactions of the Asiatic Society of Japan* 36(3); Chamberlain. 1932. *Ko-ji-ki Records of Ancient Matters.* Pp. xliii, xliv.

30. However, this does not explain the additional infixed phonemes in Zuni: /o/ and /w/, as in *showita. (Shita* without /ow/ clearly sounds more like the Japanese *shika.)* Four alternative explanations might be considered: (1) The /ow/ used to be in the Japanese word for "deer," and was dropped; (2) the /ow/ was later added in the Zuni language (less likely); (3) the two words share a protoform and changed in different directions, Zuni keeping the protoform including the /ow/ and modern Japanese dropping it; and finally, (4) perhaps these words for "deer" were never related, and this is simply an accidental sequence of very similar phonemes linked together in a very similar sequence for a word that means the same thing: deer.

31. What about the other Zuni clan names? Are they derived from other tribes speaking other languages who joined en route? Or are they names derived from ancient Japanese words yet to be found and analyzed?

32. Yamamoto, Yoshiko. 1978. *Namahage. A Festival in the Northeast of Japan.* Philadelphia: Institute for the Study of Human Issues.

33. Wright, Barton. 1985. *Kachinas of the Zuni.* Flagstaff, Ariz.: Northland Press. Pp. 27–28. References to Zuni monster kachinas also appear in Roediger, Virginia More. 1941 (1991). *Ceremonial Costumes of the Pueblo Indians. Their Evolution, Fabrication, and Significance in the Prayer Drama.* Berkeley: University of California Press; Bunzel, Ruth

L. 1932a (1984). Zuni Katcinas. An Analytical Study. Pp. 837–1108 in *47th Annual Report of the Bureau of American Ethnology for the Years 1929–1930.* Gloreita, N.M.: Rio Grande Press. Pp. 936–941; Fewkes, Jesse Walter. 1990a (1903). *Hopi Katcinas.* New York: Dover Publications.

The Hopi kachinas are similar to the Zuni ones *(kokkos),* but the Hopi seem to have more of them, and more names associated with the monsters that are called on to frighten and whip the children. Fewkes (1990a) identified a whole series of fierce kachinas including Tunwup (Plate VII), who has a white mask with black, prominent eyes, and two horns. Tunwup's Uncle (taamu) also has two horns, great goggle-eyes, and carries whips (Plate VIII).

Soyoko are other Hopi monsters, also called Natackas, that appear at Powamu. The Kumbi Natacka (Plate IX) has a black mask with goggle eyes and two horns, with black locks of hair. A whole series of Natackas go on begging trips, too. Awatpbo Soyok (Plate XII) has a protuberant snout, goggle eyes, and hair hanging down over his face. On his back hangs a basket containing a child whom he has captured. Fewkes 1990a:74.

34. There used to be a peach orchard near Matsaki, one of the original 6 villages, now in ruins, about 2 miles from the present-day Pueblo of Zuni. Matsaki is a common place name in Japan, referring to pine trees, which also figure importantly in Buddhism.

35. This small motif is embedded in the larger questions of similarities and functions of masked impersonators of deities. Are the similarities best explained as the result of the psychic unity of humankind? Or might they be better explained as a borrowing of ideas? Could all the commonalities be the consequence of a simple convergence of ideas, masks, rituals, and social functions in two separate areas of the world?

If a society is going to mask the ancestors and frighten children into proper behavior, there may be a limited number of ways to do this. But how many do it in this way and in this exact sequence?

36. This raises the question, Are the Zuni (and other Pueblo) elaborate kachina regalia and ceremonies Native American versions of formerly widespread customs in Japan? Are records available about other deities in Japan that have been "lost," or perhaps incorporated in traditional dramas? What might a comparison of Noh masks with Zuni and other Pueblo masks reveal?

What about the masking traditions of Austronesia? Yamamoto (1978:22–23) noted Masao Oka suggested that the masking of the strangers *(ijin)* may be a Melanesian custom that came to Japan with the Austronesia language before the Yayoi influences. Might the Namahage monsters of Japan be remnants of old Japanese Shinto *kami?* Are Japanese *kojin* related to Hopi and Zuni kachina? Do they possibly share origins in Southeast Asia? And with Melanesian and Polynesian masks?

37. For numerous references to the assumed Spanish introduction of, specifically, peaches, see *Handbook of North American Indians.* Vol. 9, *Southwest.* Pp. 458 (Acoma), 472 (Zuni), 594 (Hopi), 303 (Santa Clara), and 403 (Santa Ana). No Spanish references to specific introduction times and places are provided.

38. Parsons, Elsie (Clews). 1939. *Pueblo Indian Religion.* Vol. II. Chicago: University of Chicago Press. P. 862.

39. Stevenson 1904:354.

40. Ferguson, T. J. 1996. *Historic Zuni Architecture and Society. An Archaeological Application of Space Syntax.* Anthropological Papers of the University of Arizona. No. 60. Tucson: University of Arizona Press. Pp. 31, 35, 37, 62.

41. Ferguson 1996:62.

CHAPTER 9

1. For a sense of the time depth, diversity of sources of religious concepts, and perspective on the unique combination of ideas that were incorporated into Japanese religions, see Hori, Ichiro. 1968. *Folk Religion in Japan. Continuity and Change.* Joseph M. Kitagawa and Alan L. Miller, eds. Chicago: University of Chicago Press.

2. Ortiz, Alfonso. 1979. Introduction. Pp. 1–4 in *Handbook of North American Indians.* Vol. 9, *Southwest.* A. Ortiz, vol. ed. W. C. Sturtevant, general ed. Washington, D.C.: Smithsonian Institution. P. 1.

3. Kitagawa, Joseph M. 1966 *Religion in Japanese History.* New York: Columbia University Press. Pp. 13–14.

4. Parsons, Elsie (Clews). 1939. *Pueblo Indian Religion.* Chicago: University of Chicago Press; Ishaikawa, Michiji. 1936. The Japanese Concept of Man. *Cultural Nippon* 5:317–328. Tokyo: Nippon Bunka Renmei. P. 319; Tsunoda, Ryusaku, William Theodore de Bary, and Donald Keene. 1958. *Sources of the Japanese Tradition.* New York: Columbia University Press; Buchanan, D. C. 1935. *Inari: Its Origin, Development and Nature.* Asiatic Society of Japan. London: Kegan Paul, Trench, Trubner; Kato, Genchi. 1924. A Study of the Development of Religious Ideas among the Japanese People as Illustrated by Japanese Phallicism. *Transactions of the Asiatic Society of Japan.* Second series. 1(Suppl.).

5. A Japanese word for a special New Year's rice cake boiled with veg-

etables is *zoni*. A comparison of the spiritual meaning of rice to Japanese and the spiritual meaning of corn to Zuni may provide additional information concerning the major staple in each society.

6. See Brandon, Reiko Mochinaga and Barbara B. Stephan. 1994. *Spirit and Symbol. The Japanese New Year*. Honolulu: Honolulu Academy of Arts in association with University of Hawaii Press; Wright, Barton. 1985. *Kachinas of the Zuni*. Flagstaff, Ariz.: Northland Press. Pp. 13–49; Stevenson, Matilda (Coxe). 1904. The Zuni Indians: Their Mythology, Esoteric Fraternities, and Ceremonies. Pp. 3–634 in *23rd Annual Report of the Bureau of American Ethnology for the Years 1901–1902*. Washington, D.C.: U.S. Government Printing Office. Pp. 227–283.

7. The Hopi word *kachina* connotes the generalized Pueblo Indian concept of "masked spirit or supernatural being," and it is associated with ancestor worship. Adams, E. Charles. 1991. *The Origin and Development of the Pueblo Katsina Cult*. Tucson: University of Arizona Press. P. 12.

   The Hopi language is linked to a large language phylum in North America called Hokan-Siouan. No attempt is made here to link other Hopi religious words or concepts to Japanese, but that certainly presents a possible research topic for someone else.

8. Eggan, Fred. 1950. *Social Organization of the Western Pueblos*. Chicago: University of Chicago Press. P. 212.

9. As noted in the last chapter, *-kwe* is a Zuni suffix that is added onto other words to connote clan, society, or fraternity. In Japanese, the word *be* is referred to as a kind of early clan or guild affiliation. The Chinese word *kwai*, which the Japanese also use, and the Japanese stem *be* are close in sound and meaning to the Zuni sound and meaning of *kwe*. All three words *(kwai, be,* and *kwe)* refer to a group of socially linked persons.

10. Stevenson 1904:384; Cushing, Frank H. 1896. Outlines of Zuni Creation Myths. Pp. 321–447 in *13th Annual Report of the Bureau of American Ethnology for the Years 1891–1892*. Washington, D.C.: U.S. Government Printing Office. Pp. 369, 372, 373, 382, 428, 430.

11. The verb *yoko* in Japanese has a meaning of traversing, to cross over side to side. Other usage includes "to travel abroad, foreign travel."

12. The word for a Zuni rainbow dancer is *ametolela;* for rainbow colors, *amitola*.

13. Later I learned that flowers, trees, and corn are also linked to the basic color-direction format.

14. Abegg, Lily. 1952. *The Mind of East Asia*. London: Thames and Hudson. P. 101; Benedict, Ruth. 1934. *Patterns of Culture*. Boston, Mass.:

Houghton Mifflin; Bellah, Robert N. 1957. *Tokugawa Religion. The Values of Pre-Industrial Japan.* Glencoe, Ill.: Free Press. P. 15.

15. Tsunoda et al 1958:60; Cushing, Frank H. 1920. *Zuni Breadstuff.* Indian Notes and Monographs 8. New York: Museum of the American Indian, Heye Foundation. Pp. 19–20.

16. Tsunoda et al 1958:60; Stevenson 1904:432.

17. Anesaki, Masaharu. 1930. *History of Japanese Religion.* London: Kegan Paul, Trench, Trubner; Chamberlain, Basil Hall. 1932. *Ko-ji-ki or Records of Ancient Matters,* transl. 2nd ed. Kobe: J. L. Thompson; Tsunoda et al. 1958; Abegg 1952.

18. Abegg 1952:76, 86.

19. Parsons 1939: I:252; Eggan 1950:213. Dennis Tedlock adds the concept of "raw" and "cooked" in association with night and day people. Tedlock, Dennis. 1979. Zuni Religion and World View. Pp. 499–508 in *Handbook of North American Indians.* Vol. 9, *Southwest.* P. 499.

20. Smith, Watson. 1952. ˙Kiva Mural Decorations at Awatovi and Kawaika-a, with a Survey of Other Wall Paintings in the Pueblo Southwest. Papers of the Peabody Museum of American Archaeology and Ethnology, Harvard University 37. Cambridge, Mass.; Mallery, Garrick. 1893. Picture-Writing of the American Indians. *Tenth Annual Report of the Bureau of Ethnology.* Washington, D.C.: Smithsonian Institution; Parsons 1939; Eggan 1950; Cushing, Frank H. 1882. Zuni Social, Mythic and Religious Systems. *Popular Science Monthly* 21; Cushing 1896, 1920; Stevenson 1904.

21. Eggan 1950:202.

22. Cushing 1896:325.

23. Parsons 1939: II:872.

24. Anesaki 1930:59.

25. Tsunoda et al. reported "the yin-yang teachings were widely accepted and remained unchallenged until modern times." Tsunoda et al. 1958:60.

26. Dobbins, James C. 1989. *Jōdo Shinshū. Shin Buddhism in Medieval Japan.* Indianapolis: Indiana University Press. P. 23.

27. Note on Table 6 that more simple correspondence occurs between the Navaho and the Java (Indonesian) system (3 pairs out of 4) than occurs between Zuni and their Navaho neighbors (1 pair out of 4).

    Peter Gold (1994) provided a remarkable comparison of Navaho and Tibetan spiritual concepts including mandalas, color, and direction orientation in *Navaho and Tibetan Sacred Wisdom. The Circle of the Spirit.* Rochester, Vt.: Inner Traditions.

    Earlier comparisons of the Tibetan and Athabaskan (Navaho) languages were made by Sapir and Swadesh. Perhaps it is time to look again at religious concepts and links in lexicon for a Navaho and Tibetan connection. Sapir, Edward. 1929. Central and North American Languages. Pp. 138–141 in *Encyclopedia Britannica*. Vol. 5. 14th ed. New York: Encyclopedia Britannica Company; Swadesh, Morris. 1952a. Review of Athapaskan and Sino-Tibetan by Robert Shafer. *International Journal of American Linguistics* 18(3):178–181.

28. Cushing 1896:343.

29. Cushing 1920:218. Note that blue is for West and white is for East in Zuni, reversing the Japanese color directions.

30. White is also associated with East in Tibet, and with longevity in Navaho. East in both religions is associated with beginning. Gold 1994:104.

31. Some of these words are ancient Japanese words that appear in the 1903 dictionary I used originally. *Atuma* for example does not appear in the current dictionaries. *To* is a modern alternative to *higashi,* meaning East

32. Cushing 1896:373, 406.

33. Kato, Genchi. 1908. The Ancient Shinto Deity Ame-no-minaka-nushi-no-kami. *Transactions of the Asiatic Society of Japan* 36:141–162. P. 141; Kato 1924.

34. Cushing 1896; Stevenson 1904:71.

35. The symbol for "middle" also appears at the White House Ruins at Canyon de Chelly and at the Lone Pine site in eastern California.

36. Bukkyo Dendo Kyokai. 1990. *The Teaching of Buddha.* Tokyo: Toppan Printing. Pp. 112–126.

37. Perhaps research by experts in medieval Japanese will reveal more Zuni clan names that derive from Old Japanese. Alternatively, perhaps some clan names were introduced by other Native American groups that joined the trek en route to Itiwanna. The oral tradition of migration refers to incorporating people who possessed different languages, knowledge, and clans; perhaps some of their words and clan names merged with Zunian, thus reflecting and preserving their different origins.

38. The Chinese concept of breath, *Qi,* was first developed by Zhuangzi, who is credited with writing one of the founding texts of Taoism perhaps as early as the fourth century B.C. Robinet, Isabelle. 1997. *Taoism. Growth of a Religion.* Phyllis Brooks, transl. Stanford: Stanford University Press. Pp. 30–35.

39. Sahara, Makoto and Hideji Harunari, eds. 1995–1996. *The Art of Bronze Bells in Early Japan.* (An exhibition catalog.) National Museum of Japanese History. Otsuka Kogei-sha, Tokyo: Mainichi Newspapers. See especially pp. 28–43, 184.

40. Mallery noted that the breath or "heart" line also appeared in Ojibwa pictographs. Mallery 1893:495, 496.
41. Stevenson 1904:25–26.
42. Parsons 1939. See especially vol. II, pp. 576, 577, 596, 598–599, 698, 699, 753.
43. Tyler, Susan C. 1992. *The Cult of Kasuga Seen through Its Art.* Michigan Monograph Series in Japanese Studies. No. 8. Center for Japanese Studies. Ann Arbor: University of Michigan. See especially p. 68.
44. Butsu represents the Chinese word at the time it was borrowed by the Japanese about A.D. 400; it has survived unchanged in the modern language. Sansom, George. 1928. *An Historical Grammar of Japanese.* Oxford: Clarendon Press. P. 11.

   The official date for the introduction of Buddhism is A.D. 538. Hall, John Whitney. 1968 [1991]. *Japan. From Prehistory to Modern Times.* Center for Japanese Studies. Ann Arbor: University of Michigan. P. 41.
45. Stevenson 1904:408.
46. Stevenson 1904:279, 281.
47. Stevenson 1904:277.
48. Wyaco, Virgil. 1988. Personal communication. Nov. 22.
49. Stevenson 1904:408.
50. Nahohai, Milford. 1988. Personal communication. Pueblo of Zuni. May 27. One of the startling experiences of my first visit to Zuni was casually asking about Bitsitsi. I had read about him in Stevenson's 1904 volume and wondered if this *kokko* was still a recognized deity. An elder spoke at great length in Zunian and his son listened carefully. Finally, the son turned to me and translated the narrative into a brief summary: "Bitsitsi is famous because he found the Corn Maidens and saved the Zuni people from famine."

   The possible significance of this statement did not register until much later when research on skeletons and settlement patterns indicated that the time for the arrival of the pilgrims from the west was probably the late 13th century, a time of great drought and famine in the Southwest.
51. Perhaps the droughts and the rainy periods in the American Southwest are linked to El Niños and La Niñas in the Pacific, yet another theme to pursue. See Ely et al. 1993
52. Ferguson, T. J. and E. Richard Hart. 1985. *A Zuni Atlas.* Norman: University of Oklahoma Press. P. 126.
53. Neither the Japanese language nor Zunian traditionally utilized the /v/ sound so it seems unlikely that *kiva* originates from them. The religious links of Hopi and other Pueblos should be investigated in

the future, including key religious words. How might Hokan-Siouan languages compare to Japanese? Hopi and Tibetan?

CHAPTER 10

1. In order to avoid the draft there was some increase in religious activity as more draft-age men were selected for ceremonial positions, and urged to participate. The men who were drafted were encouraged to request furloughs to attend important events, such as Shalako. Some ceremonies that had been dropped were revived, including one called "the scalp dance," performed only once since 1921. Another called "owinahaiya" was last performed in 1910.
2. Adair, John J. and Evon Z. Vogt. 1949. Navaho and Zuni Veterans: A Study of Contrasting Modes of Culture Change. *American Anthropologist* 51:547–561.
3. Adair and Vogt 1949:549.
4. Wyaco, Virgil. 1998. *A Zuni Life. A Pueblo Indian in Two Worlds.* Albuquerque: University of New Mexico Press. Especially Chapter 4, pp. 25–39.
5. Japanese has a verb, *hanasu,* which means "let go, release," and a noun, *ishu,* which means "hatred, malice or enmity." The Zuni phrase *hanasema isuwaha* could translate to "let go of hatred," which is what the cleansing ceremony was intended to do. However, the verb "let go" should appear at the end: *isuwaha hanasema* (hatred let go). Is this an example of syntax change in response to the influence of English?
6. At least one Zuni veteran survived the Bataan death march in the Philippines.
7. Some veterans never returned to live in the pueblo, though they occasionally come for the Shalako ceremonies, or the Memorial Day Parade.
8. Primarily she consulted Reo Fortune's *Sorcerer's of Dobu* and Franz Boas's multivolume works on the Kwakuitl published between 1897 and 1930.
9. Ruth Benedict's publications on the Zuni include: 1930. Psychological Types in the Cultures of the Southwest. Pp. 572–581 in *Proceedings of the Twenty-third International Congress of Americanists.* New York: The Science Press; 1935. *Introduction to Zuni Mythology.* Columbia University Contributions to Anthropology 21. New York: Columbia University.

   Bunzel's work with the Zuni was much more extensive than Benedict's and her publications include: 1932a (1984). Zuni Katcinas.

An Analytical Study. Pp. 843–1108 in *47th Annual Report of the Bureau of American Ethnology for the Years 1929–1930*. Gloreita, N.M.: Rio Grande Press; 1932b (1984). Zuni Origin Myths. Pp. 545–609 in *47th Annual Report of the Bureau of American Ethnology for the Years 1929–1930;* 1933. *Zuni Texts.* Publications of the American Ethnological Society, New York. Publication 15; 1935. Zuni. Pp. 385–515 in *Handbook of American Indian Languages,* Part 4. New York: J.J. Austin.

10. For historical perspective on the discussion of diffusion, psychic unity of mankind, parallel evolution, and independent innovation, see Langness, L. L. 1987. Historicalism and Diffusion. Pp. 50–73 in *The Study of Culture.* Novato, Calif.: Chandler and Sharp.

11. Arts, P. L. W. 1983. *Japanese Porcelain. A Collector's Guide to General Aspects and Decorative Motifs.* Lochem, Netherlands: Uitgevers-maatschappij De Tijdsroom Lochem-Poperinge. P. 144.

12. Arts 1983:145.

13. Arts 1983:166.

14. Turnbull 1982. *The Warrior Class of Japan.* A Bison Book. New York: Arco Publishing. P. 249.

15. Matsuya, Gofakuten. 1972. *Japanese Design Motifs.* 4,260 Illustrations of Japanese Crests. Compiled by the Matsuya Piece-Goods Store. Fumie Adachi, transl. New York: Dover Publications. Pp. v–vi.

16. Hardin, Margaret Ann. 1985. *Gifts of Mother Earth: Ceramics in the Zuni Tradition.* Phoenix, Ariz.: Heard Museum.

17. Stevenson, James. 1883. *Illustrated Catalogue of the Collections Obtained from the Indians of New Mexico and Arizona in 1879.* (Extract from the *2nd Annual Report of the Bureau of American Ethnology.*) Washington, D.C.: U.S. Government Printing Office. P. 537.

18. The Hopi have a "sunflower" design that has a large center and indeed looks like a sunflower. The Zuni medallion has a small center and usually has more "petals" than the Hopi sunflower.

19. Cushing, Frank H. 1896. Outlines of Zuni Creation Myths. Pp. 321–447 in *13th Annual Report of the Bureau of American Ethnology for the Years 1891–1892.* Washington, D.C.: U.S. Government Printing Office. P. 338.

20. Kenegy, Susan G. 1978. Deer-and-Medallion Style Pottery at Zuni Pueblo: Iconography and Iconology. *New Mexico Studies in the Fine Arts* (3):46–52.

21. Stevenson, J. 1883:322, 344.

22. Kroeber, A. L. 1916a. Zuni Potsherds. Anthropological Papers of the American Museum of Natural History, New York. Vol. 18, No. 1. P. 13.

23. Tanner, Clara L. 1968. *Southwest Indian Craft Arts.* Tucson: University of Arizona Press. P. 96.

24. See Chapman, K. M. 1938. Pajaritan Pictography, the Cave Pictographs of the Rito de Frijoles. Pl. IVa in *Pajarito Plateau and Its Ancient People.* E. L. Hewett, ed. Albuquerque: University of New Mexico Press.

25. See Hibben, Frank C. 1975. *Kiva Art of the Anasazi at Pottery Mound.* Las Vegas, Nev.: KC Publications. P. 74. Smith, Watson. 1952. Kiva Mural Decorations at Awatovi and Kawaika-a, with a Survey of Other Wall Paintings in the Pueblo Southwest. Papers of the Peabody Museum of American Archaeology and Ethnology, Harvard University 37. Cambridge, Mass. P. 134.

26. Carlson, R. L. 1977. Eighteenth Century Painted Pottery from the Governador District of New Mexico. *American Indian Art* 2(4):41.

27. Kenegy 1978:52.

28. Frank, Larry and Francis H. Harlow. 1974. *Historic Pottery of the Pueblo Indians 1600–1880.* Photographs by Bernard Lopez. Boston, Mass.: New York Graphic Society. P. 145.

29. Wright, Barton. 1985. *Kachinas of the Zuni.* Flagstaff, Ariz.: Northland Press. Plates 2, 9, 13, 16, 20, 31, 36, 47, 51, 52, 53.

30. Cushing, Frank H. 1886. A Study of Pueblo Pottery as Illustrative of Zuni Cultural Growth. Pp. 467–521 in *Fourth Annual Report of the Bureau of Ethnology, 1882–1883.* Washington, D.C.: U.S. Government Printing Office. Pp. 512–513.

31. Stinchecum, Amanda Mayer. 1984. *Kosode. 16th–19th Century Textiles from the Nomura Collection.* With essays by Monica Bethe and Margo Paul. Naomi Noble Richard and Margo Paul, eds. New York: Japan Society and Kodansha International; Noma, Seiroku. 1974. *Japanese Costume and Textile Arts.* Armins Nikovskis, transl. New York: Weatherhill; Shaver, Ruth M. 1966. *Kabuki Costume.* Illustrations by Sōma Akira and Ōta Gakō. Rutland, Vt.: Charles E. Tuttle.

32. Southwest ceramic enthusiasts are challenged by the complexity of the potsherds, and the named types are characteristic of highly technical research. Knowledgeable specialists can recognize, date, and locate the original sources for types called, for example, black on white, black on yellow, red on brown, red on buff, and the many polychromes: El Paso polychrome, Gila polychrome, Jeddito polychrome, Matsaki polychrome, Ramos polychrome, St. Johns polychrome, Sikyatki polychrome, Casa Grandes polychrome, and Rio Grande glazes.

33. Kintigh, Keith W. 1996. The Cibola Region in the Post-Chacoan Era. Pp. 131–144 in *The Prehistoric Pueblo World A.D. 1150–1350.* Michael A. Adler, ed. Tucson: University of Arizona Press. P. 136.

34. Haury, Emil W. 1932. The Age of Lead Glaze Decorated Pottery in the

Southwest. *American Anthropologist* 34:418–425; Danson, Edward B. 1957. *An Archaeological Survey of West Central New Mexico and East Central Arizona.* Papers of the Peabody Museum of American Archaeology and Ethnology, Harvard University 44(1). Cambridge, Mass.; Gladwin, Harold S. 1957. *A History of the Ancient Southwest.* Portland, Me.: Bond Wheelwright; Wormington, H. Marie. 1959. *Prehistoric Indians of the Southwest.* (4th printing.) Denver: Denver Museum of Natural History.

35. Spier, Leslie. 1917. An Outline for a Chronology of Zuni Ruins. Anthropological Papers of the American Museum of Natural History, New York. Vol. 18, No. 3. Pp. 207–332.

36. Spier 1917:296.

37. Spier 1917:328.

38. Spier 1917:316.

39. Haury 1932. Especially see pp. 418, 422.

40. Reed, Erik K. 1955. Painted Pottery and Zuni History. *Southwestern Journal of Anthropology* 11:178–193. See p. 184.

41. Shepard, Anna O. 1956. *Ceramics for the Archaeologist.* Publication 906. Washington, D.C.: Carnegie Institution of Washington.

42. Shepard 1956:48.

43. Brody, J. J. 1991. *Anasazi and Pueblo Painting.* A School of American Research Book. Albuquerque: University of New Mexico Press. Pp. 95–96. Brody further reported that between about A.D. 1300 and 1700, the Rio Grande polychrome styles in the Eastern Pueblo area included black, green, and purple glaze paints. The Rio Grande glazes are much more thoroughly studied than the short-lived Western Pueblo glazes.

44. Hough, Walter. 1928. The Lead Glaze Decorated Pottery of the Pueblo Region. *American Anthropologist* 30:243–249. Pp. 245, 248.

45. Mellott, Richard L. 1990. Ceramics of the Asuka, Nara, and Heian Periods (AD 552–1185). Pp. 57–66 in *The Rise of a Great Tradition: Japanese Archaeological Ceramics from the Jomon through Heian Periods (10,500 BC–AD 1185).* Agency for Cultural Affairs, Government of Japan. New York: Japan Society.

46. In March 1998, I was startled to see two ceramic bowl fragments, one with black glaze paint and the other with a very dark-green glaze, at a major exhibit at the National Museum of Japanese History at Sakura. The quality of the glaze looked identical to Zuni glaze sherds. The sign identified them both as 13th-century vintage. A comparison of glaze technique is clearly called for—and also an analysis of glaze content on pieces from both sides of the Pacific.

BIBLIOGRAPHY

Abegg, Lily. 1952. *The Mind of East Asia.* London: Thames and Hudson.

Adair, John J. and Evon Z. Vogt. 1949. Navaho and Zuni Veterans: A Study of Contrasting Modes of Culture Change. *American Anthropologist* 51:547–561.

Adams, E. Charles. 1991. *The Origin and Development of the Pueblo Katsina Cult.* Tucson: University of Arizona Press.

Adler, Michael A., ed. 1996. *The Prehistoric Pueblo World, A.D. 1150–1350.* Tucson: University of Arizona Press.

Akin, Marjorie Helen Kleiger. 1992. Asian Coins in the North American West: A Behavioral System Approach to Numismatic Analysis. Unpublished Ph.D. thesis. University of California, Riverside.

——1998. When Wen Wasn't Money. *The Numismatist* 111:1258–1263.

——n.d. The Noncurrency Functions of Chinese *Wen* in America.

Anesaki, Masaharu. 1930. *History of Japanese Religion.* London: Kegan Paul, Trench, Trubner.

——1963. *History of Japanese Religion. With Special reference to the social and Moral Life of the Nation.* Rutland, Vt.: Charles E. Tuttle.

Arnold, Jeanne E. 1995. Transportation Innovation and Social Complexity among Maritime Hunter-Gatherer Societies. *American Anthropologist* 97:733–747.

Arnon, Nancy S. and W. W. Hill. 1979. Santa Clara Pueblo. Pp. 296–307 in *Handbook of North American Indians.* Vol. 9, *Southwest.* A. Ortiz, vol. ed. W. C. Sturtevant, general ed. Washington, D.C.: Smithsonian Institution.

Arts, P. L. W. 1983. *Japanese Porcelain. A Collector's Guide to General Aspects and Decorative Motifs.* Lochem, Netherlands: Uitgeversmaatschappij De Tijdsroom Lochem-Poperinge.

Associated Press. 1995. "Ocean Crossing." *Anchorage Daily News,* September 26, p. 2.

Aston, W. G., transl. 1972. *Nihongi. Chronicles of Japan from the Earliest Times to A.D. 697.* Two volumes in one. Tokyo, Japan: Charles E. Tuttle.

Atlas, Allan W. 1991. Belasco and Puccini: "Old Dog Tray" and the Zuni Indians. *Musical Quarterly* 75(3):362–398.

Baker, Herbert G. 1971. Commentary: Section III. Pp. 428–444 in *Man across the Sea. Problems of Pre-Columbian Contacts.* Carroll L. Riley et al., eds. Austin: University of Texas Press.

Bandelier, Adolph F. A. 1892. An Outline of the Documentary History of the Zuni Tribe. *Journal of American Ethnology and Archaeology* 3(1):1–115.

Barnes, Gina L. 1988. Protohistoric Yamato. Archaeology of the First Japanese State. The University of Michigan Center for Japanese Studies. Michigan Papers in Japanese Studies, No. 17. Anthropological Papers. No. 78. Museum of Anthropology, University of Michigan, Ann Arbor.

Batten, Bruce Loyd. 1989. State and Frontier in Early Japan. The Imperial Court and Northern Kyushu, 645–1185. Unpublished dissertation. Stanford University.

Beardsley, Richard K. 1954. *Temporal and Areal Relationships in Central California Archaeology.* University of California Archaeological Survey Reports 24–25. Berkeley: University of California.

Belich, Mônica P., J. Alejandro Madrigal, William H. Hildebrand, Jacqueline Zemmour, Robert C. Williams, Roberto Luz, Maria Luiza Petzl-Erler, and Peter Parham. 1992. Unusual HLA-B Alleles in Two Tribes of Brazilian Indians. *Nature* 357:326–329.

Bellah, Robert N. 1957. *Tokugawa Religion. The Values of Pre-Industrial Japan.* Glencoe, Ill.: Free Press.

Benedict, Ruth. 1930. Psychological Types in the Cultures of the Southwest. Pp. 572–581 in *Proceedings of the 23rd International Congress of Americanists.* New York: Science Press.

——1934. *Patterns of Culture.* Boston, Mass.: Houghton Mifflin.

——1935. *Introduction to Zuni Mythology.* Columbia University Contributions to Anthropology 21. New York: Columbia Press.

——1940. *Race: Science and Politics.* New York: Modern Age.

——1989 (1949). *The Chrysanthemum and the Sword: Patterns of Japanese Culture.* Boston, Mass.: Houghton Mifflin.

Benedict, Paul K. 1990. *Japanese/Austro-Tai.* Ann Arbor, Mich.: Karoma Publishing.

Bennett, John W., Herbert Passin, and Robert K. McKnight. 1958. *In Search of Identity. The Japanese Overseas Scholar in America and Japan.* Minneapolis: University of Minnesota Press.

Blaudschun, Mark. 1994. "Native Americans Ready to Make Another Run." *Boston Globe,* April 15, p. 45.

Bloomfield, Andrew and Yanki Tshering. 1987. *Tibetan Phrasebook.* Ithica, N.Y.: Snow Lion Publications.

Bloomfield, Leonard. 1933. *Language.* New York: Holt, Rinehart and Winston.

Borden, Charles A. 1967. *Sea Quest: Global Blue-Water Adventuring in Small Craft.* Philadelphia: MacRae Smith.

Bourke, John G. 1884. *The Snake-dance of the Moquis of Arizona.* New York: Charles Scribner's Sons.

Bowen, B. W., F. A. Abreu-Grobois, G. H. Balazs, N. Kamezaki, C. J. Limpus, and R. J. Ferl. 1995. Trans-Pacific Migrations of the Loggerhead Turtle *(Caretta caretta)* Demonstrated with Mitochondrial DNA Markers. *Proceedings of the National Academy of Sciences, USA* 92:3731–3734.

Brady, William. 1995. Personal communication.

Brandon, Reiko Mochinaga and Barbara B. Stephan. 1994. *Spirit and Symbol. The Japanese New Year.* Honolulu: Honolulu Academy of Arts in association with University of Hawaii Press.

Brody, J. J. 1977. *Mimbres Painted Pottery.* Santa Fe: School of American Research. Albuquerque: University of New Mexico Press.

——1991. *Anasazi and Pueblo Painting.* A School of American Research Book. Albuquerque: University of New Mexico Press.

Brooks, Charles Wolcott. 1964. *Japanese Wrecks Stranded and Picked Up Adrift in the North Pacific Ocean.* Fairfield, Wash.: Ye Galleon Press. (Originally printed in 1876 in *Proceedings of the California Academy of Sciences,* No. 6.)

Brown, K. S., B. L. Hanna, A. A. Dahlberg, and H. H. Strandskov. 1958. The Distribution of Blood Groups Alleles among Indians of Southwest North America. *American Journal of Human Genetics* 10:175–195.

Buchanan, D. C. 1935. *Inari: Its Origin, Development and Nature.* Asiatic Society of Japan. London: Kegan Paul, Trench, Trubner.

Bukkyo Dendo Kyokai. 1990. *The Teaching of Buddha.* Tokyo: Toppan Printing.

Bunzel, Ruth L. 1932a (1984). Zuni Katcinas. An Analytical Study. Pp. 837–1108 in *47th Annual Report of the Bureau of American Ethnology for the Years 1929–1930.* Gloreita, N.M.: Rio Grande Press.

——1932b (1984). Zuni Origin Myths. Pp. 545–609 in *47th Annual Report of the Bureau of American Ethnology for the Years 1929–1930.* Glorieta, N.M.: Rio Grande Press.

——1933. *Zuni Texts.* Publications of the American Ethnological Society, New York. Publication 15. (Reprinted by AMS Press, New York, 1974.)

——1935. Zuni. Pp. 385–515 in *Handbook of American Indian Languages,* Part 3. New York: J. J. Austin.

——1972. *The Pueblo Potter: A Story of Creative Imagination in Primitive Art [1929].* New York: Dover.

Callaghan, Catherine A. and Geoffrey Gamble. 1996. Borrowing. Pp. 111–116 in *Handbook for North American Indians.* Vol. 17, *Languages.*

Ives Goddard, vol. ed. W. C. Sturtevant, general ed. Washington, D.C.: Smithsonian Institution.

Campbell, Lyle and Marianne Mithun, eds. 1979. *The Languages of Native America: Historical and Comparative Assessment.* Austin: University of Texas Press.

Carlson, R. L. 1977. Eighteenth Century Painted Pottery from the Governador District of New Mexico. *American Indian Art* 2(4):38–43.

Carter, George F. 1971. Pre-Columbian Chickens in America. Pp. 178–218 in *Man across the Sea. Problems of Pre-Columbian Contacts.* Carroll L. Riley et al., eds. Austin: University of Texas Press.

Cavalli-Sforza, L. Luca, Paolo Menozzi, and Alberto Piazza. 1994. *The History and Geography of Human Genes.* Princeton, N.J.: Princeton University Press.

Chamberlain, Basil Hall, transl. 1932. *Ko-ji-ki Records of Ancient Matters.* 2nd ed. Kobe: J. L. Thompson. P. xxviii.

——1981. *The Kojiki. Records of Ancient Matters.* Rutland, Vt.: Charles E. Tuttle.

Chapman, K. M. 1938. Pajaritan Pictography, the Cave Pictographs of the Rito de Frijoles. Pl. IVa in *Pajarito Plateau and Its Ancient People.* E. L. Hewett, ed. Albuquerque: University of New Mexico Press.

Chartkoff, Joseph L. and Kerry Kona Chartkoff. 1984. *The Archaeology of California.* Stanford: Stanford University Press.

Chinese Academy of Sciences. 1983. *Ancient China's Technology and Science.* Institute of the History of Natural Sciences. China Knowledge Series. Beijing: Foreign Languages Press.

Cho-Yang. 1991. *The Voice of Tibetan Religion and Culture.* Year of Tibet Edition. Occasional publication of the Council for Religious and Cultural Affairs of H. H. the Dalai Lama. Pedron Yeshi and Jeremy Russell, eds. Kuala Lumpur, Malaysia: Graphic Press.

Collcutt, Martin, Marius Jansen, and Isao Kumakura. 1988. *Cultural Atlas of Japan.* New York: Facts on File.

Colton, Harold S. 1932. Sunset Crater: The Effect of a Volcanic Eruption on an Ancient Pueblo People. Reprinted in R. I. Ford, ed. 1987. *The Prehistoric American Southwest. A Source Book. History, Chronology, Ecology, and Technology.* New York: Garland Publishing.

——1941. Prehistoric Trade in the Southwest. *Scientific Monthly* 52 (April):308–319.

Colwell, Rita. 1996. "Global Climate: Emerging Diseases and New Epidemics." American Association for the Advancement of Science Presidential Address. Baltimore, Md. February 10.

Cook, C. D. 1974. *Zuni Language Learning Manual.* Gallup, N.M.: Gallup-McKinley County Schools.

——1975. Nucleus and Margin of Zuni Clause Types. *Linguistics* 13:5–37.

Corruccini, Robert S. 1972. The Biological Relationships of Some Prehistoric and Historic Pueblo Populations. *American Journal of Physical Anthropology* 37:373–388.

Crowell, Aron L. and Daniel H. Mann. 1996. Sea Level Dynamics, Glaciers, and Archaeology along the Central Gulf of Alaska Coast. *Arctic Anthropology* 33(2):16–37.

Culin, Stewart. 1920. Japanese Discovery of Alaska, "Kwankai-ibun", the Wonderful News of Circumnavigation. *Asia Monthly* 20:365–372, 436.

Cushing, Frank H. 1882. Zuni Social, Mythic and Religious Systems. *Popular Science Monthly* 21 (June):186–192.

——1886. A Study of Pueblo Pottery as Illustrative of Zuni Cultural Growth. Pp. 467–521 in *Fourth Annual Report of the Bureau of Ethnology, 1882–1883.* Washington, D.C.: U.S. Government Printing Office.

——1896. Outlines of Zuni Creation Myths. Pp. 321–447 in *13th Annual Report of the Bureau of American Ethnology for the Years 1891–1892.* Washington, D.C.: U.S. Government Printing Office.

——1901 [1986]. *Zuni Folk Tales.* Tucson: University of Arizona Press.

——1920. *Zuni Breadstuff.* Indian Notes and Monographs 8. New York: Museum of the American Indian, Heye Foundation.

Danson, Edward B. 1957. *An Archaeological Survey of West Central New Mexico and East Central Arizona.* Papers of the Peabody Museum of American Archaeology and Ethnology, Harvard University 44(1). Cambridge, Mass.

Davis, Emma Lou. 1965. Small Pressures and Cultural Drift as Explanations for Abandonment of the San Juan Area, New Mexico and Arizona. *American Antiquity* 30:353–355.

Davis, Irvine. 1979. The Kiowa-Tanoan, Keresan, and Zuni Languages. Pp. 390–443 in *The Languages of Native America: Historical and Comparative Assessment.* L. Campbell and M. Mithun, eds. Austin: University of Texas Press.

Davis, Nancy Yaw. 1992. The Zuni Enigma. New England Antiquities Research Association. *NEARA Journal* 27(1–2):39–55. (Reprinted in *Across before Columbus? Evidence for Transoceanic Contact with the Americas prior to 1492.* Donald Y. Gilmore and Linda S. McElroy, eds. New England Antiquities Research Association. Edgecomb, Me.: NEARA Publications, 1998. Pp. 125–140.)

De Visser, M. W. 1908. The Fox and Badger in Japanese Folklore. *Transactions of the Asiatic Society of Japan* 36(3).

Dillehay, Tom. 1997. *Monte Verde: A Late Pleistocene Settlement in Chile.* Washington, D.C.: Smithsonian Institution Press.

Dixon, E. James. 1993. *Quest for the Origins of the First Americans.* Albu-querque: University of New Mexico Press.

Dobbins, James C. 1989. *Jodō Shinshū. Shin Buddhism in Medieval Japan.* Indianapolis: Indiana University Press.

Donnelly, Ivon A. 1987. *Chinese Junks and Other Native Craft.* Shanghai, China: Kelly & Walsh, Lo.

Doran, Edwin, Jr. 1971. The Sailing Raft as a Great Tradition. Pp. 115–138 in *Man across the Sea. Problems of Pre-Columbian Contacts.* Carroll L. Riley et al., eds. Austin: University of Texas Press.

Ebbesmeyer, Curtis C. and W. James Ingraham, Jr. 1992. Shoe Spill in the North Pacific. *EOS, Transactions, American Geophysical Union* 73(34):361–365.

——1994a. Pacific Toy Spill Fuels Ocean Current Pathways Research. *EOS, Transactions, American Geophysical Union* 75(37):425–427.

——1994b. *Drifting Objects. Atlas of Pilot Charts. North Pacific Ocean.* 3rd ed. Washington, D.C.: Defense Mapping Agency, U.S. Department of Defense. NV Publication 108.

Eggan, Fred. 1950. *Social Organization of the Western Pueblos.* Chicago: University of Chicago Press.

——1972. Summary. Pp. 287–305 in *New Perspectives on the Pueblos.* A. Ortiz, ed. A School of American Research Book. Albuquerque: University of New Mexico Press.

——1979. Pueblos: Introduction. Pp. 224–235 in *Handbook of North American Indians.* Vol. 9, *Southwest.* A. Ortiz, vol. ed. W. C. Sturtevant, general ed. Washington, D.C.: Smithsonian Institution.

Eggan, Fred and T. N. Pandey. 1979. Zuni History, 1850–1970. Pp. 474–481 in *Handbook of North American Indians.* Vol. 9, *Southwest.* A. Ortiz, vol. ed. W. C. Sturtevant, general ed. Washington, D.C.: Smith-sonian Institution.

Ekholm, G. F. 1953. A Possible Focus of Asiatic Influence in the Late Classic Cultures of Mesoamerica. Memoirs of the Society for Amer-ican Archaeology, No. 9. 18:72–89.

Ely, Lisa L., Yehouda Enzel, Victor R. Baker, and Daniel R. Cayan. 1993. A 5000-Year Record of Extreme Floods and Climate Change in the Southwestern United States. *Science* 262:410–412.

Emmons, George Thornton. 1991. *The Tlingit Indians.* Edited with addi-tions by Frederica de Laguna and a biography by Jean Low. Seattle: University of Washington Press and American Museum of Natural History.

Epstein, Jeremiah F. 1990. Sails in Aboriginal Mesoamerica: Reevaluat-ing Thompson's Argument. *American Anthropologist* 92:187–192.

Epstein, Paul R., ed. 1999. *Extreme Weather Events: The Health and Eco-nomic Consequences of the 1997/98 El Niño and La Niña.* The Center for Health and the Global Environment. Boston, Mass.: Harvard Medical School.

Estrada, Emilio and Betty J. Meggers. 1961. A Complex of Traits of Probable Transpacific Origin on the Coast of Ecuador. *American Anthropologist* 63:913–939.

Ferguson, T. J. 1996. *Historic Zuni Architecture and Society. An Archaeological Application of Space Syntax.* Anthropological Papers of the University of Arizona. No. 60. Tucson: University of Arizona Press.

Ferguson, T. J. and E. Richard Hart. 1985. *A Zuni Atlas.* Norman: University of Oklahoma Press.

Ferguson, William M. and Arthur H. Rohn. 1986. *Anasazi Ruins of the Southwest in Color.* Foreward by Richard B. Woodbury. Albuquerque: University of New Mexico Press.

Fewkes, Jesse Walter. 1896. Pacific Coast Shells from Tusayan Pueblos. *American Anthropologist* 9:359–367.

——1990a (1903). *Hopi Katcinas.* (First published in 1903 as a paper contained in the 21st annual report of the Bureau of American Ethnology.) New York: Dover Publications.

——1990b (1914–1924). *The Mimbres Art and Archaeology.* With an introduction by J. J. Brody. Albuquerque: Avanyu Publishing.

Fink, Colin G. 1941. Division of Electrochemistry, Department of Chemical Engineering, Columbia University. Personal correspondence to Allen L. Chickering of Chickering and Gregory in San Francisco. July 3. Berkeley: Phoebe Hearst Museum Archives.

Finney, Ben. 1976. *Pacific Navigation and Voyaging.* Polynesian Society Memoir No. 39. Wellington, New Zealand: Polynesian Society.

——1985. Anomalous Westerlies, El Niño, and the Colonization of Polynesia. *American Anthropologist* 87:9–26.

——1994. *Voyage of Rediscovery. A Cultural Odyssey through Polynesia.* Berkeley: University of California Press.

Fischman, Joshua. 1993. Going for the Old: Ancient DNA Draws a Crowd. *Science* 262:655–656.

Fitzhugh, William W. 1988. Comparative Art of the North Pacific Rim. Pp. 294–312 in *Crossroads of Continents. Cultures of Siberia and Alaska.* William Fitzhugh and Aron Crowell, eds. Washington, D.C.: Smithsonian Institution Press.

Fladmark, K. R. 1979. Routes: Alternative Migration Corridors for Early Man in North America. *American Antiquity* 44:55–69.

——1983. Times and Places: Environmental Correlates of Mid-to-Late Wisconsin Human Population Expansion in North America. Pp. 13–42 in *Early Man in the New World.* Richard Shutler, ed. Beverly Hills: Sage Publications.

Ford, Richard I. 1983. Inter-Indian Exchange in the Southwest. Pp.

711–722 in *Handbook of North American Indians.* Vol. 9, *Southwest.* A. Ortiz, vol. ed. W. C. Sturtevant, general ed. Washington, D.C.: Smithsonian Institution.

Ford, Richard I., Albert H. Schroeder, and Stewart L. Peckham. 1972. Three Perspectives on Puebloan Prehistory. Pp. 19–39 in *New Perspectives on the Pueblos.* A. Ortiz, ed. Albuquerque: University of New Mexico Press.

Ford, R. I., ed. 1987. *The Prehistoric American Southwest. A Source Book. History, Chronology, Ecology and Technology.* New York: Garland Publishing.

Fox, Robin. 1972. Some Unsolved Problems of Pueblo Social Organization. Pp. 71–85 in *New Perspectives on the Pueblos.* A. Ortiz, ed. Albuquerque: University of New Mexico Press.

Frank, Larry and Francis H. Harlow. 1974. *Historic Pottery of the Pueblo Indians 1600–1880.* Boston, Mass.: New York Graphic Society.

Frazier, Kendrick. 1986. *People of Chaco. A Canyon and Its Culture.* New York: W. W. Norton.

Fuller, Richard E. 1960. *Japanese Art in the Seattle Art Museum. A Historical Sketch.* Seattle: [s.n.].

Furuta, Ryoichi and Yoshikazu Hirai. 1967. *A Short History of Japanese Merchant Shipping.* Duncan Macfarlane, transl. and annot. Tokyo: Tokyo New Service.

Garn, Stanley M. 1961 (1969 ed.). *Human Races.* Springfield, Ill.: Charles C. Thomas.

Gernet, Jacques. 1972 (1982). *A History of Chinese Civilization.* J. R. Foster, transl. Cambridge: Cambridge University Press.

Gilmore, Donald Y. and Linda S. McElroy, eds. 1998. *Across before Columbus? Evidence for Transoceanic Contact with the Americas prior to 1492.* New England Antiquities Research Association. Edgecomb, Me.: NEARA Publications.

Gladwin, Harold S. 1957. *A History of the Ancient Southwest.* Portland, Me.: Bond Wheelwright.

Goddard, Ives. 1987. Comments on book review of *Language in the Americas. Current Anthropology* 28:656–657.

——1996a. Introduction. Pp. 1–16 in *Handbook of North American Indians.* Vol. 17, *Languages.* I. Goddard, vol. ed. W. C. Sturtevant, general ed. Washington, D.C.: Smithsonian Institution.

——1996b. The Classification of the Native Languages of North America. Pp. 290–323 in *Handbook of North American Indians.* Vol. 17, *Languages.* I. Goddard, vol. ed. W. C. Sturtevant, general ed. Washington, D.C.: Smithsonian Institution.

Gold, Peter. 1994. *Navajo and Tibetan Sacred Wisdom. The Circle of the*

Spirit. With a message from H. H. the Dalai Lama. Rochester, Vt.: Inner Traditions.

Goodenough, Ward H. 1953. *Native Astronomy in the Central Carolines.* Philadelphia: University Museum, University of Pennsylvania.

Granberry, J. 1967. Zuni Syntax. Ph.D. dissertation. SUNY Buffalo.

Green, Jesse, ed. 1979. *Zuni. Selected Writings of Frank Hamilton Cushing.* Foreword by Fred Eggan. Lincoln: University of Nebraska Press.

——1990. *Cushing at Zuni. The Correspondence and Journals of Frank Hamilton Cushing. 1879-1884.* Albuquerque: University of New Mexico Press.

Greenberg, Joseph H. 1953. Historical Linguistics and Unwritten Languages. Pp. 265–286 in *Anthropology Today. An Encyclopedic Inventory.* A. L. Kroeber, chair. Chicago: University of Chicago Press.

——1971. Unpublished notebooks. Vol. 8. Penutian. Stanford University Library.

——1987. *Language in the Americas.* Stanford: Stanford University Press.

——1990. The American Indian Language Controversy. *Review of Archaeology* 11(2):5–14.

Greenberg, Joseph H., Christy G. Turner, II, and Stephen L. Zegura. 1986. The Settlement of the Americas: A Comparison of the Linguistic, Dental, and Genetic Evidence. *Current Anthropology* 27:477–497.

Grierson, Philip. 1975. *Numismatics.* New York: Oxford University Press.

Gumerman, George J., ed. 1994. *Themes in Southwest Prehistory.* Santa Fe: School of American Research Press.

Hale, Kenneth and David Harris. 1979. Historical Linguistics and Archeology. Pp. 170–177 in *Handbook of North American Indians. Vol. 9, Southwest.* A. Ortiz, vol. ed. W.C. Sturtevant, general ed. Washington, D.C.: Smithsonian Institution.

Hall, John Whitney. 1968 [1991]. *Japan from Prehistory to Modern Times.* Center for Japanese Studies. Ann Arbor: University of Michigan.

Hall, John W. and Jeffrey P. Mass, eds. 1988 (1974). *Medieval Japan. Essays in Institutional History.* Stanford: Stanford University Press.

Hammer, Michael F. and Satoshi Horai. 1995. Y Chromosomal DNA Variation and the Peopling of Japan. *American Journal of Human Genetics* 56:951–962.

Hamp, E. P. 1975. On Zuni-Penutian Consonants. *International Journal of American Linguistics* 41:310–312.

Hanna, Warren L. 1979. *Lost Harbor. The Controversy over Drake's California Anchorage.* Berkeley: University of California Press.

Hardin, Margaret Ann. 1985. *Gifts of Mother Earth: Ceramics in the Zuni Tradition.* Phoenix, Ariz.: Heard Museum.

Harrell, Debera C. 1994. "Toys Drift into Ice." Seattle Post-Intelligencer in *Anchorage Daily News,* November 28, Pp. B1, B2.

Hattori, Shiro. 1948. The Relationship of Japanese to Ryukyu, Korean, and Altaic Languages. *Transactions of the Asiatic Society.* Third Series. 1:101–133.

Haury, Emil W. 1932. The Age of Lead Glaze Decorated Pottery in the Southwest. *American Anthropologist* 34:418–425.

———1950. *The Stratigraphy and Archaeology of Ventana Cave Arizona.* Tucson: University of Arizona Press; Albuquerque: University of New Mexico Press. (Part VII by Norman E. Gabel.)

Hawley, Florence M. 1937. Pueblo Social Organization as a Lead to Pueblo History. *American Anthropologist* 39:504–522.

Hayden, F. V. 1878. *Colorado and Parts of Adjacent Territories. Report of Progress of the Exploration for the Year 1876. Tenth Annual Report of the United States Geological and Geographical Survey of the Territories.* Washington, D.C.: U.S. Government Printing Office.

Hazard, Benjamin Harrison, Jr. 1967. Japanese Marauding in Medieval Korea: The *Wakō* Impact on Late Koryo. Ph.D. dissertation in history. University of California, Berkeley.

Heil, Celia. 1998. The Significance of Metallurgy in the Purhépecha Religion. Pp. 43–51 in *Across before Columbus? Evidence for Transoceanic Contact with the Americas prior to 1492.* Donald Y. Gilmore and Linda S. McElroy, eds. New England Antiquities Research Association. Edgecomb, Me.: NEARA Publications.

Heizer, Robert Fleming. 1941. Archaeological Evidence of Sebastian Rodriguez Cermeño's California Visit in 1595. *California Historical Society Quarterly* 20:315–328.

———1978a. Introduction. Pp. 1–5 in *Handbook of North American Indians.* Vol. 8, *California.* R. F. Heizer, vol. ed. W. C. Sturtevant, general ed. Washington, D.C.: Smithsonian Institution.

———1978b. Trade and Trails. Pp. 690–692 in *Handbook of North American Indians.* Vol. 8, *California.* R. F. Heizer, vol. ed. W. C. Sturtevant, general ed. Washington, D.C.: Smithsonian Institution.

Heizer, Robert F. and William C. Massey. 1953. Aboriginal Navigation off the Coasts of Upper and Baja California. Pp. 285–312 in Anthropological Papers, No. 39. Bureau of American Ethnology. Bulletin 151. Washington, D.C.: Smithsonian Institution.

Heizer, Robert F. and McCown, Theodore D. 1950. *The Stanford Skull: A Probable Early Man from Santa Clara County, California.* Report No. 6, The University of California Archaeological Survey. Berkeley: University of California Press.

Hepburn, James Curtis. 1903. *A Japanese-English, English-Japanese Dictionary,* abridged. 2nd ed. London: Truber. Tokyo: Z. P. Maruya.

Heyerdahl, T. 1950. *Kon-Tiki: Across the Pacific by Raft.* New York: Rand McNally.

Hibben, Frank C. 1975. *Kiva Art of the Anasazi at Pottery Mound.* Las Vegas, Nev.: KC Publications.

Hockett, Charles F. 1987. Personal communication. Letter, 4 pp. June 17.

Hooton, Ernest Albert. 1930. *The Indians of Pecos Pueblo: A Study of Their Skeletal Remains.* New Haven: Yale University Press.

Hori, Ichiro. 1968. *Folk Religion in Japan. Continuity and Change.* Joseph M. Kitagawa and Alan L. Miller, eds. Chicago: University of Chicago Press.

Hori, Kyotsu. 1967. The Mongol Invasions and the Kamakura Bakufu. Ph.D. dissertation in political science. Columbia University.

Hornung, Clarence, ed. 1986. *Traditional Japanese Crest Designs.* New York: Dover Publications.

Hosler, Dorothy. 1988. Ancient West Mexican Metallurgy: South and Central American Origins and West Mexican Transformations. *American Anthropologist* 90:832–855.

Hough, Walter. 1928. The Lead Glaze Decorated Pottery of the Pueblo Region. *American Anthropologist* 30:243–249.

Hoy, Wendy E., Donald M. Megill, and Michael D. Hughson. 1987. Epidemic Renal Disease of Unknown Etiology in the Zuni Indians. *American Journal of Kidney Diseases* 9 (June):485–496.

Hrdlička, Aleš. 1927. *Catalogue of Human Crania in the United States National Museum Collections: The Algonkin and Related Iroquois; Siouan, Caddoan, Salish and Sahaptin, Shoshonean, and California Indians.* Washington: United States Government Printing Office.

Hughson, Michael D., Don M. Megill, Suzanne M. Smith, Kenneth S. K. Tung, Gerald Miller, and Wendy E. Hoy. 1989. Mesangiopathic Glomerulonephritis in Zuni (New Mexico) Indians. *Archives Pathological Laboratory Medicine* 113:148–157.

Hughte, Phil. 1994. *A Zuni Artist Looks at Frank Hamilton Cushing.* Zuni, N.M.: Pueblo of Zuni Arts and Crafts and the A:shiwi A:wan Museum and Heritage Center.

——1995. Four Cartoons. From *A Zuni Artist Looks at Frank Hamilton Cushing. American Anthropologist* 97:10–13.

Hurst, G. Cameron, III. 1988 (1974). The Structure of the Heian Court: Some Thoughts on the Nature of "Familial Authority" in Heian Japan. Pp. 39–59 in *Medieval Japan. Essays in Institutional History.* John W. Hall and Jeffrey P. Mass, eds. Stanford: Stanford University Press.

Hymes, Dell H. 1960. Lexicostatistics So Far. *Current Anthropology* 1(1):3–34; 41–44.

Imamura, Keiji. 1996. *Prehistoric Japan. New Perspectives on Insular East Asia.* Honolulu: University of Hawai'i Press.

Ishaikawa, Michiji. 1936. The Japanese Concept of Man. *Cultural Nippon* 5:317–328. Tokyo: Nippon Bunka Renmei.

Jacobsen, William H., Jr. 1989. The Pacific Orientation of Western North American Languages. Paper presented at the Circum-Pacific Prehistory Conference. Seattle, Wash.

Jeancon, Jean A. 1923. *Excavations in the Chama Valley, New Mexico.* Bureau of American Ethnology Bulletin 81. Washington, D.C.: U.S. Government Printing Office.

Jett, Stephen C. 1964. Pueblo Indian Migration: An Evaluation of the Possible Physical and Cultural Determinants. *American Antiquity* 29:281–300.

——1971. Diffusion versus Independent Development: The Bases of Controversy. Pp. 5–53 in *Man across the Sea. Problems of Pre-Columbian Contacts.* Carroll L. Riley et al., eds. Austin: University of Texas Press.

——1993. Dyestuffs and Possible Early Contacts between Southwestern Asia and Nuclear America. New England Antiquities Research Association. *NEARA Journal* 28(1–2):31–38.

Jett, Stephen C. and Peter B. Moyle. 1986. The Exotic Origins of Fishes Depicted on Prehistoric Mimbres Pottery from New Mexico. *American Antiquity* 51:688–720.

Johannessen, Carl L. 1998. Maize Diffused to India before Columbus Came to America. Pp. 111–125 in *Across before Columbus? Evidence for Transoceanic Contact with the Americas prior to 1492.* Donald Y. Gilmore and Linda S. McElroy, eds. New England Antiquities Research Association. Edgecomb, Me.: NEARA Publications.

Josenhans, Heiner, Daryl Fedje, Reinhard Pientiz, and John Southon. 1997. Early Humans and Rapidly Changing Holocene Sea Levels in the Queen Charlotte Islands-Hecate Strait, British Columbia, Canada. *Science* 277:71–74.

Kakubayashi, Fumio. 1981. Japanese Drift Records and the Sharp Hypothesis. *Journal of Polynesian Society* 90:515–524.

Kato, Genchi. 1908. The Ancient Shinto Deity Ame-no-minaka-nushi-no-kami. *Transactions of the Asiatic Society of Japan.* 36:141–162.

——1924. A Study of the Development of Religious Ideas among the Japanese People as Illustrated by Japanese Phallicism. *Transactions of the Asiatic Society of Japan.* Second Series. 1 (Suppl.).

Keddie, Grant R. 1990. *The Question of Asiatic Objects on the North Pacific Coast of America: Historic or Prehistoric?* Contributions to Human History, No. 3. Pp. 1–26. Victoria, British Columbia: Royal British Columbia Museum.

Kehoe, Alice B. 1971. Small Boats upon the North Atlantic. Pp. 275–292 in *Man across the Sea. Problems of Pre-Columbian Contacts.* Carroll L. Riley et al., eds. Austin: University of Texas Press.

Kenegy, Susan G. 1978. Deer-and-Medallion Style Pottery at Zuni Pueblo: Iconography and Iconology. *New Mexico Studies in the Fine Arts* 3:46–52.

Kennedy, K. A. R. 1959. *The Aboriginal Population of the Great Basin.* Report No. 45. Berkeley: University of California Archaeological Survey.

Kent, Kate Peck. 1983. *Pueblo Indian Textiles. A Living Tradition.* Santa Fe.: School of American Research Press.

Kidder, J. Edward. 1959. *Japan before Buddhism.* New York: Frederick A. Praeger.

——1964. *Early Japanese Art. The Great Tombs and Treasures.* Princeton, N.J.: D. Van Nostrand.

——1965. *The Birth of Japanese Art.* New York: Frederick A. Praeger.

Kintigh, Keith W. 1985. *Settlement, Subsistence, and Society in Late Zuni Prehistory.* Anthropological Papers of the University of Arizona. No. 44. Tucson: University of Arizona Press.

——1996. The Cibola Region in the Post-Chacoan Era. Pp. 131–144 in *The Prehistoric Pueblo World A.D. 1150–1350.* Michael A. Adler, ed. Tucson: University of Arizona Press.

Kirk, Ruth and Richard D. Daugherty. 1974. *Hunters of the Whale: An Adventure in Northwest Coast Archaeology.* New York: William Morrow.

——1978. *Exploring Washington Archaeology.* Seattle: University of Washington Press.

Kitigawa, Joseph M. 1966. *Religion in Japanese History.* New York: Columbia University Press.

——1987. *On Understanding Japanese Religion.* Princeton, N.J.: Princeton University Press.

Kitka, Herman. 1997. Speech at the opening of the Sitka Tribe's Community Center. May 23.

Kotler, Jared. 1999. "Oceangoing Raft Crew Seeks to Prove Point." The Associated Press. *Anchorage Daily News,* January 6, p. A6.

Koyama, Fujio. *The Heritage of Japanese Ceramics.* New York: Weatherhill/Tankosha.

Kroeber, Alfred L. 1916a. Zuni Potsherds. Anthropological Papers of the American Museum of Natural History, New York. Vol. 18, No. 1. Pp. 1–37.

——1916b. The Speech of a Zuni Child. *American Anthropologist* 18(4):529–534.

——1919. Zuni Kin and Clan. Anthropological Papers of the American Museum of Natural History, New York. Vol. 18, No. 2. Pp. 39–204.

——1925. *Handbook of the Indians of California.* Bureau of American Ethnology Bulletin 78. Washington, D.C.: U.S. Government Printing Office.

——1928. Native Culture in the Southwest. University of California Publications in American Archaeology and Ethnology Vol. 23, No. 9. Pp. 375–398. Berkeley: University of California.

——1948. *Anthropology. Race. Language. Culture. Psychology. Prehistory.* New York: Harcourt, Brace.

——1951. Elements of Culture in Native California. Pp. 3–68 in *The California Indians. A Source Book.* R. F. Heizer and M. A. Whipple, eds. Berkeley: University of California Press.

Kroskrity, Paul V. 1983. On Male and Female Speech in the Pueblo Southwest. *International Journal of American Linguistics* 49:88–91.

Ladd, Edmund J. 1979a. Zuni Social and Political Organization. Pp. 482–491 in *Handbook of North American Indians.* Vol. 9, *Southwest.* A. Ortiz, vol. ed. W. C. Sturtevant, general ed. Washington, D.C.: Smithsonian Institution.

——1979b. Zuni Economy. Pp. 492–498 in *Handbook of North American Indians.* Vol. 9, *Southwest.* A. Ortiz, vol. ed. W. C. Sturtevant, general ed. Washington, D.C.: Smithsonian Institution.

Langness, L. L. 1987. *The Study of Culture.* Novato, Cal.: Chandler and Sharp.

Laughlin, William S. 1980. *Aleuts: Survivors of the Bering Land Bridge.* Case Studies in Cultural Anthropology. New York: Holt, Rinehart and Winston.

LeBlanc, Steven A. 1983. *The Mimbres People. Ancient Pueblo Painters of the American Southwest.* London: Thames and Hudson.

Levy, Matthys and Mario Salvadori. 1995. *Why the Earth Quakes. The Story of Earthquakes and Volcanoes.* New York: W. W. Norton.

Lewis, Governor Robert. 1989. Personal communication. Pueblo of Zuni. November 22.

Lister, Robert H. and Florence C. Lister. 1981. *Chaco Canyon. Archaeology and Archaeologists.* Albuquerque: University of New Mexico Press.

Long, Jeffrey C. 1991. The Genetic Structure of Admixed Populations. *Genetics* 127:417–428.

Lowie, Robert H. 1935. *The Crow Indians.* New York: Rinehart.

Luomala, Katharine. 1978. Tipai and Ipai. Pp. 592–609 in *Handbook of North American Indians.* Vol. 8, *California.* R. F. Heizer, vol. ed. W. C. Sturtevant, general ed. Washington, D.C.: Smithsonian Institution.

Mack, Joanne M. 1991. Ceramic Figurines of the Western Cascades of

Southern Oregon and Northern California. Pp. 99–110 in *The New World Figurine Project*. Vol. 1. Terry Stocker, ed. Provo, Utah: Research Press.

Mack, Joanne M., ed. 1990. *Hunter-Gatherer Pottery from the Far West*. Anthropological Papers No. 23. Carson City: Nevada State Museum.

Makah Tribal Council. n.d. "Welcome Brochure."

Mallery, Garrick. 1893. Picture-Writing of the American Indians. *Tenth Annual Report of the Bureau of Ethnology*. Washington, D.C.: Smithsonian Institution.

Mann, Daniel H., Aron L. Crowell, Thomas D. Hamilton, and Bruce P. Finney. 1998. Holocene Geologic and Climatic History around the Gulf of Alaska. *Arctic Anthropology* 35(1):112–131.

Mass, Jeffrey P. 1974. *Warrior Government in Early Medieval Japan*. New Haven: Yale University Press.

——1979. *The Development of Kamakura Rule, 1180–1250*. Stanford: Stanford University Press.

Mass, Jeffrey P., ed. 1982. *Court and Bakufu in Japan. Essays in Kamakura History*. New Haven: Yale University Press.

Matisoff, James A. 1990. Discussion Note. On Megalocomparison. *Language* 66:106–120.

Matisoff, Susan. 1978. *The Legend of Semimaru. Blind Musician of Japan*. New York: Columbia University Press.

Matsuya, Gofukuten. 1972. *Japanese Design Motifs*. 4,260 Illustrations of Japanese Crests. Compiled by the Matsuya Piece-Goods Store. Fumie Adachi, transl. New York: Dover Publications.

McCartney, Allen P., Hiroaki Okada, Atsuko Okada, and William B. Workman. 1998. Introduction. North Pacific and Bering Sea Maritime Societies. The Archaeology of Prehistoric and Early Historic Coastal Peoples. *Arctic Anthropology* 35(1):1–5.

McEwan, Gordon F. and D. Bruce Dickson. 1978. Valdivia, Jomon Fishermen, and the Nature of the North Pacific: Some Nautical Problems with Meggers, Evans, and Estrada's (1965) Transoceanic Contact Thesis. *American Antiquity* 43:362–371.

McNitt, Frank, ed. 1964. *Navaho Expedition. Journal of a Military Reconnaissance from Santa Fe, New Mexico to the Navaho Country Made in 1849 by Lieutenant James H. Simpson*. Norman: University of Oklahoma Press.

Meggers, Betty J. 1975. The Transpacific Origin of Mesoamerican Civilization: A Preliminary Review of the Evidence and Its Theoretical Implications. *American Anthropologist* 77:1–27.

——1976. Yes If by Land, No If by Sea: The Double Standard in Interpreting Cultural Similarities. *American Anthropologist* 78:637–639.

——1998. Jomon-Valdivia Similarities: Convergence or Contact? Pp. 11–22 in *Across before Columbus? Evidence for Transoceanic Contact with the Americas prior to 1492.* Donald Y. Gilmore and Linda S. McElroy, eds. New England Antiquities Research Association. Edgecomb, Me.: NEARA Publications.

Meggers, Betty J., Clifford Evans, and Emilio Estrada. 1965. Early Formative Period of Coastal Ecuador; The Valdivia and Machalilla Phases. *Smithsonian Contributions to Anthropology.* Vol. 1. Washington, D.C.: Smithsonian Institution.

Meighan, Clement W. 1950. *Excavations in Sixteenth Century Shellmounds at Drake's Bay, Marin County.* University of California Archaeological Survey Report #9. Pp. 27–32. Berkeley: University of California.

——1955. *Archaeology of the North Coast Ranges, California.* University of California Archaeological Survey Report 30. Pp. 1–39. Berkeley: University of California.

Mellot, Richard L. 1990. Ceramics of the Asuka, Nara, and Heian Periods (AD 552–1185). Pp. 56–66 in *The Rise of a Great Tradition: Japanese Archaeological Ceramics from the Jomon through Heian Periods (10,500 BC–AD 1185).* Agency for Cultural Affairs, Government of Japan. New York: Japan Society.

Meltzer, David J. 1997. Monte Verde and the Pleistocene People of the Americas. *Science* 276:754–755.

Merbs, Charles F. 1992. ABO, MN and RH Frequencies among the Havasupai and Other Southwest Indian Groups. *Kiva* 58(1):67–88.

Merrien, Jean. 1954. *Lonely Voyagers.* J. H. Watkins, transl. New York: Putnam.

Merrill, William L., Edmund J. Ladd, and T. J. Ferguson. 1993. The Return of the Ahayu:da: Lessons for Repatriation from Zuni Pueblo and the Smithsonian Institution. *Current Anthropology* 34(5):523–568.

Mertz, Henriette. 1953. *Pale Ink. Two Ancient Records of Chinese Exploration in America.* Chicago: Ralph Fletcher Seymour.

Michaels, Davis. 1971. A Note on Some Exceptions in Zuni Phonology. *International Journal of American Linguistics* 37(3):189–192.

Miller, Laura. 1989. The Japanese Language and Honorific Speech: Is There a Nihongo without Keigo? *Penn Linguistics Review* 13:38–46.

——1994. The Discourse of Japanese Workers and Folklinguistic Theories of Honorifics. Presented at a meeting of the American Anthropological Association.

——1995a. Two Aspects of Japanese and American Co-worker Interaction: Giving Instructions and Creating Rapport. *Journal of Applied Behavioral Science* 31:141–161.

Miller, Roy Andrew. 1967. *The Japanese Language.* Chicago: University of Chicago Press.

——1971. *Japanese and the Other Altaic Languages.* Chicago: University of Chicago Press.

——1980. *Origins of the Japanese Language. Lectures in Japan during the Academic Year 1977–78.* Seattle: University of Washington Press.

Mills, Barbara J. and Patricia L. Crown, eds. 1995. *Ceramic Production in the American Southwest.* Tucson: University of Arizona Press.

Mills, Barbara J. and T. J. Ferguson. 1998. Preservation and Research of Sacred Sites by the Zuni Indian Tribe of New Mexico. *Human Organization* 57(1):30–42.

Mindeleff, Victor. 1989. *A Study of Pueblo Architecture in Tusayan and Cibola.* Introduction by Peter Nabokov. Classics of Smithsonian Anthropology. Washington, D.C.: Smithsonian Institution Press. (Reprint of Pp. 3–228 in the *Eighth Annual Report of the Bureau of Ethnology to the Secretary of the Smithsonian Institution 1886–87 by J. W. Powell.* Washington, D.C.: U.S. Government Printing Office, 1891.)

Miner, Kenneth L. 1986. Noun Stripping and Loose Incorporation in Zuni. *International Journal of American Linguistics* 52:242–254.

Montreal Museum of Fine Arts. 1989. *The Japan of the Shoguns.* The Tokugawa Collection.

Moriarty, James R. and Neil F. Marshal. 1965. The History and Evolution of Anchors. San Diego Science Foundation, Occasional Paper No. 3. San Diego.

Morris, Ivan. 1966. *Dictionary of Selected Forms in Classical Japanese Literature.* New York: Columbia University Press.

Munsterberg, Hugo. 1963. *The Arts of Japan. An Illustrated History.* Rutland, Vt.: Charles E. Tuttle.

Murdock, George P. 1953. *Ethnographic Bibliography of North America.* 2nd ed. New Haven: Human Relations Area Files.

Murray, Dian H. 1987. *Pirates of the South China Coast 1790–1810.* Stanford: Stanford University Press.

Nahohai, Milford. 1988. Personal communication. Pueblo of Zuni. May 27.

Nahohai, Milford and Elisa Phelps. 1995. *Dialogues with Zuni Potters.* Photography by Dale W. Anderson. Zuni, N.M.: Zuni A:Shiwi Publishing.

Newman, Marshall T. 1962. Evolutionary Changes in Body Size and Head Form in American Indians. *American Anthropologist* 64:237–257.

Newman, Russell W. 1957. *A Comparative Analysis of Prehistoric Skeletal Remains from the Lower Sacramento Valley.* Report No. 39. Berkeley: University of California Archaeological Survey.

Newman, Stanley. 1954a. A Practical Zuni Orthography. In *Zuni Law. A*

Field of Values. J. M. Roberts and W. Smith, eds. Papers, Peabody Museum of American Archaeology and Ethnology, Harvard University 43(1) Appendix B. Cambridge, Mass.

——1954b. American Indian Linguistics in the Southwest. *American Anthropologist* 56:626–634.

——1955. Vocabulary Levels: Zuni Sacred and Slang Usage. *Southwestern Journal of Anthropology* 11:345–354.

——1958. Zuni Dictionary. *International Journal of American Linguistics* 24(1):1–117.

——1964. Comparison of Zuni and California Penutian. *International Journal of American Linguistics* 30:1–13.

——1965. *Zuni Grammar.* University of New Mexico Publications in Anthropology. No. 14. Albuquerque: University of New Mexico Press.

——1967. Zuni Grammar: Alternative Solutions versus Weaknesses. *International Journal of American Linguistics* 33:187–192.

——1996. Sketch of the Zuni Language. Pp. 483–506 in *Handbook of North American Indians. Vol. 17, Languages.* Ives Goddard, vol. ed. W. C. Sturtevant, general ed. Washington, D.C.: Smithsonian Institution.

Nichols, Johanna. 1992. *Linguistic Diversity in Space and Time.* Chicago: University of Chicago Press.

——1994. Language at 40,000 BC. Paper presented at the American Association for the Advancement of Science annual meeting, San Francisco, February 21. Panel on "Comparative Linguistics and Historical Relationships."

Noma, Seiroku. 1974. *Japanese Costume and Textile Arts.* Armins Nikovskis, transl. New York: Weatherhill.

Nuttall, Zelia. 1901. The Fundamental Principles of Old and New World Civilizations: A Comparative Research Based on a Study of the Ancient Mexican Religion, Sociological and Calendrical Systems. Archaeological and Ethnological Papers of the Peabody Museum, Harvard University Vol. II. Cambridge, Mass.

——1906. *The Earliest Historical Relations between Mexico and Japan (from Original Documents Preserved in Spain and Japan).* University of California Publications in American Archaeology and Ethnology. Vol. 4, No. 1. Pp. 1–45. Berkeley: University of California Press.

Ohno, Susumu. 1970. *The Origin of the Japanese Language.* Tokyo: Kokusai Bunka Shinkokai. Japan Cultural Society.

Ohnuki-Tierney, Emiko. 1993. *Rice as Self. Japanese Identities through Time.* Princeton, N.J.: Princeton University Press.

Olsen, John W. 1983. An Analysis of East Asian Coins Excavated in Tucson, Arizona. *Historical Archaeology* 17:41–55.

Olson, Ronald L. 1930. *Chumash Prehistory*. University of California Publications in American Archaeology and Ethnology. Vol. 28, No. 1. Pp. 1–21. Berkeley: University of California Press.

Ortiz, Alfonso. 1979. Introduction. Pp. 1–4 in *Handbook of North American Indians*. Vol. 9, *Southwest*. A. Ortiz, vol. ed. W. C. Sturtevant, general ed. Washington, D.C.: Smithsonian Institution.

Ostler, James, Marian Rodee, and Milford Nahohai. 1996. *Zuni. A Village of Silversmiths*. Photography by Michael Mouchette and Dale W. Anderson. Zuni, N.M.: Zuni A:Shiwi Publishing and the University of New Mexico.

Ostler, Jim. 1995. Pueblo of Zuni Arts and Crafts. Unpublished report. 4 pp. January 12.

Owen, Roger C. 1965. The Patrilocal Band: A Linguistically and Culturally Hybrid Social Unit. *American Anthropologist* 67:675–791.

Palmer, J. W., M. G. Hollander, P. S. Z. Rogers, T. M. Benjamin, C. J. Duffy, J. B. Lambert, and J. A. Brown. 1998. Pre-Columbian Metallurgy: Technology, Manufacture, and Microprobe Analysis of Copper Bells from the Greater Southwest. *Archaeometry* 40(2):361–382.

Parsons, Elsie (Clews). 1939. *Pueblo Indian Religion*. 2 vols. Chicago: University of Chicago Press.

Patterson, Alex. 1994. *Hopi Pottery Symbols. Based on Work by Alexander M. Stephen*. Boulder: Johnson Books.

Pearson, Richard. 1968. Migration from Japan to Ecuador: The Japanese Evidence. *American Anthropologist* 70:85–86.

Pierson, Larry J. 1979. New Evidence of Asiatic Shipwrecks off the California Coast. Independent research in anthropology, 34 pp. Unpublished manuscript. University of San Diego.

Pierson, Larry J. and James R. Moriarty. 1980. Stone Anchors: Asiatic Shipwrecks off the California Coast. *Anthropological Journal of Canada* 18:17–23.

Pinto-Cisternas, Juan and Hernan Figueroa. 1968. Genetic Structure of a Population of Valparaiso. II. Distribution of Two Dental Traits with Anthropological Importance. *American Journal of Physical Anthropology* 29:339–348.

Plog, Fred. 1979. Prehistory: Western Anasazi. Pp. 108–130 in *Handbook of North American Indians*. Vol. 9, *Southwest*. A. Ortiz, vol. ed. W. C. Sturtevant, general ed. Washington, D.C.: Smithsonian Institution.

Plummer, Katherine. 1991. *A Japanese Glimpse at the Outside World 1839–1843. The Travels of Jirokichi in Hawaii, Siberia and Alaska*. Adapted from a translation of *Bandan*. Richard A. Pierce, ed. Alaska History No. 36. Kingston, Ontario, and Fairbanks, Alaska: Limestone Press.

Powell, John Wesley. 1891. Indian Linguistic Families of America North of Mexico. Pp. 1–142 in *7th Annual Report of the Bureau of American Ethnology for the Years 1885–1886.* Washington, D.C.: U.S. Government Printing Office.

Quam, Alvina, transl. 1972. *The Zunis: Self-portrayals by the Zuni People.* Albuquerque: University of New Mexico Press.

Quimby, George I. 1948. Culture Contact on the Northwest Coast. 1785–1795. *American Anthropologist* 50:247–255.

——1985. Japanese Wrecks, Iron Tools, and Prehistoric Indians of the Northwest Coast. *Arctic Anthropology* 22(2):7–15.

Ramage, Colin S. 1994. El Niño. Pp. 78–85 in *The Enigma of Weather.* A Collection of Works Exploring the Dynamics of Meteorological Phenomena. New York: Scientific American.

Ramer, Alexis Manaster. 1996. Tonkawa and Zuni: Two Test Cases for the Greenberg Classification. *International Journal of American Linguistics* 62:264–288.

Redman, Charles L. 1993. *People of the Tonto Rim. Archaeological Discovery in Prehistoric Arizona.* Washington, D.C.: Smithsonian Institution Press.

Reed, Erik K. 1955. Painted Pottery and Zuni History. *Southwestern Journal of Anthropology* 11:178–193.

Renfrew, Colin. 1987. *Archaeology and Language. The Puzzle of Indo-European Origins.* London: Jonathan Cape.

Riley, Carroll L., J. Charles Kelley, Campbell W. Pennington, and Robert L. Rands. 1971. *Man across the Sea. Problems of Pre-Columbian Contacts.* Austin: University of Texas Press.

Ringe, Donald A., Jr. 1992. On Calculating the Factor of Chance in Language Comparison. *Transactions of the American Philosophical Society* 82:1–110.

Roberts, Frank H. H., Jr. 1931. *The Ruins at Kiatuthlanna Eastern Arizona.* Smithsonian Institution. Bureau of American Ethnology Bulletin 100. Washington, D.C.: U.S. Government Printing Office.

——1932. *The Village of the Great Kivas on the Zuni Reservation, New Mexico.* Bureau of American Ethnology Bulletin 111. Washington, D.C.: U.S. Government Printing Office.

Rogers, Spencer L. 1954. *The Physical Type of the Paa-ko Population.* School of American Research Monograph 19, Part VI. Santa Fe: School of American Research.

Robinet, Isabelle. 1997. *Taoism. Growth of a Religion.* Phyllis Brooks, transl. Stanford: Stanford University Press.

Rodee, Marian and James Ostler. 1990. *The Fetish Carvers of Zuni.* Maxwell Museum of Anthropology and Pueblo of Zuni Arts and

Crafts. Albuquerque: Maxwell Museum of Anthropology, University of New Mexico.

Roediger, Virginia More. 1941 (1991). *Ceremonial Costumes of the Pueblo Indians. Their Evolution, Fabrication, and Significance in the Prayer Drama.* New Introduction by Fred Eggan. Berkeley: University of California Press.

Rogers, Spencer L. 1963. *The Physical Characteristics of the Aboriginal La Jollan Population of Southern California.* San Diego Museum Papers. No. 4. San Diego: Museum of Man.

Roney, John R. 1996. Eastern San Juan Basin, Acoma-Laguna Area. Pp. 145–169 in Michael A. Adler, ed. *The Prehistoric Pueblo World A.D. 1150–1350.* Tucson: University of Arizona Press.

Roscoe, Will. 1991. *The Zuni Man-Woman.* Albuquerque: University of New Mexico Press.

Ross, Philip E. 1991. Trends in Linguistics. Hard Words. *Scientific American* 264(4):138–147.

Rowen, Lee, Gregory Mahairas, and Leroy Hood. 1997. Sequencing the Human Genome. *Science* 278:605–607.

Ruby, Jay W. 1964. Occurrence of Southwestern Pottery in Los Angeles County, California. *American Antiquity* 30:209–210.

——1970. Culture Contact between Aboriginal Southern California and the Southwest. Unpublished Ph.D. dissertation in anthropology. University of California, Los Angeles.

Rudolph, John H. 1998. An Ancient Solar Observatory at Willow Creek, California. Pp. 71–84 in *Across before Columbus? Evidence for Transoceanic Contact with the Americas prior to 1492.* Donald Y. Gilmore and Linda S. McElroy, eds. New England Antiquities Research Association. Edgecomb, Me.: NEARA Publications.

Ruhlen, Merritt. 1987. *A Guide to the World's Languages.* Vol. 1, *Classification.* Stanford: Stanford University Press.

Sahara, Makoto and Hideji Harunari, eds. 1995–1996. *The Art of Bronze Bells in Early Japan.* (An exhibition catalog.) National Museum of Japanese History. Otsuka Kogei-sha, Tokyo: Mainichi Newspapers.

Sando, Joe S. 1979. The Pueblo Revolt. Pp. 194–197 in *Handbook of North American Indians.* Vol. 9, *Southwest.* A. Ortiz, vol. ed. W. C. Sturtevant, general ed. Washington, D.C.: Smithsonian Institution.

Sansom, George. 1928. *An Historical Grammar of Japanese.* Oxford: Clarendon Press.

——1958. *A History of Japan to 1334.* Stanford: Stanford University Press.

Sapir, Edward. 1929. Central and North American Indian Languages. Pp. 138–141 in *Encyclopedia Britannica.* Vol. 5. 14th ed. New York: Encyclopedia Britannica Company. (Reprinted in 1949 in pp. 169–178 in

Selected Writings of Edward Sapir in Language, Culture, and Personality. David G. Mandelbaum, ed. Berkeley: University of California Press.)

Schneider, David M. and John M. Roberts. 1956. *Zuni Kin Terms.* University of Nebraska, Laboratory of Anthropology Notebook 3. Lincoln: University of Nebraska. (Reprinted by Human Relations Area Files Press, New Haven, Conn.)

Schneider, Harold K. 1977. Prehistoric Transpacific Contact and the Theory of Culture Change. *American Anthropologist* 79:9–25.

Schroeder, Albert H. 1979. Pueblos Abandoned in Historic Times. Pp. 236–254 in *Handbook of North American Indians.* Vol. 9, *Southwest.* A. Ortiz, vol. ed. W. C. Sturtevant, general ed. Washington, D.C.: Smithsonian Institution.

Schwerin, Karl H. 1970a. The Mechanisms of Culture Change. Pp. 283–305 in *The Social Anthropology of Latin America. Essays in Honor of Ralph Leon Beals.* W. Goldschmidt and H. Hoijer, eds. Latin American Center. Los Angeles: University of California.

——1970b. *Winds across the Atlantic. Mesoamerican Studies.* No. 6. University Museum. Carbondale, Ill.: Southern Illinois University.

Scott, G. Richard, Rosario H. Yap Potter, John F. Noss, Albert A. Dahlberg, and Thelma Dahlberg. 1983. The Dental Morphology of Pima Indians. *American Journal of Physical Anthropology* 61:13–31.

Scott, G. R., S. Street, and A. A. Dahlberg. 1986. The Dental Variation of Yuman Speaking Groups in an American Southwest Context. Pp. 305–319 in *Teeth Revisited: Proceedings of the VIIth International Symposium on Dental Morphology,* Paris 1986. D. E. Russell, J.-P. Santoro, and D. Sigogneau-Russell, eds. *Mémoires du Muséum National d'Histoire Naturelle, Paris* (série C) 53:305–319.

Scott, G. Richard and Christy G. Turner, II. 1997. *The Anthropology of Modern Human Teeth. Dental Morphology and Its Variation in Recent Human Populations.* Cambridge: Cambridge University Press.

Seltzer, Carl. 1944. *Racial Prehistory in the Southwest and the Hawikuh Zunis.* Papers of the Peabody Museum of American Archaeology and Ethnology, Harvard University 23(1). Cambridge, Mass.

Shao, Paul. 1976. *Asiatic Influences in Pre-Columbia American Art.* Ames: Iowa State University Press.

——1983. *The Origin of Ancient American Cultures.* Ames: Iowa State University Press.

Shaver, Ruth M. 1966. *Kabuki Costume.* Illustrations by Sōma Akira and Ōta Gakō. Rutland, Vt.: Charles E. Tuttle.

Shepard, Anna O. 1956. *Ceramics for the Archaeologist.* Publication 906. Washington, D.C.: Carnegie Institution of Washington.

Shibatani, Masayoshi. 1990. *The Languages of Japan.* (Cambridge Language Surveys.) Cambridge: Cambridge University Press.

The Shiwi Messenger 1994–. A Biweekly Newspaper Forum. P.O. Box 1502. Zuni, New Mexico 87327.

Simmons, Marc. 1979. History of Pueblo-Spanish Relations to 1821. Pp. 178–193 in *Handbook of North American Indians.* Vol. 9, *Southwest.* A. Ortiz, vol. ed. W. C. Sturtevant, general ed. Washington, D.C.: Smithsonian Institution.

Smith, Watson. 1952. *Kiva Mural Decorations at Awatovi and Kawaika-a, with a Survey of Other Wall Paintings in the Pueblo Southwest.* Papers of the Peabody Museum of American Archaeology and Ethnology, Harvard University 37. Cambridge, Mass.

So, Kwan-wai. 1975. *Japanese Piracy in Ming China during the 16th Century.* East Lansing: Michigan State University Press.

Sofaer, J. A., J. D. Niswander, C. J. MacLean, and P. L. Workman. 1972. Population Studies on Southwestern Indian Tribes. V. Tooth Morphology as an Indicator of Biological Distance. *American Journal of Physical Anthropology* 37:357–366.

Sorenson, John L. and Martin H. Raish. 1996. *Pre-Columbian Contact with the Americas across the Oceans. An Annotated Bibliography.* 2nd ed., revised. 2 vols. Provo, Utah: Research Press.

Sowell, Thomas. 1996. *Migrations and Cultures. A World View.* New York: Basic Books.

Spencer, Robert F., Jesse D. Jennings, et al. 1965. *The Native Americans.* New York: Harper & Row.

Spier, Leslie. 1917. An Outline for a Chronology of Zuni Ruins. Anthropological Papers of the American Museum of Natural History, New York. Vol. 18, No. 3. Pp. 207–332.

Spuhler, James N. 1979. Genetic Distances, Trees, and Maps of North American Indians. Pp. 135–183 in *The First Americans: Origins, Affinities, and Adaptations.* W. S. Laughlin and A. B. Harper, eds. New York: Gustav Fischer.

Steiner, Stan. 1977. China's Ancient Mariners. *Natural History* 86(10):48–63.
——1979. *Fusang. The Chinese Who Built America.* New York: Harper & Row.

Stenger, Alison T. 1991. Japanese-Influenced Ceramics in Precontact Washington State: A View of the Wares and Their Possible Origin. Pp. 111–122 in *The New World Figurine Project.* Vol. 1. T. Stocker, ed. Provo, Utah: Research Press.

Stevenson, James. 1883. *Illustrated Catalogue of the Collections Obtained from the Indians of New Mexico and Arizona in 1879.* (Extract from the *2nd Annual Report of the Bureau of American Ethnology.*) Washington, D.C.: U.S. Government Printing Office.

Stevenson, Matilda (Coxe). 1904. The Zuni Indians: Their Mythology, Esoteric Fraternities, and Ceremonies. Pp. 3–634 in *23rd Annual Re-*

port of the Bureau of American Ethnology for the Years 1901–1902. Washington, D.C.: U.S. Government Printing Office.

——1915. Ethnobotany of the Zuni Indians. Pp. 35–102 in *Thirtieth Annual Report of the Bureau of American Ethnology. 1908–1909.* Washington, D.C.: U.S. Government Printing Office.

Steward, Julian H. 1953. Evolution and Process. Pp. 313–326 in *Anthropology Today.* A. L. Kroeber, ed. Chicago: University of Chicago Press.

Stinchecum, Amanda Mayer. 1984. *Kosode. 16th–19th Century Textiles from the Nomura Collection.* With essays by Monica Bethe and Margo Paul. Naomi Noble Richard and Margo Paul, eds. New York: Japan Society and Kodansha International.

Stocker, Terry, ed. 1991. *The New World Figurine Project.* Vol. 1. Provo, Utah: Research Press.

Storry, Richard. 1978. *The Way of the Samurai.* Photographs by Werner Forman. New York: G.P. Putnam's Son.

Stout, C. C. 1972. Zuni Transitivity: A Generative Approach. Ph.D. dissertation. University of New Mexico.

——1973. Problems of a Chomskyan Analysis of Zuni Transitivity. *International Journal of American Linguistics* 39:207–223.

Strong, William D. 1927. An Analysis of Southwestern Society. *American Anthropologist* 29:1–61.

Sullivan, Walter. 1992. "If the Shoe Floats, Follow it." Science Times. *New York Times,* September 22, P. B5.

Suzuki, Makoto and Takuro Sakai. 1964. Shovel-shaped Incisors among the Living Polynesians. *American Journal of Physical Anthropology* 22:65–72.

Swadesh, Morris 1952a Review of Athapaskan and Sino-Tibetan by Robert Shafer. *International Journal of American Linguistics* 18(3):178–181.

—— 1952b. Lexico-statistic Dating of Prehistoric Ethnic Contacts; With Special Reference to North American Indians and Eskimos. *Proceedings of the American Philosophical Society* 96:452–463.

——1956. Problems of Long-Range Comparison in Penutian. *Language: Journal of the Linguistic Society of America* 32(1):17–41.

——1966. Personal communication. Letters dated February 20 and March 18.

——1967a. Lexicostatistic Classification. Pp. 79–115 in *Handbook of Middle American Indians.* Vol. 5, *Linguistics.* Norman McQuown, vol. ed., Robert Wanchope, general ed. Austin: University of Texas Press.

——1967b. Linguistic Classification in the Southwest. Pp. 281–309 in *Studies in Southwestern Ethnolinguistics.* Dell Hymes and William Bittle, eds. Thettaque, Netherlands: Mouton.

Syromiatnikov, N. A. 1981. *The Ancient Japanese Language. Central Department of Oriental Literature.* Moscow: Nauka Publishing House.

Szathmary, Emoke J. E. 1993. Genetics of Aboriginal North Americans. *Evolutionary Anthropology* 1:202–220.

Tannen, Deborah. 1990. *You Just Don't Understand: Women and Men in Conversation.* New York: Morrow.

Tanner, Clara L. 1968. *Southwest Indian Craft Arts.* Tucson: University of Arizona Press.

Tedlock, Dennis, transl. 1969. The Problem of k in Zuni Phonemics. *International Journal of American Linguistics* 35:67–71.

——1972. *Finding the Center: Narrative Poetry of the Zuni Indians, from Performances in Zuni, by Andrew Peynetsa and Walter Sanchez.* New York: Dial Press. Lincoln: University of Nebraska Press.

——1979. Zuni Religion and World View. Pp. 499–508 in *Handbook of North American Indians.* Vol. 9, *Southwest.* A. Ortiz, vol. ed. W. C. Sturtevant, general ed. Washington, D.C.: Smithsonian Institution.

Thompson, Gunnar. 1989. *Nu Sun. Asian-American Voyages 500 B.D.* Fresno, Cal.: Pioneer Publishing.

——1994. *America Discovery. Our Multicultural Heritage.* Seattle, Wash.: Argonauts Misty Isles Press.

Thompson, J. Eric S. 1951. Canoes and Navigation of the Maya and Their Neighbors. *Journal of the Royal Anthropological Institute* 79:69–78.

Tokyo National Museum. 1988. Japanese Archaeology. History and Achievements. Special Exhibition.

Tolstoy, Paul. 1991. Paper Route. Were the Manufacture and Use of Bark Paper Introduced into Mesoamerica from Asia? *Natural History* 6(7):6–14.

Torroni, Antonio, Theodore G. Schurr, Margaret F. Cabell, Michael D. Brown, James V. Neel, Merethe Larsen, David G. Smith, Carlos M. Vullo, and Douglas C. Wallace. 1993. Asian Affinities and Continental Radiation of the Four Founding Native American mtDNAs. *American Journal of Human Genetics* 53:563–590.

Trager, George L. and Felicia E. Harben. 1958. North American Indian Languages. Classification and Maps. Studies in Linguistics, Occasional Papers 5. Buffalo, NY.

Troup, G. M., R. L. Harvey, R. L. Walford, G. S. Smith, and P. Sturgeon. 1973. Analysis of the HL-A, Erythrocyte and Gamma Globulin Antigen Systems in the Zuni Indians of New Mexico. Pp. 339–344 in *Histocompatibility Testing 1972.* J. Dausset and J. Colombani, eds. Copenhagen Munksgaard.

Tsuji, Tadashi. 1958. Incidence and Inheritance of the Carabelli's Cusp in a Japanese Population. *Japanese Journal of Human Genetics* 3:21–31.

Tsunoda, Ryusaku and L. Carrington Goodrich. 1951. *Japan in Chinese Dynastic Histories.* Perkins Asiatic Monograph No. 2. South Pasadena, Cal.: P.D. and Ione Perkins.

Tsunoda, Ryusaku, William Theodore de Bary, and Donald Keene, comp. 1958. *Sources of the Japanese Tradition.* New York: Columbia University Press.

Tucci, Giuseppe. 1980. *The Religions of Tibet.* Geoffrey Samuel, transl. Berkeley: University of California Press.

Turnbull, Stephen R. 1977. *The Samurai. A Military History.* New York: Macmillan.

——1982. *The Book of the Samurai. The Warrior Class of Japan.* A Bison Book. New York: Arco.

Turner, Christy G., II. 1969. Microevolutionary Interpretation from the Dentition. *American Journal of Physical Anthropology* 30:421–426.

——1985. Expression Count: A Method for Calculating Morphological Dental Trait Frequencies by Using Adjustable Weighting Coefficients with Standard Ranked Scales. *American Journal of Physical Anthropology* 68:263–267.

——1987. Late Pleistocene and Holocene Population History of East Asia Based on Dental Variation. *American Journal of Physical Anthropology* 73:305–321.

Turner, Christy G. and Jacqueline A. Turner. 1999. *Man Corn. Cannibalism and Violence in the Prehistoric American Southwest.* Salt Lake City, Utah: University of Utah Press.

Tyler, Susan C. 1992. *The Cult of Kasuga Seen through Its Art.* Michigan Monograph Series in Japanese Studies. No. 8. Center for Japanese Studies. Ann Arbor: University of Michigan.

Underhill, Ruth. 1954. Intercultural Relations in the Greater Southwest. *American Anthropologist* 56:645–656.

Ushijima, Yoichi. 1954. The Human Skeletal Remains from the Mitsu Site, Saga Prefecture, a Site Associated with the 'Yayoishiki' Period of Prehistoric Japan. *Quarterly Journal of Anthropology* 1(3–4):273–303.

Vargas, Victoria D. 1995. *Copper Bell Trade Patterns in the Prehispanic U.S. Southwest and Northwest Mexico.* Arizona State Museum Archaeological Series 187. Tucson: University of Arizona.

Vermeij, Geerat J. 1991. When Biotas Meets: Understanding Biotic Interchange. *Science* 253:1099–1104.

von Bonin, Gerhardt and G. M. Morant. 1938. Indian Races in the United States. A Survey of Previously Published Cranial Measurements. *Biometrica* 30 (Parts I and II):94–129.

Wakabayashi, K. 1891. Pictures of Dōkatu or so-called bronze bell. *Anthropological Society of Tokyo Journal* (Tokyo Jinrui Gakkai Zasshi) 7(67–69).

Walker, Willard. 1964. Reference, Taxonomy and Inflection in Zuni. Ph.D. dissertation. Cornell University.

——1966. Inflectional Class and Taxonomic Structure in Zuni. *Interna-*

tional Journal of American Linguistics 32:217–227.

——1972. Toward the Sound Pattern of Zuni. *International Journal of American Linguistics.* 38:240–259.

——1979. Zuni Semantic Categories. Pp. 509–513 in *Handbook of North American Indians.* Vol. 9, *Southwest.* A. Ortiz, vol. ed. W. C. Sturtevant, general ed. Washington, D.C.: Smithsonian Institution.

Watanabe, S., S. Kondo, and E. Matsunagi, eds. 1975. *Anthropological and Genetic Studies on the Japanese. Human Adaptability.* Vol. 2. Japanese Committee for the International Biological Program. Tokyo: University of Tokyo Press.

Watkins, David I., Stephen N. McAdam, Xiaomin Liu, Clarice R. Strang, Edgar L. Milford, Cindy G. Levine, Theodore L. Garber, Alex L. Dogon, Carol I. Lord, Steven H. Ghim, Gary M. Troup, Austin L. Hughes, and Norman L. Letvin. 1992. New Recombinant HLA-B Alleles in a Tribe of South American Amerindians Indicate Rapid Evolution of MHC Class I Loci. *Nature* 357:329–333.

Watts, Linda K. 1988. Relational Terminology and Household-Group Role Structure at Zuni. Paper read at the 87th annual meeting of the American Anthropological Association, November 19.

Weatherford, Jack. 1994. *Savages and Civilization. Who Will Survive?* New York: Fawcett Columbine.

Webber, Bert. 1984. *Wrecked Japanese Junks Adrift in the North Pacific Ocean.* Fairfield, Wash.: Ye Galleon Press.

Wheeler, Post, ed. and transl. 1952 (1976). *The Sacred Scriptures of the Japanese.* Westport, Conn.: Greenwood Press.

Whitaker, Thomas W. 1970. Endemism and Pre-Columbian Migration of the Bottle Gourd, *Lagenaria siceraria* (Mol.) Standl. Pp. 320–327 in *Man across the Sea. Problems of Pre-Columbian Contact.* Carroll L. Riley et al., eds. Austin: University of Texas Press.

Whorf, Benjamin and George L. Trager. 1937. The Relationship of Uto-Aztecan and Tanoan. *American Anthropologist* 39:609–624.

Wilford, John Noble. 1992. Case for Other Pre-Columbian Voyagers. *New York Times,* July 7, p. B10.

Willey, Gordon R. 1966. *An Introduction to American Archaeology.* Vol. 1, *North and Middle America.* Englewood Cliffs, N.J.: Prentice-Hall.

Winchester, Simon. 1991. *Pacific Rising. The Emergence of a New World Culture.* New York: Prentice Hall.

Wood, Jim. 1980. Early Asians May Have Sailed to West. *San Francisco Sunday Examiner & Chronicle,* July 13, Section A, p. 8.

Woodbury, Richard B. 1956. The Antecedents of Zuni Culture. *Transactions of the New York Academy of Sciences.* Second series. 18(6):557–563.

——1979. Zuni Prehistory and History to 1850. Pp. 467–473 in *Handbook of North American Indians.* Vol. 9, *Southwest.* A. Ortiz, vol. ed. W. C. Sturtevant, general ed. Washington, D.C.: Smithsonian Institution.

Woodward, Arthur. 1932. A Modern Zuni Pilgrimage. *The Masterkey* 6:44–51.

Workman, P. L., J. D. Niswander, K. S. Brown, and W. C. Leyshon. 1974. Population Studies on Southwestern Indian Tribes. IV. The Zuni. *American Journal of Physical Anthropology* 41:119–132.

Workman, William B. and Allen P. McCartney. 1998. Coast to Coast: Prehistoric Maritime Cultures in the North Pacific. *Arctic Anthropology* 35(1):361–370.

Wormington, H. Marie. 1959. *Prehistoric Indians of the Southwest.* (4th printing.) Denver: Denver Museum of Natural History.

Wright, Barton. 1985. *Kachinas of the Zuni.* Original paintings by Duane Dishta. Flagstaff, Ariz.: Northland Press.

Wright, Barton, ed. 1988. *The Mythic World of the Zuni. Written by Frank Hamilton Cushing.* Albuquerque: University of New Mexico Press.

Wyaco, Virgil. 1988. Personal communication. Pueblo of Zuni. November 22.

——1998. *A Zuni Life. A Pueblo Indian in Two Worlds.* J. A. Jones, transcr. and ed. Historical sketch by Carroll L. Riley. Albuquerque: University of New Mexico Press.

Xu, Mike. 1996. *Origin of Olmec Civilization.* Edmund, Okla.: University of Central Oklahoma Press.

Yamamoto, Yoshiko. 1978. *Namahage. A Festival in the Northeast of Japan.* Philadelphia: Institute for the Study of Human Issues.

Yoshida, Nobuhiro. 1991. Personal communication. February 6.

——1992. Personal communication. January 5.

Yoshitake, Saburo. 1934. *The Phonetic System of Ancient Japanese.* Vol. XII. London: Royal Asiatic Society.

Yoshitaro, Takenobu, general ed. 1942. *Kenkyusha's New Japanese-English Dictionary.* American ed. Cambridge, Mass.: Harvard University Press.

Young, M. Jane. 1988. *Signs from the Ancestors. Zuni Cultural Symbolism and Perceptions of Rock Art.* Albuquerque: University of New Mexico Press.

Zengel, Majorie Smith. 1962. Literacy as a Factor in Language Change. *American Anthropologist* 64:132–139.

Zunie, Willard. 1999. Personal communication. May 5.

CREDITS

FIGURE CREDITS

1. Courtesy of the author
2. Photograph by Ben Wittick, courtesy of the Museum of New Mexico, Santa Fe, #16059
3. Photograph by E. G. Curtis, courtesy of the Denver Public Library, Western History Collection
4. Photograph by Sarbo, reprinted with permission
5. Courtesy of the Zuni Arts and Crafts Cooperative
6. Courtesy of the author
7. Photograph by E. G. Curtis, courtesy of the Denver Public Library, Western History Collection
8. Courtesy of the National Anthropology Archives, Smithsonian Institution
9. Reprinted with permission of Arco Press from *The Book of the Samurai* by Stephen Turnbull (1982)
10. Illustrations by Duane Dishta, reproduced with permission of Barton Wright from his book *Kachinas of the Zuni*
11. Photograph by George H. H. Huey, #0202-1049, reprinted with permission
12. Photograph by George H. H. Huey, #0204-1029, reprinted with permission
13. Courtesy of J. W. Palmer, reprinted with permission
14. Courtesy of the National Anthropology Archives, Smithsonian Institution
15. Courtesy of the Maxwell Museum of Anthropology, the University of New Mexico, Albuquerque
16. Reprinted with permission of National Geographic Society Cartographic Division/Image Collection
17. Reprinted with permission of the Field Museum, Chicago, Illinois, #CSA38922
18. Courtesy of the National Museum of Japanese History
19. Courtesy of the Arctic Studies Center, Smithsonian Institution
20. Photograph by Ruth Kirk, reprinted with permission of the photographer
21. Courtesy of the Phoebe Hearst Museum of Anthropology, Berkeley, California, and the Regents of the University of California
22. Courtesy of the Phoebe Hearst Museum of Anthropology, Berkeley, California, and the Regents of the University of California
23. Courtesy of the Phoebe Hearst Museum of Anthropology, Berkeley, California, and the Regents of the University of California
24. Courtesy of Larry Pierson
25. Courtesy of the Phoebe Hearst Museum of Anthropology, Berkeley, California, and the Regents of the University of California
26. Illustration by S. S. Ling, reproduced with permission of the Science and Society Picture Library, Science Museum, London, England

27. Reproduced by permission of the American Anthropological Association from *American Anthropologist* 97:4, December 1995. Not for further reproduction.

28. Reproduced with permission of the Tokyo National Museum

29. Courtesy of the National Museum of Japanese History

30. Reprinted by permission of the University of Wisconsin Press, from *Arctic Anthropology,* Vol. 22, No. 2, copyright 1985

31. Illustrations by Tadashi Tsuji, reprinted from *Japanese Journal of Genetics* 3:21–31(1958)

32. Courtesy of the author

33. Courtesy of the author

34. Courtesy of the National Museum of the American Indian, Smithsonian Institution, #N7472

35. Reproduced with permission of the San Diego Museum of Man, #19243 (front)

36. Reproduced with permission of the San Diego Museum of Man, #19243 (craniogram)

37. Courtesy of the author

38. Courtesy of the author

39. Courtesy of the author

40. Courtesy of the Maxwell Museum of Anthropology, the University of New Mexico, Albuquerque

41. Courtesy of the author

42. Courtesy of the author

43. Photograph by Yoshiko Yamamoto

44. Illustration by Duane Dishta, reproduced with permission of Barton Wright from his book *Kachinas of the Zuni*

45. Illustration by Duane Dishta, reproduced with permission of Barton Wright from his book *Kachinas of the Zuni*

46. Reproduced with permission of the Senri Foundation, Tokyo, Japan

47. Courtesy of the author

48. Photograph by Ben Wittick, courtesy of the Museum of New Mexico, Santa Fe, #16055

49. Courtesy of the School of American Research, Santa Fe, SAR T.11

50. Courtesy of the author

51. Courtesy of the author

52. Courtesy of the author

53. Courtesy of the National Park Service, #5260, G2376

54. Courtesy of the Tokyo National Museum

55. Courtesy of the National Anthropology Archives, Smithsonian Institution

56. Courtesy of the Taylor Museum at the Colorado Springs Fine Arts Center, Colorado Springs, TM4364

57. Courtesy of the author

58. Courtesy of the National Anthropology Archives, Smithsonian Institution

59. Photograph by George H. H. Huey, #0121-1041, reprinted with permission

60. Courtesy of Virgil Wyaco

61. Courtesy of the author

62. Courtesy of the author

63. Adapted from Brooks, 1876 *Proceedings of the California Academy of Sciences*, No. 6

64. Courtesy of the Seattle Art Museum, Eugene Fuller Memorial Collection, 60.84

65. Reprinted with permission of Dover Publications from *Japanese Design Motifs* by Gofukuten Matsuya, copyright 1972

66. Illustration by Randy Nahohai, reproduced with permission of the artist

67. Courtesy of the Department of Anthropology, Smithsonian Institution, 77-11245

68. Courtesy of the School of American Research, Santa Fe, New Mexico, SAR P.91

69. Courtesy of the Library, American Museum of Natural History, New York, New York, Neg. #312257

70. Illustrations by Duane Dishta, reproduced with permission of Barton Wright from his book *Kachinas of the Zuni*

71. Courtesy of the Bureau of American Ethnology

72. Zuni rosette illustration by Randy Nahohai, reproduced by permission of the artist. Japanese emblem from Brooks, 1876 *Proceedings of the California Academy of Sciences*, No. 6.

MAP CREDITS

1. Source: *A Zuni Atlas.* T. J. Ferguson and E. Richard Hart. University of Oklahoma Press, 1985. P. 2.

2. Source: Map of the Four Corners Area (drawn by Dennis Roberts) in *Beauty from the Earth.* J. J. Brody. University of Pennsylvania Press, Museum of Archaeology and Anthropology, 1990. P. xii.

3. Source: *A Zuni Atlas.* T. J. Ferguson and E. Richard Hart. University of Oklahoma Press, 1985. P. 34.

4. Source: *A Zuni Atlas.* T. J. Ferguson and E. Richard Hart. University of Oklahoma Press, 1985. P. 20.

5. By the author

6. Source: *A Zuni Atlas.* T. J. Ferguson and E. Richard Hart. University of Oklahoma Press, 1985. P. 52.

7. Source: *A Zuni Atlas.* T. J. Ferguson and E. Richard Hart. University of Oklahoma Press, 1985. P. 5.

8. Source: *Handbook of North American Indians.* Vol. 8. Smithsonian Institution, 1978. P. ix.

9. Source: *Cultural Atlas of Japan.* Martin Collcutt, Marius Jansen, and Isao Kumakura. Facts on File, 1988.

10. Source: Anomalous Westerlies, El Niño, and the Colonization of Polynesia. Ben Finney. *American Anthropologist* 87 (1), 1985.

11. Source: Jomon-Valdivia Similarities: Convergence or Contact? Pp. 11–22 in *Across before Columbus? Evidence for Transoceanic Contact with the Americas prior to 1492.* Donald Y. Gilmore and Linda S. McElroy, eds. New England Antiquities Research Association, 1998.

12. Source: *Quest for the Origins of the First Americans*. E. James Dixon. University of New Mexico Press, 1993. P. 122.
13. Source: *Cultural Atlas of Japan*. Martin Collcutt, Marius Jansen, and Isao Kumakura. Facts on File, 1988.
14. Source: *Handbook of North American Indians*. Vol. 17. Smithsonian Institution, 1997. Pocket insert.
15. Source: *Language of the Americas*. Joseph H. Greenberg. Stanford University Press. P. 388.
16. Source: *The Languages of Japan*. Masayoshi Shibatani. Cambridge University Press, 1990. P. 189.
17. Source: Asian Museum of San Francisco map series.

INDEX

Page numbers in *italics* refer to illustrations and tables.